Our task must be to free ourselves from prison by widening our circle of compassion to embrace all living beings and all of nature.

—Albert Einstein

Widening the Circle

Inspiration and Guidance
FOR COMMUNITY LIVING

DEBORA HOGELAND

HOHM PRESS
Prescott, Arizona

Cover design:
Kim Johansen, San Francisco, California

Layout and design:
Hope Sinatra, Hope Graphics, San Diego, California

Special thanks to Riane Eisler at the Center for Partnership
Studies, Pacific Grove, California, for permission to reprint the
chart of the Partnership Model vs. the Dominator Model that
appears on pp. 116–117. Originally from her book: *The
Partnership Way: New Tools for Living and Learning* San
Francisco: Harper San Francisco, 1990, p. 183.

Library of Congress Cataloging-in-Publication Data

Hogeland, Debora, 1964-
    Widening the circle : inspiration and guidance for community living / Debora Hogeland.
        p. cm.
    ISBN 1-890772-03-8 (alk. paper)
    1. Community life. 2. Community organization. I. Title

    HM761 .H64 2000
    307--dc21

                                                                        00-044894

HOHM PRESS
P.O. Box 2501, Prescott, AZ 86302
800-381-2700 • http://www.hohmpress.com

This book was printed in the U.S.A.
on acid-free paper using soy ink.

DEDICATION

To my Teacher and the sangha who graciously share their company with me, giving me a place to serve and be served.

ACKNOWLEDGEMENTS

To my Teacher, who has brought to life in me all that is alive, I am eternally grateful. I thank Regina Sara Ryan for all her efforts in spreading the word. For all the efforts of those who helped me write and live this book, I am thankful. For the children, who remind me to be present.

CONTENTS

Introduction

Chapter One   The Relocation of Culture 1

Chapter Two   At the Roots of Things—
Food, Gardens, Hospitality
& Sacred Spaces 24

Chapter Three   Working Together 51

Chapter Four   Context and Culture—
The Vision and the Commitment 69

Chapter Five   Power and Participation—
Types of Leadership 94

Chapter Six   Diversity, Conflict and Communication....135

Chapter Seven At the Heart of Community—
Good Company, Bonding and Intimacy 161

Chapter Eight   On Men and Women—
The Gender Cultures................................186

Chapter Nine   The Continuity of Life—
Children and Elders 216

Chapter Ten   The Healing Power of Community............252

Chapter Eleven Celebration and Ritual 270

Chapter Twelve Of Spirit and Soul....................................282

Endnotes 333

Bibliography..339

Community is one of the great concerns of our times. Experiments in community have gone through many changes in the past twenty-five years—intentional communities; Christian, Buddhist and Hindu monasteries, centers and ashrams; hippie communes; gay and lesbian communities; artists' co-ops; back-to-the-earth communities; cooperatives; recovery and psychotherapeutic groups and communities; and work collectives running businesses like bakeries and publishing companies. Some have dissolved or fallen apart while others have endured and flourished. That communities persevere and continue to spring to life is a sign of our collective need and hunger for a return to the wisdom of community life.

Those of us who have tried diligently but failed to create community have been disillusioned at times, even deeply disheartened, by our thwarted or stumbling efforts. Yet, many have also found the quest for community to be enlivening, revolutionary and transformational in their individual lives. Living in an intentional community in the U.S. Southwest for the past seventeen years has given me a passion for sharing the breakthroughs and insights of my own process and experience in community, and that of others.

Many excellent books contain an abundance of practical information about community—the "nuts and bolts" of finding, starting and sustaining community; how to solve problems; how to run a meeting; how to develop management structures; how to communicate; how to create rituals; how to sustain a cross-cultural and multi-racial mix, and so on. This book takes a different approach by going straight to the heart of what community is— the living experience of the delights, challenges, possibilities and heartbreaks of human relatedness which transcend our differences and unify us. Instead of offering ABC's of how to "do" community, *Widening the Circle* focuses on community as a dynamic, evolving process through which the individual and the world can be effectively transformed.

My own experience has compelled me to articulate this possibility for transformation through community. But this would not have been possible without the community of family and friends who have shared their earthy, poignant, sometimes shocking, funny or sad, and often inspirational stories and insights with me. These friends, who speak from many different perspectives and experiences of community life, have had the courage to live community fully, and to commit to its moment-to-moment creation. Their commitment to push on through to the heart of community has tremendously enriched my life and this book, and I am indebted to them. Most of their names and the places they lived have been changed to afford them anonymity. A conscious relationship to the shadow side of human nature and community is of tremendous value in our search for the transforming path of living together. Consequently, many of the stories in this book are drawn from the familiar "hard knocks" school of life, in which confrontation with the shadow side of human frailty and woundedness was the necessary evolutionary step encountered personally within community. Conflict, power struggles, violence, anger, fear, addiction and dysfunction within family systems are all concerns of community that must be honestly faced and worked through if community is to become the organic vessel—the container or matrix—from which the individual may explore spiritual dimensions and self-realization.

Many communitarians, myself among them, believe that a resurgence—a virtual renaissance—of community spirit is necessary for human life to continue on this planet. A large number of communities have been formed based on the belief that technological culture is doomed to crumble in the next fifty years, and that new tools—a much softer technology and return to sustainable agriculture, for example—are needed. Experience has taught me that the single most necessary ingredient of any "survival" of the human species and society is the development of an all-pervading culture based on relatedness and wholeness. The bond of human relationship is the promise and possibility of community, but community must develop a true culture that spans the breadth and depth of human life and encompasses a complete context for how we live. When this context has at its roots the principles of conscious and sacred relationship among all beings, then the deep spiritual and psychological bonds among humans naturally connect us into the vast, interpenetrating patterns of nature. Thus connected, we experience a natural way of living in harmony with the Earth. Living in conscious, organic relatedness with others—individuals and small groups—leads us to recognize our interconnectedness on a global and universal scale. I see the successful development of intentional communities—which are essentially tribal in nature, but not necessarily in form—as the most powerful counteraction against the dehumanizing effects of modern technological culture. Yet, I also know that creating community is extraordinarily difficult for any group of people. In this regard we have much to learn from indigenous, tribal cultures.

Underlying our training, our cultural and psychological biases—and regardless of whatever wounds we may carry through life—each human being has an unerring instinctual sense of what is appropriate and beneficial in life. Stripping away the overlay of modern culture upon this instinctual sense reveals an innate way of knowing that can lead us through the questions that living in community invariably raises. Although there are no easy answers, a growing body of wisdom is developing about the subject of community today. This book is my attempt to underline the need for a greater sense of belonging and the possibility for transformation and purpose within the human family that community may provide.

CHAPTER ONE

The Relocation of Culture

It is curious to me when I hear people say they are interested in spiritual development but do not want to be involved in a group. They are willing to receive the teaching but they are not willing to learn to love others, especially if those others do not share their own likes and dislikes, tastes, interests, and so forth. This is usually a clear sign of being stuck in one's own separateness, the very separateness that must be melted in order to know one's essential Self. We cannot do the work alone; we need to learn from the experience of others; we need others to show us to ourselves and help us become complete.

—Kabir Helminski

What is the yearning we feel for human relatedness? At the deepest level it arises from our desire to realize that we are not separate from the life we see all around us. Somewhere in us, maybe in the nuclei of our cells, we have some vague stirring of a memory: of sitting around a fire with others, or of sweating in the fields, tending flocks, hunting for food, sharing in celebration, making tools, pounding corn or wheat, cooking, dancing to a drum or a fiddle, worshipping together, birthing our children and caring for them with others, attending to our elders and burying our dead.

Since the beginning of time human beings have gathered together in the company of their own kind to create culture. We have sought each other initially for practical, physical survival, but underlying the drive to survive has also been the impulse for

1

our evolution as conscious beings. A yearning for individual and collective wholeness is somehow tied up in this longing for the togetherness, reciprocity and bonded unity that is community. When we begin to discover these possibilities, we enter into a life of meaning and purpose. This is poignantly echoed in the sense of incompleteness and emptiness that most of us feel when our lives are lived outside of the bond of community—outside of full relationships with other human beings. We are not isolated, separate individuals; we are profoundly and organically interconnected and interdependent creatures.

If we look, we find that community exists here and now within each of us; it is a fact of our essential nature. We are all born of woman and man, will live and die, eat and sleep, laugh and cry. We have profound commonality regardless of any superficial differences. The fact that we are human transcends differences in race, sex, nationality or religious preferences. We are a part of a global community. There really are no strangers here.

This commonality is never more obvious than when we travel to other countries. The language and/or the culture may be quite different, but delighting in children is universally understood among adults, and can be communicated in a simple smile or glance. This ubiquitous connectedness comes to the foreground also in areas like birth, death, food, sickness and simple acts of daily maintenance. The forms may vary, but the necessity is the same. There is a direct correlation between the degree to which we experience a basic commonality in our shared humanity, and the degree of closeness that we feel with another. The recognition of that commonality is one of the fundamentals of building community.

A Culture of Separation

We can tap into and pursue a more conscious relationship with one another or we can simply allow our

2

underlying connectedness to fade into the background of awareness. This is what has happened in modern technological culture. The fact is that the great majority of Westerners live in a culture of separation and isolation. When we forget that we are organically interconnected we become psychologically isolated and separated. Life takes on a very lonely hue. We begin to feel misunderstood, forsaken, alone, bereft or just terribly bored or scared. Our lives become empty, meaningless and abstract rather than potent, resonant and vibrant with a meaty and tangible sense of purpose. We may feel like we are living in exile and carrying a tremendous weight by ourselves. Our potential becomes limited and thwarted in the repetitive daily ennui of a closed and narrowly defined life. We are buffered from real feeling and separated from the core of authentic human experience.

Many of us can remember growing up with the feeling that no one really understood us. Raised on the fables and fairy tales of old Europe reinterpreted by Walt Disney, we longed for and dreamt of someone who would know us deeply. We wanted a hero or a fairy godmother who would heal us and make our wounds, our disappointments and our separation from life itself—represented by the wicked stepmother, the evil sorcerer, the cruel siblings, the witches, the poisoned apple—go away. In this mythical person's presence we would become whole. Most of us were taught to believe that a husband or wife and children would fill this empty space, but have been sadly disillusioned in realizing that the narrow confines of the nuclear family are simply not meeting our needs.

When the nuclear family exists as a natural subset within a larger matrix—extended family, community, tribe—with which it interacts freely in a reciprocal flow of mutual support, then it is a healthy, functioning part of a natural social order. In times past it was common to live as an extended family, which included mothers, fathers and children, as well as grandmothers, grandfathers, aunts, uncles and cousins, even distant cousins. This was a family based on a sense of continuity between generations, and it allowed for a wide range and variety of relationships, potentials and resources to be experienced and exchanged. In the extended family, one had a tremendous support system and many avenues of skill sharing and affection, besides the sharing of sorrow and tears.

Rather than the extended family growing toward greater cohesion and evolution, our separation and isolation from each other and the Earth has grown in direct proportion to the burgeoning economic strength, technological power and material possessions of the Western world. And so, in this age of information and mass communication, a strong parallel exists between our separation from the Earth and our separation from the heart and spirit of the extended human family and the community.

Not only have we lost the warmth and sustenance of friendship, kinship, belonging, acceptance and the gratification that comes from caring for a wide range of others, but we have lost the synergy that takes place in community—a synergy that seeds and catalyzes the inherent potential of individual members. We can easily see why so many prominent sociologists and contemporary psychologists have said that the majority of the social problems rampant in civilized culture today stem from our failure to acknowledge and deal with this fragmentation and emptiness.

In the past thirty years we have become more globally aware that what we create has an effect on all the systems of the environment in which we live. In spite of this, most Westerners still carry on as if they were separate from their environment; as if there were no connection between their actions and the state of the world or the decay of culture. Human beings are killing the Earth—or destroying various ecosystems, many of which are already damaged beyond repair. The state of our planet is a reflection of the condition of the human race, and in the same way the individual's body is the reflection of the inner life or the soul.

We sit upon landfills of our undigested waste, vastly more than the Earth can process. Living in the carefully defined personal territory of our separate houses or apartments, we are buffered from one another by the conveniences and harried pace of modernity. Distracted from the truth and the impact of the dire circumstances of contemporary life, we are lulled into sleep by consumerism, the media—especially television—and the gratification of over-feeding ourselves in every possible way: with money, sex, food, a multitude of entertainment, possessions, material objects, power or fame. The present population is, on the average, nearly five-times richer than their great grandparents were at the turn of the century, but they are not five-times happier. Psychological research has clearly indicated that the relationship between consumerism and personal happiness is weak. An added negative side effect is that two major sources of human fulfillment—social relations and leisure—seem to have withered or stagnated in the rush to riches. We have been unwisely attempting to satisfy needs that are essentially social, psychological and spiritual by amassing more things, including money.[1]

Measured in constant dollars, the world's people have consumed as many goods and services since 1950 as all previous generations put together.[2] Mutual interdependence for day-to-day sustenance—a basic characteristic of life for those who have not achieved middle-class consumer status—bonds people much more than close proximity alone ever can. Yet, those bonds are disintegrating with the onslaught of the commercial mass market into neighborhoods and communities once cultured by family members and local enterprises. Immense malls crammed with consumer goods, superhighways, and "strips" of more stores, 24-plex movie theatres and fast-food businesses have replaced corner stores, local restaurants, and neighborhood cinemas—those elements of daily life that help create a sense of common identity and community in an area.

5

Members of the consumer class have a degree of personal independence that is unprecedented in human history, but at a high cost: the decline in our attachments to each other. Informal visits between neighbors and friends, family conversation, and time spent at family meals have all diminished in the United States since mid-century.[3] Many neighborhoods are called "bedroom communities" for good reason: their inhabitants use them for little more than a place to sleep. Being "neighbors" means that the only thing shared in common are a video rental franchise and a convenience store. Americans move, on the average, every five years, and develop little attachment to those who live near them.[4]

We have so lost touch with the natural cycles of growing our own food in the U.S. that the typical mouthful of food travels over 1500 miles from farm field to dinner plate.[5] Where we once had the bustling life of the village or town marketplace in which people could daily greet, share the news in the jostling throng, argue, gossip, admire the vendors' wares and buy vegetables and fruits that were grown only miles away, we now have the often antiseptic, media- and marketing-glitzed atmosphere of immense supermarkets and impersonal warehouse buying clubs, supplied by long-distance trucking and air freight, at the great consumption of the Earth's fossil fuels.

All the basics of life in Western culture have become depersonalized. Now the construction company builds the house or the barn rather than the community. The harvest is brought in before the weather changes or the storm hits by the technology of mechanized agribusiness rather than the combined, superhuman efforts of the extended family or community working together in the face of the raw elements of nature. The simple exchange or bartering of goods has been replaced by industry, high-level economics, and the slick strategic planning of the marketing approach to consumer sales—all driven by the profit motive.

Death itself has become an unnatural and technologized event. The family no longer cares for its own dead. Instead, the funeral home takes charge of the body, the laying in state and usually the final rituals. The majority of us have never touched a dead body much less bathed and prepared a deceased loved-one's body for burial. Many of us are even unwilling to gather together in our family's home in the presence of the dead to mourn, cry, pray, sing, dance, laugh, feast and celebrate the life of the beloved deceased. In fact, these experiences—which were a natural part of daily life even fifty years ago—are considered not only archaic and obsolete today, but repulsive and even frightening.

Because modern culture has failed to replace these deeply bonding and therefore community-building events which are rooted in the Earth, it is continually leading us further away from our natural human social structure. The media and a plethora of false values have convinced the mass populace to fear what is primal, earthy, physical—dimensions of life that are connected with the body. The more we eschew and ignore these basics of life, the more we become disconnected from our instinctual knowing of how to care for our bodies and the body of the Earth. As we become more disconnected as a race, and especially as we lose our natural sense of community and relationship, we lose touch with the meaning of self-respect, respect for others, respect for all of life. As respect diminishes our social structures break down, and human interactions become increasingly cheapened and violent. The onslaught of this decline and decay is becoming harder and harder to ignore.

The antidote to this scenario of destruction and despair is a reorientation of culture from one of separation to one of wholeness. African tribal spokesman Malidoma Somé describes culture in terms of the four alchemical elements: water, earth, air and fire. He suggests that modern Western society is a culture of only fire, lacking in the balance of water (which he calls "wisdom

7

of the elders," and other ancient traditions might call *feeling, receptivity and heart*) and other elements. As a result, we are burning ourselves up, meanwhile forgetting our inherent awareness of and respect for the Earth. It is community, according to Somé, that is the missing link. Sooner or later we may discover that in order to have an inner culture of wholeness, we need our fellow beings to help create a societal or collective culture of wholeness.

Widening the Circle

Westerners psychologists are only just beginning to realize how deeply severed we are from our own ancestral wisdom and psyche, and what a great loss that may prove to be. When we acknowledge and deal with our pain about the culture of separation, then we can begin to relocate our lives in the vicinity of cohesion and wholeness—a process that often leads through many circuitous routes toward the center of things where past and present meet. Many tribal people believe that life is sustained by a relationship of honor and respect with the tribal and familial ancestors.

Each individual has a unique gift to offer in community—a gift that has come down through the ancestral ages to this moment. The coming together of these diverse streams of humanity not only generates the individual wholeness we may experience now, but also infuses human culture with wholeness. We feel a sense of rightness reconnecting with the ancestral roots of life, a rightness that comes from living and working together in the service of something that is greater than ourselves. In this way, engaging community at the most fundamental levels brings renewal and purpose back into our daily tasks, our self-esteem and our sense of possibility. We begin to draw the scattered threads back together to re-weave the fabric of life, and to connect us back to

our ancestral relationship with the Earth. Albert
the point when he said:

> A human being [sometimes] experiences himself, his
> thoughts and feelings, as something separated from the
> rest—a kind of optical illusion of his consciousness. This
> illusion is a prison for us, restricting us to our personal
> desires and to affection for only the few people near us.
> Our task must be to free ourselves from prison by widen-
> ing our circle of compassion to embrace all living beings
> and all of nature.

The fact that we are so disconnected from our own ancestry,
and therefore our wholeness, is mirrored in the desecration and
genocide of indigenous cultures, the disappearing rain forests,
the destruction of the ozone layer, the toxicity of our air, water
and soil. When we hear about the decay and decline that is still
happening in native cultures in the world, we feel a pain; sometimes we cry bitter tears of remorse and helplessness. And yet,
what has happened to the Native American tribes of North,
Central and South America, or what is happening today to traditional culture in India or Africa has *already happened* to people
of European descent. If we study our history books we find that
European tribal and clan roots were destroyed hundreds of years
ago by the onslaughts of Rome. What Rome started in its colo-
nization and subjugation of Europe was finished in subsequent
centuries by the combined forces of the Romanized, militaristic
monarchies of Europe fueled by the aggressive political involvement of the sovereign Catholic Church.

Several years ago my friend Mary attended a pow wow in
the U.S. Southwest where several tribes—Yavapai-Apache,
Papago and others—had gathered to dance some of their social
dances for the enrichment not only of their own communities, but
for the greater community of the local populace. Mary was struck

9

by the fact that the master of ceremonies referred to the Caucasian Americans who were present as "European Americans." This is, of course, quite true—a fact of our ancestral history that the descendants of European immigrants would just as soon forget.

One important way to reconnect with our roots in community is to accept our European heritage and even embrace it. Those of European descent have also descended from a tribal way of life! This birthright to community has been slowly trained out of us over many generations, and we may feel a certain grief for what has been lost of our ancient tribal culture—regardless of our race, nationality or circumstance. If we allow ourselves to acknowledge our grief, we can begin to revision and rebuild. Such acknowledgement requires the kind of self-honesty that is ultimately an act of community. A self-honesty that generates personal vulnerability allows us to look compassionately at each other and see that, indeed, we are simply two or more human beings, suffering together.

If we stay vulnerable in that sadness, and stay open to what is happening in tribal and indigenous cultures today, we have a chance to rebuild community culture for ourselves and maybe even help stop the momentum of decay in existing Third World cultures.

LEARNING FROM INDIGENOUS CULTURES

The Bribri of Costa Rica

Author Mariana Caplan spent many months living with an Indian tribe in Costa Rica in the early 1990s.[6] In the following story she describes expanding her connection to the human family by bringing together European and indigenous American Indian roots under one roof called *community*.

10

My initial inspiration to travel and study for my bachelor's degree in cultural anthropology in Central America was inspired by the search for other lifestyles—another way of people relating to each other than how they did in my hometown. I wanted to know what it was like to live in community, to live from the land, to live naturally, with natural rhythms, without electricity and all the modern conveniences that tend to make our lives artificial and insanely paced. I wanted to operate from a paradigm other than success, power and material wealth. Granted, I was naive. When I was dropped off at the Kekoldi Indian Reservation on the southwest coast of Costa Rica, I knew I would have to work to find acceptance within the tribal community there. I expected to find myself in a small village of homes where I could hang out with different families, working and learning from them. What a surprise when my Indian companion took my too-large luggage out of the car, and hiked through knee-deep mud in the rain up to a small, wooden building where I was to live with three other native women, one of whom was widowed; the other two had decided not to marry—an unusual choice in their community. He wished me well and left.

How awkward it was! I soon learned that although I was in a native community, people there lived in homes and huts scattered throughout many hectares in the rain forest, so that houses were often a one or two hour hike away from each other. This is the form that community took for the Bribris, whose traditional culture was in a state of significant decline due to the pressures of technology, alcoholism and tourism. Curious spectators of indigenous cultures contribute to their decline as much as the ideals of Western industrialization.

I immediately found myself immersed in a three-week monsoon season where there was rarely a time in which I could leave the house. There we were—Juanita, Gloria, Doña Catalina and I—their native language Bribri, mine English, and a shared knowledge of broken Spanish. Hour by hour we burned in a shared un-ease. None of us could think of anything to talk about—a month-long mental block! Weeks went by and I was counting the days until the end of my two-month commitment. Occasionally the villagers would come by and stare in my open window, or watch me wash my clothes at the well, while they giggled amongst themselves; but few would ever speak to me.

Sitting around in hammocks by candlelight one evening, when my time was nearly over and my high goals unfulfilled, the house began to shake. It took some moments to recognize that this rumbling was an earthquake. None of us had any idea how serious it would be! In a single moment, all of the cultural, class, language, and racial barriers were gone; the differences between us suddenly negligible in relationship to the reality of life and death and our uncertain future. We sat together quietly, powerless, looking at one another and sharing in true intimacy as we awaited our shared destiny.

The earthquake subsided, but things were never the same. We had broken through and come out the other side. Slowly, this began to happen with the others in the community. I had interpreted their response, or lack of response, to me as negative feelings, as our racial and cultural differences, but it was really fear and suspicion of each other as strangers that was standing between us. They simply did not talk to me because they were afraid of me, and as soon as I started understanding that I could drop my own defenses and approach them, things changed. Once the barriers were down, the language of human friendship and shared community took over.

I decided to extend my visit one more month, and then another, and then another. We found a way to live together, each sharing our very distinct knowledge and resources. Evenings in the home became joyful—the four of us sitting around talking and laughing for hours after the sun went down. I wanted to hear their traditional stories and about how village families worked (and didn't work) together; they wanted to hear about how rockets could make it up into space and about how laundry machines worked, and why when you're in the middle of a car accident you don't just turn the engine off. One night while sitting around in the glow of the dying fire and the burning candles, sitting on tree stumps that served as benches or hammocks, my Bribri friends asked me where our water comes from in North America. They were shy, and I could tell they had been thinking about it for a long time.

Having lived with them for several months and knowing how basic water was to them, I was embarrassed because I didn't know the answer. I started thinking about the reservoirs and rivers around where I lived in California, and trying to come up with an answer. At last I told them that I didn't know, because that was the truth. Then they asked me where my electricity came from, and I knew even less—I really had no idea! What I felt inside was shame; not that I was ashamed of myself, but that the culture that I was a part of is so ignorant concerning the most basic aspects of life.

As my relationships within the community developed, the children began to come over in the morning to show me the gourds they had carved, or the fruits they had picked from their farms. There was a window without any glass in it by my bed, and every morning when I woke up there was a child perched up in the tree right outside, watching me sleep. As soon as they realized that I valued their artistry and oral history and the traditions that they were rapidly losing, people began to arrive at my house with baskets, bags and stories. One morning an eight-year-old boy, Coqui, excitedly knocked on my door and proudly showed me the bow and arrow he had made by himself.

The differences between us never went away, and there were many misunderstandings that came up in our daily lives together, but there was mutual acceptance between us—qualities of care and respect that transcended the previous obstacles.

I loved to visit Don Alejandro's farm—a magical pocket amid a larger community. From the amount of visitors, you would never imagine than Don Alejandro's farm was a thirty-minute walk down the beach from the center of the village and another fifteen-minute walk into the jungle. With his large belly and hearty laugh, he always had food cooking over the fire, and people would come—with or without excuses—to visit him at any hour of the day. Walking over the plank that served as a bridge to cross the swamp, you would inevitably be greeted with a bright smile that made you feel instantly welcome. He would sit on the hammock, feeding his pigs and chickens, and tell stories about the elders or about a dog they used to have, or about the alligators that ate the chickens. As for myself, I came for the communion, for the company. Time stood still at Don Alejandro's, and before I knew it the sun would be going down and I'd have to run through the forest in the remaining light to avoid any snakes, tarantulas, or other surprises.

Some months after returning to the States, I planned a return trip to Costa Rica, and sent a letter to let my friends know I would like to come, and to ask if it was all right to visit. I received no response. Knowing that the postal system in the rain forest is unreliable, and trusting the bond that had grown between us over the years, I got on the plane and went anyway. En route to the area, the bus had a flat tire, and by the time it dropped me off at the nearest stop to their home—which was about three miles away—it was dark and rainy. I arrived at the house soaked, and called the customary, "Oopee!" to inform them that a visitor had come.

They opened the door as though they had been waiting for me all evening, and within minutes I was sipping hot coffee and eating a delicious plate of beans and rice. "So you knew I was coming?" I asked. "Oh no, we never received your letter." Nonetheless, before I even knew what they were doing, they had cleared out my old room and made my bed. The next afternoon when I returned from visiting friends in the forest, there was a pile of clean clothes on my bed. I immediately recognized them as the clothes I had left there two years before for them to distribute to others. When I asked them about this, they said, "We thought you'd come back to visit sometime, and we wanted to make sure you had enough clothes to wear when you got here!" That was hospitality! That is evidence of a living bond, which extends far beyond the ordinary limits of manners and protocol to true community.

One of the things that has saddened me the most in my travels in the Third World is that Western ideals are taking over, and there is a general loss of respect for tradition, the wisdom of the elders, the oral history, and a basic spirituality that is the connecting thread for the community. For example, one day I was deep in the rain forest in Costa Rica, hiking up very steep trails, when I came across a friend of mine with a huge boom box with cassette deck and radio on his shoulder, and his machete in the other hand. The obvious juxtaposition of the two cultures impacted me deeply in the moment; I found it truly bizarre and unsettling.

Amid all this cultural and traditional decline, in almost every place I visited there were one or two people, or a small group of people—sometimes elders and sometimes children—who had an implicit understanding of the value of their traditional culture, along with the wisdom to acknowledge that some Western ideas and technological advancements are useful and should be allowed in, while maintaining the integrity of traditional life. They often thanked me for what I contributed to their community, and years later all I can think of is how much I benefited in a lasting way from living in close proximity with these different cultures. Whatever benefits they gained from me must be small in comparison to what they gave. In retrospect, I can see that what they valued from me more than knowledge of the technological world which I brought was that a person from North America came as a friend, and interacted in very ordinary human terms with them.

Tewa of New Mexico

One of the religious ceremonies of Tewa people of New Mexico contains encoded wisdom of the profound web of relationship between human life and nature. Every morning and evening at the San Juan Pueblo, the winter chief—who has the sacred duty to lead and care for the people during the winter—stands outside and observes the exact point where the sun intersects with the mountains to the east and west. This is an activity that has enormous implications for him and his people. As soon as he determines that the sun's seasonal drift has reached its southernmost limit, the winter chief announces that it is time again for the Tewa to celebrate the winter solstice and to make preparations for the solar new year.

As the living descendents of ancient holy people whose existence is completely intertwined with the creation myth of their people, the winter chief and other designated guardians of the community known as *Towa é* trace their ancestry to the twelve brothers whom the original Corn Mothers—the first mothers of all the Tewa—sent up from the depths to watch over the people. This is their ancestral lineage, one that brings respect and meaning to a life dedicated to serving the well being of their people.

After this announcement of the winter solstice is made, the Tewa people enter into a flurry of activity to prepare for feasting and celebration in honor of "our elder the Sun."[7] All this is based on the innate, even cellular, knowledge held by so many tribal people who still cling to their spiritual traditions: that we are not separate from nature, and that our lives depend on our interconnectedness with all of the cycles and systems of nature. This ritual time indicates a very specific knowledge of the power and energy of the Sun itself, considered a deity, and the fact that all life is dependent upon this energy.

Many tribal people have an ecological sophistication equal to the most current understanding of Western science.

For example, the Desana of the Northwestern Amazon say that "the Sun's energy makes women conceive and give birth, makes the animals reproduce and the plants grow and causes the fruits to ripen," while James Lovelock, chemist, has said, "Without the decay of the Universe there could have been no Sun, and without the superabundant consumption of its energy store the sun could never have provided the light that let us be."[8]

The traditional native understanding goes even further. As one Tewa woman said, "I am holding on the sash of our elder the Sun," a metaphor for her relationship with the Sun—a relationship of awe and reverence and conscious interconnectedness, which increases her chances for well being and health.[9]

If we choose to participate in the great drama of the annual seasons of nature through gardening, hiking or camping (or by living close to the ground, so to speak); if we lie on the Earth and feel the light of the sun or moon upon our faces, we become connected with the activities that sustain life. It becomes harder to forget about their importance. Simply because our relationship to the Sun is alive, activated, we become less apathetic about the disintegration of the ozone layer. When our relationship to the grand web of life is tapped, we become informed by the wisdom of knowing that we have a place in the universe—knowledge that is received through both practical and subtle relationships to the natural world. These are the lessons we learn from indigenous, tribal people. As Bill Devall and George Sessions note in their book *Deep Ecology:*

> This is the work we call cultivating ecological consciousness. This process involves becoming more aware of the actuality of rocks, wolves, trees, and rivers—the cultivation of the insight that everything is connected. Cultivating ecological consciousness is a process of learning to appreciate silence and solitude and rediscovering how to listen. It is learning how to be more receptive, trusting, holistic in

perception . . . This process involves being honest with ourselves and seeking clarity in our intuitions, then acting from clear principles. It results in taking charge of our actions, taking responsibility, practicing self-discipline and working honestly within our community. It is simple but not easy work.[10]

People of highly technological cultures do not intend to destroy the Earth; we have just been so far removed from our relationship to it that we have forgotten that our interdependence with the Earth makes us responsible for it. If we slow down long enough to be in community and communion with the Earth, to hear our conversation with the Earth—these environmental and social issues begin to have a vitality, an applicability to the passion and meaning of daily life. As author Peter Russell maintained in his book *The Global Brain,* we are the extended body of the planetary being that is the Earth, so that human beings represent the nervous system, or consciousness, of the vast organism that is our planet Earth. Russell refers to this being as Gaia, drawing upon the ancient Greek mythology of a goddess who is the symbol of the Earth. The Gaia Hypothesis assumes that the Earth is a whole living system of which we are a part. And as physicist Fritjof Capra reflects, this holistic ecological view has spiritual or religious implications:

> Ecological awareness and ecological consciousness goes far beyond science, and at the deepest level it joins with religious awareness and religious experience. Because at the deepest level, ecological awareness is an awareness of the fundamental interconnectedness and interdependence of all phenomena and of this embeddedness in the cosmos . . . This is where ecology and religion meet . . . The worldview now emerging from modern science is an

ecological view, and ecological awareness at its deepest level is spiritual or religious awareness.[11]

A Growing Compassion

In our commitment to live a conscious, productive, affirming and spiritually-inspired life, our actions become more important because we know they affect more than just ourselves and our immediate environment. We realize that we are responsible not only for ourselves, but to others, to our environment and to the cosmos. Most people think of personal freedom as doing whatever they want to do, based on media images of self-centered pleasures: "getting away from it all," "taking the phone off the hook," or "being rich enough not to care what others think," and so on. But, as author and activist Bo Lozoff points out, "Human beings exist in relation to each other. Real personal freedom is being able to respond to whatever our situation or circumstances require from us. Ability to respond. Respond-ability. Responsibility." [12]

The Native American view is that whenever one makes a decision, one should think of its effect down to the seventh generation. Robert Bly calls this a vertical thought, the opposite of which would be a decision based on immediate or short-term profits. According to Bly, in vertical thought there is no distinction between men and women, and one becomes an elder when one learns to think vertically. As we are transformed by the power of community to broaden our perspective beyond that of the isolated individual, we begin to link our lives to the greater whole, going toward both the ancestral past and future relations.

The impetus to become fully responsible individuals doesn't stem from guilt, but from compassion—for ourselves, for others, for the suffering that is experienced in the "human condition." When we see the faces of starving children throughout the world, perhaps we feel we "should" do something about their hunger. But do our donations make a real difference? I am not suggesting that we neglect to share financially, but I am advocating that we question what will be most effective in healing our world.

Entering a greater field of compassion may be the first prerequisite for answering this question. Growing a capacity for compassion is a conscious act that actively draws one into authentic relatedness. Compassion means to "suffer with" another, and we can only do that if we are in relationship, feeling into our common human bond at the most basic bodily levels—feeling into the community that exists at the heart of the world.

Community—A Way of Transformation

Many people have come to the conclusion, after years of social activism that real change begins within the individual. They have found that the greatest means to achieve world peace, to end hunger, protect children and the environment, and to preserve the life forms and ecological systems that comprise the planet Earth is to seek personal transformation, and that personal transformation is more accessible in the bonded company of others—in *community*.

Once we find ourselves living in community, we are challenged to become more compassionate and receptive, more able to listen, to hear, to be physically connected with all of existence. Regardless of how we arrive at the relocation of culture, we find that our experience in community leads us deeper into a transformational journey that is bigger than our individual selves. The way opens out into more global, spiritual and humanitarian considerations. The personal feeds the transpersonal in a pattern of reciprocal flow, so that the more "enlightened" and conscious one's interaction with the world becomes, the more enlightened and conscious the individual becomes.

The impetus for personal transformation urges us to align ourselves to a higher vision—a way of life that is affirming, joyful, compassionate and wise; a way of life that springs from our inherent knowledge of how to best serve, beginning with our own families, friends and acquaintances, and spreading out to the world at large. When we align ourselves to make a contribution to the world and serve others, we align ourselves to our rightful purpose. That is what we are really hungry for and what fulfills our longing for meaning. Community and the company of others is the rich and fertile arena in which we may discover and live out that purpose. Anne's story, which follows, is a testimony to the transformational possibility that service in community affords.

Anne Speaks About Service and Transformation

When my mother was diagnosed with inoperable cancer, it was a shock to us all. She was, after all, still young and vibrant—only sixty-two years old—and had an irrepressible exuberance and great enjoyment of life. Everyone loved her for this enthusiasm and for the heart-felt empathy that was completely natural to her.

During the last two months of her life she was completely bedridden and suffering profoundly. Her body was in a state of degeneration; all of its systems were expiring slowly, and she required twenty-four hour care. My sister and I were both married with children, working and living in other states, but clearly our stepfather was not able to handle her care by himself. We made the decision to do whatever we had to in order to keep our mother at home. Taking some leave from our jobs we came to Georgia to care for Mother in the last of her days so that she wouldn't have to spend them in the local hospital. We knew only too well how much it meant to her to be able to lay in the rented hospital bed which we set up in the den by the fireplace, where she could look out the window through the wintry pine trees to see the sun shining on the lake like diamonds only a hundred feet away.

Our last days with her were incredibly bittersweet as we watched and cared for her during her final struggle in life. We had

21

tremendous moments of communion between us and with her, and we shared as much laughter as we shared tears. As Mother struggled with letting go, we gained our strength from each other as a family, with the help of the local hospice nurse and visiting volunteer. Without their steady, firm and caring presence, we would have been lost in moments when Mother's pain became unmanageable; or when we were still holding on too tightly for her to be able to let go; or when she became angry and denied the fact that she was days or hours away from death. They guided us with sensitivity and real concern not only for Mother, but for ourselves—the bereaved. The physical support and experience, which they shared so freely with us, made it possible for our family to embrace and serve our mother in her dying and death in a way that was extraordinarily enriching to us as human beings and as a family.

A few months after Mother's death, I moved to another state. In my new city I discovered a large and successful hospice organization with an excellent training program for volunteers. I enrolled immediately, and found that not only was my own grieving for the death of my mother supported and nurtured in this process of connecting with the hospice community, but that something even more significant happened as I graduated from their training program and began to serve a family with a ten-year-old girl who had terminal leukemia. My horizons on the world had suddenly broadened; I began to consider in a whole new way the nature of compassion, what it meant to serve others and what tremendous benefits are reaped by the one who is serving. I began to realize in an immediate, practical way how truly we do feel the suffering of others. In hospice, the volunteer—as well as the trained professionals, the nurses and social workers—walks into the family home as a stranger, and in most cases becomes a bonded part of the family very quickly because of the intensity of the circumstance and the great need which is being met. It is a humbling experience to be able to meet another person in that extreme moment of human suffering, and to be able to serve that person. I found out that it was a great blessing to me to have the opportunity to help in even the smallest way. A glass of water, a gentle word, a quiet, understanding presence—these are the things the dying accept from us. And it is really all we can do, because they journey on alone. For the living, it is as simple as running an errand, taking some small responsibility off of the shoulders of the bereaved, reading a book to a child, sitting and listening, saying and doing nothing but holding a hand while tears fall. These moments forge unforgettable bonds, and for the volunteers and professionals and the dying and the bereaved family and friends who make up the community of hospice, these shared realities and experiences create a common link in which our mutual humanity—our fragility, strength, beauty and dignity—is made conscious, appreciated, tasted, absorbed and then fed back into the stream of life.

The death of her mother became Anne's connecting link to community and sparked a personal transformation for Anne. Less than a year after her mother died, Anne joined an intentional community where she has continued to live and thrive for over ten years.

For the great majority of people in the Western world today, living in an intentional residential community will not be a life choice, unless cultural and environmental change forces such a return to a village or communal life. Instead, most people will find community through the many different avenues they traverse in their daily lives. They will align with communities that are resonant with their basic interests and concerns about life. Community will be experienced in group worship, in a neighborhood project, in meetings with co-workers, in therapy sessions or 12-Step programs. But for those who have tasted the fruits of both struggle and joy in a bonded, intentional community over a period of years, or those who have lived in a culture seeking true wholeness, the recognition is clear that community is the only sane alternative in a world steeped in confusion, violence and profound separation.

CHAPTER TWO

At the Roots of Things

A single protein molecule or a single finger print, a single syllable on the radio or a single idea of yours, implies the whole historical reach of stellar and organic evolution. It is enough to make you tingle all the time.
—John Platt, biophysicist

It is the story of all life that is holy and is good to tell, and of us two-leggeds, sharing in it with the four-leggeds and the wings of the air and all green things; for these are children of one mother and their father is one Spirit.
—Black Elk, Sioux elder

Community has its roots at the foundation of life, for which the body is both a workable metaphor and a practical reality. Our bodies, the Earth and the concrete structures of practical daily life are the underpinnings of all that we can dream, create or aspire to be. We begin our exploration into community as transformational possibility with the body, therefore, because it represents that matrix from which all else becomes possible.

The creation of a life-positive culture that sustains its people starts at the roots of things. Creating sacred spaces, gardening, cooking, providing hospitality for guests, song, dance and art all of these are the domain of culture within community. These are the simple daily events in a continuum of life that have the potential to transform us, to teach us how to grow, mature and live in wisdom and compassion.

Food and Feast

He who is rooted in the soil endures. —Carl Jung

We take a big step toward community when we begin to share food with others. Sometimes this community-building aspect of food shows up in the most ordinary or unexpected circumstances. When I visited my parents recently, my father casually expressed his love for a certain food. I knew I could make this dish for him and make it better than any restaurant, so I offered to do so. I didn't realize the extent to which this gesture would become an extraordinary medium for sharing love within my family. My mother and I spent time together in the local markets gathering the ingredients, my brother managed the charcoal grill for the vegetables and my nephews joined in by helping me prepare the meal. The kitchen was full of warmth, laughter and fun as all of us worked together. When we sat down together the food tasted extraordinary, not because of the ingredients necessarily, but because of the mood that was generated around it. We had created something more than the usual familial bond over supper; we had created community.

Food is about as basic and fundamental to human life as one can get. Traditionally, community life revolved around the planting, growing, harvesting, preserving, preparing, cooking, serving and cleaning up of food. Most of the great tribal (or shamanistic) and pagan sacred days were marked with feasting as a symbolic act, a tradition that we see reflected in popular modern holidays like Thanksgiving, Christmas and Easter. Food is the obvious, physical manifestation of the emotional and spiritual nurturing that human beings need. It has been honored as such since the beginning of human life.

Many of us intuit that our holiday celebrations and feasts and even our daily meals are sacred. Native peoples have an instinctual and yet spiritually profound knowledge of the subtle relationships between food and that which eats it. Every time we eat, there is a sacrifice underlying that act; another life form has been sacrificed so that we human beings may live and thrive.

> By accepting the warm, energy- and nutrient-laden carcass as a supreme gift, and by honoring its willing sacrifice by respectfully handling its physical remains, the hunter confirms and revitalizes the sacred contract between human beings and kindred animals. His empathy for the elegant creature and his sense of its place in the cosmos compels him to communicate with the deceased deer and its unborn descendants with the same reverence with which he addresses his own family members and ancestors . . . In the end, this minute interspecies bond is dwarfed by the sheer size and grandeur of [a] larger, fluid, yet orderly universe, in which the fates of countless other elements are destined daily to intersect.[1]

This "interspecies bond" is equally true with the plant world as it is for the animal world, for native peoples all over the world acknowledge that animals and plants, as well as rocks, wind, water and sky are all imbued with spiritual force and are therefore alive and sacred. Whatever we take from nature to sustain our lives is "sacrificed" for us. This is perhaps the most basic form of hospitality: the Earth provides all, and human beings are the most fortunate recipients of this bounty.

Gardens are sacred spaces, and they contribute to our quality of life in ways that are intangible and unmeasurable. In my community we garden organically, grow our own sprouts, make our own yogurt from raw milk, bake bread occasionally and adhere to a simple vegetarian diet—with the exception of certain feasting days. There is tremendous satisfaction and richness of spirit in our daily diet. Our attention to food begins with our garden, which is a group effort, with one person at "source."

Not only does the garden produce high-quality vegetables, herbs and beautiful flowers for our table, it also provides an opportunity for working together in cooperation and even delight toward our mutual good, and in a way that is in harmony with the rhythms of the Earth. Sister Miriam MacGillis, the founder and director of Genesis Farm, and a spokesperson for ecological awareness, shares how growing food relates to one's spiritual life:

> It [growing food] puts you right in touch with the miracle of existence, that life comes so gratuitously . . . that we even exist. Why do we exist? Why were we called into being? Why is life the way it is? Why is existence the way it is? And of course I do believe in a Divine Being, for whom I have no name, no image. 'God' just is not adequate anymore . . . But the wonder of existence, the joy of it, the total gratuitousness of it; it nurtures my soul, opens it; it wants to burst into song at why or how God [started it off]. And why shouldn't it be in the future? Why shouldn't all species . . . all people . . . everyone hold communion? It's Eucharist . . . touching the very mystery by which God creates. You are touching that creation by taking that food in. You are participating at one level in the wonder of the whole thing . . . That kind of conscious eating is very important.[2]

Gardening in itself is a big part of many if not most intentional communities, as well as neighborhood communities who pool resources to garden together on empty city lots. Gardening cares for the body of the community—our individual and collective body and health—by providing fresh, wholesome food, homegrown with conscious care and attention. Gardening also cares for the Earth—when we garden organically, for example. Organic gardening has been likened to a form of meditation or spiritual practice, in fact, because its implications reach out in many directions. We re-establish and sustain a conscious, supportive relationship with the Earth by gardening in a way that replenishes the soil through composting (which makes use of kitchen scraps and unused food, as well as manure, leaves, grass clippings and other organic refuse) and planting in harmony with seasonal and cyclic flows of the Earth. And such gardening provides physical exercise for the body and also has a contemplative dimension to it as well. Gardening can instill a deep peace within the gardener; it gives us time and space to reflect and know ourselves. Gardening is a form of intimacy—with oneself and with that Being who cradles and sustains us all, the Earth. Gardening also lends itself to ritual and creating beauty. Many gardens are like sculptures or altars by both intentional and natural design; to walk or work in them nourishes the soul in many intangible ways.

Flower gardens are found in most world cultures. We cannot measure the importance of beauty in the maintenance or transformation of the human spirit. Who doesn't like to rest their eyes on a full bouquet of flowers, rampant with color and the inspired designs of nature, and fragrant with perfume? This too is a kind of food that satisfies the hunger of the senses, and can be an integral part of the whole picture of a transformational culture in community.

The following reflections on community gardening are from Laramie, a long-time gardener and community resident.

Laramie Speaks About the Garden

There is a lot more to growing food together in our community garden than just the pleasure and practical use of the food that might come from our labors. Physical food is one type of food that comes out of the garden to feed the community, but there are some subtle types of food that the gardeners are also responsible for. There is an emotional or energetic component of food that impacts the community. Whenever people are working and communicating together on any project a energetic or electromagnetic field that has psychic and emotional components comes into play. When we are growing food we are actually imprinting the ground itself as we interact with it, and that applies also to the seeds that we plant. The vegetables that we harvest and carry up to the kitchen to be cleaned and used for food, all the different stages of growing a garden—digging up the ground, meeting together to work on the project—create very complex psychic and emotional relationships between the people working in and on the garden, and in anyone who comes in contact with the garden via eating the food. In this way gardens can become healing places, so that even someone coming to look at the garden can receive a healing, strengthening communication from the "food" that exists in the garden at all these levels.

Any good gardener can make a garden produce food. The next step up from ordinary gardening would be organic gardening, which creates a reciprocal relationship with the Earth. As our relationship to the garden evolves, another step could be to take into account these subtle and physical forces, and how they work together. That includes how the forces of moon and sun work together with the land and soil, and the heightened growing influences that arise from our conscious relationship to the garden and between the people who are working in the garden. I try to be attuned to these physical and subtle forces that are part of the total food-growing experience in the community garden. In this way, a community garden can produce much more than simply the tangible and physical fruits from it that one sees with the ordinary eye.

Simply producing food is a huge asset and contribution to the life of the community, but as we become more interested in the possibilities of personal transformation in community, these other factors become more important and apparent to us. Relationships between people, and between people and things, affect the total picture of the environment and work synergistically to create something; this is exactly the same principle as how community on a larger scale can generate something intangible that is beneficial for the world at large.

Every person on the garden crew is an important part of creating this possibility of subtle "food" in the garden. If I am an enlightened gardener, then what I am doing—my mood and attitudes becomes impregnated in the essence of the food. Of course this principle applies to any work that is being done in community, whether it is dishwashing or working in the community cottage industry. We all have the opportunity, because of the synergy and transformational possibility in community, to contribute to our lives together and to the health of the community in general.

In her book Passionate Enlightenment, *Miranda Shaw tells the story of a woman, a Buddhist teacher, who set three tasks for people who wanted to become her students: to build a stupa, or religious shrine for the community and maintain it; to heal a schism within the community and to be a active healing force for healing schisms within the community; and thirdly they had to provide a garden for their community, whether small or large.[3] These tasks created a receptivity and sensitivity in people that made it possible for them to really absorb her teaching. But more importantly, gardening was considered a profound healing activity of the Bodhisattva, or enlightened being, who works tirelessly for the benefit of all sentient beings.*

I am inspired by this idea because I know how far-reaching the effects of a community garden can be. Too often those of us living in community get caught up in all the other important business of the day—generating money for the community, taking care of crises and just maintaining the daily schedule of work that must be done. When this happens, we need to remember the vital importance of the garden as a healing force on many levels for the community, and even for the world.

The Mood of the Food

Food is a symbol of nurturance, of the archetypal Great Mother, of the bounty and abundant blessings of the Divine. In modern times, much of what passes for food is laden with chemicals, overly processed, and virtually poisonous to the human body and spirit. On the other hand, food can be a kind of manna or nectar. This transformational possibility for food that is begun in our garden is continued in how our food is handled and prepared and in how mealtimes are conducted. The inherent elegance and order and protocol of spaces where food is served is important to honor, as is the protocol of relationship during meals. A meal in which the latest tragedy or act of violence being touted on television or in which a cruel piece of gossip is the main topic of discussion will be very different in mood and bodily impact than a meal in which the discussion turns to fine literature, or something inspiring that happened during the day, or the children's exciting projects.

When people in community have their own individual food "stashes" or personal preferences which are indulged privately, it sooner or later leads to isolation and separation from others, whereas sharing food, and agreeing on dietary guidelines brings people together. This important dynamic is exemplified in most tribal cultures that have maintained their integrity against the onslaught of Western intervention: the same foods are cultivated, gathered or hunted together, food is shared and everyone eats basically the same thing. In modern intentional community, food and dietary considerations must be an expression of the shared context of the community, to which its members have agreed in principle. This does not mean that the community should not also have the wisdom to allow for necessary differences, for example in the instance of specific health needs; this too requires thoughtful discernment and individual integrity as to what is really needed.

Some of the most important celebratory events of all communities center around food. The excitement builds as fragrant smells waft through the house, or are borne on the breeze through open windows. Anticipation of the feast and the attendant communion between bonded friends and loved ones and guests makes the eyes shine with pleasure. On many occasions I have chosen to fast prior to the meal on a particular feast day in order to build a certain receptivity and sensitivity within myself. A mood of celebration and communion opens the possibility of invoking a particular group energy that is ecstatic and provides a sumptuous "feast" of the spirit. We come away from such a meal fulfilled in a way that is almost inexpressible. On these happy occasions when the heart has been so touched, we may feel "drunk" just on the "wine" of good company, when we have imbibed nothing stronger than water or herb tea!

The following comments on food and cooking were contributed by Joli, a passionate enthusiast of the culinary arts, who has lived and cooked in community for over fifteen years.

A Cook Speaks About Food

Food is the body and the blood of the Divine. We commonly know this as a metaphor, but many cultures consider this to be literally so—all the way from Adam and Eve eating the first apple to holy communion in Christianity, in which the food is a symbol of the body and blood of Christ, to eating certain animal parts because they have a way of healing or infusing that same part in your body with strength and vitality. For example, when I had hepatitis, my naturopathic doctor recommended that I eat raw liver to strengthen my own liver. Some tribes say if you eat brains it directly feeds the mind, or if you eat the heart then your own heart is strengthened. In Judaism there are also foods that are eaten as representations of specific qualities that represent aspects of human relationship with the Divine: bitter, sweet, salty and so on. The Native Americans have a sacred relationship to corn, or to the buffalo, such that these living substances or creatures are deified as Corn Mother or White Buffalo Woman. In Hinduism, food is used as prasad, *or a sacred gift that has the power to bless. This attitude toward food encompasses a relationship of reciprocity and gratitude to the Divine for providing sustenance and abundance.*

Reverence is a big part of this kind of relationship to food, which can extend to all spaces and actions and objects having to do with food—tools, knives, chopsticks, wooden spoons. One begins to cultivate this kind of reverence toward all of life. When I pick flowers, for example, I always thank the plant for its gift, and I tell the plant how the flower is going to be used. When I take food from the garden, I do the same, and when I cook, I thank the food, even out loud sometimes, for its offering or sacrifice—not just for me and my hungry stomach, so to speak, but for its contribution to the ongoing evolution of the Divine in the world.

One thing I have experimented with is being mindful of my relationship to food in many different ways. When I go to the store or market I like to take the first piece of fruit or vegetable that I handle. What that does is strengthen my focus in choosing the food, rather than mindlessly handling, picking up and putting down anything and everything I see without thought or care for the food.

Another principle I work with is to not taste at all while I am cooking. The purpose of this is very similar; I've found that it forces me to focus with intention about what it is I am wanting to prepare, and to stop and be present with what I'm going to make and connect to what the food is speaking. It encourages simplicity and elegance, so that if I am going to make a vegetable soup, I can prepare my broth, prepare the vegetables, and come up to the point at which I am ready to spice the soup. Then I can either go to the spice cabinet and wildly start pulling out every spice that I think would be good in a soup—savory, rosemary, basil, dill, marjoram, etc. Or, I can be present with the soup as it is, and attempt to listen, to feel into what the vegetables, in the richness of their own

33

flavor and essence, have created in this harmonious chemistry with each other. From there, I might just choose basil.

I've been cooking and managing kitchens for many years—both professionally in a popular restaurant and in the community I live in—and I've developed a passion for the subtle possibilities of cooking for others and of food in general. A good example of what I'm talking about was depicted in the popular art film, Like Water For Chocolate, *some years ago, in which the main character, a young woman, cooks one magical meal that transforms the petty problems and bickering of her family and friends. I've tried to be a vehicle for those subtle possibilities while cooking, rather than cooking from my own self-centered insular motivation.*

If the tenzo *(a Zen term for the cook or primary person who manages the kitchen) has prepared the meal with this kind of intention, the logical progression would be that the guests or the community-at-large would then partake of the very mood that has infused his or her actions all along the way. The soup then has the possibility to contribute the same simplicity, intention and elegance in the dining space and within the individuals who eat it, rather than fickleness and chaos and frantic, scattered energy or scarcity. I've seen the latter approach of cooking contribute to a loud, inelegant, indigestible dining experience riddled with competition, greed and scarcity. On the other hand, a meal that is prepared with intention, consciousness, quiet self-reflection, contemplation and that is relational with the food itself (as a reminder or aspect of the Divine), contributes to a mood of joyous celebration, sanctity and gratitude. This latter mood might be full of laughter, conversation, children telling stories and delighting over a large plate of spaghetti, or it could be very still, quiet and contemplative. It is not a question of form, but one of subtle presence or mood.*

Food is one avenue of our lives where we tend to exhibit scarcity, greed, indulgence, fear, addiction etc. If those qualities or tendencies show up in our relationship to food, then you can be

*sure that they also show up in relationship to other aspects of life—
to our spouses and children, to money, to work and projects and so
on. When one begins to focus this kind of intention in relationship
to food, then the scarcity, greed and indulgence begins to be transformed, which then affects other areas of our lives as well.*

Food is a primary element in how we build a rich culture
together. Living in community we must remember to return again
and again to an attitude of sacredness around food and the sharing of food. When meals become too institutionalized, food loses
its quality of soul and becomes empty, unsatisfying. The intimacy
of bonded relationships and communion suffers or is lost alto-
gether. The community begins to lose its buoyancy and vibrancy.
When the food that is served in community is full of life force and
imbued with love and care, it is reflected in the physical, psychological and spiritual health of the members of the community.

Hospitality

Food is only one aspect of hospitality, and yet
these two are intertwined. The law of hospitality is one of the
most ancient principles known to civilization, and in many cultures it takes precedence over all other considerations. To provide hospitality to another is a great blessing and boon to the
host, and is not only an act of kindness and generosity, but a
sacred act.

In India, the guest is honored as an expression and individual spark of that totality which is the Divine, seen as living
within all beings; to provide food and hospitality for a guest is
therefore considered an auspicious privilege and spiritual boon
in the Hindu tradition. This tradition comes to life today in places
like Anandashram in Kerala State, Western India. There, until
her death in 1988, Mataji Krishnabai, who was the devoted disciple and feminine counterpart of Swami Papa Ramdas, a revered

35

holy man and teacher who established Anandashram—made it her life's work to feed the poor, the untouchables and the wandering *sadhus* or holy people of India. Today, that tradition is continued on. Anandashram remains one of the places in India where food is freely distributed to the hungry and destitute.

Another example of hospitality is witnessed in the life of the Indian saint, Ramana Maharshi, whose devotees always tried to serve him first and to give him the best of what was available. Ramana Maharshi made a point, however, by refusing to eat until everyone else had been served, including his disciples, the beggars and even the ashram animals—cows, monkeys and peacocks. Once he was given a large mango to eat, but when he noticed that others weren't served mango he refused to eat it and gave it to the crowd.

Ashrams, monasteries and the hospices of old Europe have provided hospitality and places for retreat for thousands of years. Tribal people have the same instinctive understanding of the nobility inherent in honoring the guest. In a contemporary culture characterized by isolation, survival angst and fear of strangers, we have forgotten the spiritual pleasure of greeting, accepting and embracing the invited or unexpected guest at the door. Once we begin to open our hearts, to widen our circle of compassion, to fling the doors open, to live from an expectation of abundance, however, we begin to rediscover the joy of sharing with and caring for others. Anyone who has traveled extensively knows how much this kind of generosity of spirit is appreciated when one is on the road—a friendly welcome, a good meal with good company, a clean bed. But hospitality must be given freely, without expectation of return, even though there is a reciprocity that is catalyzed when one begins to live according to the laws of hospitality. One always receives in kind, in return, but not necessarily in a linear or rational manner.

The law of hospitality applies to the guest as well, and there are many ways in which one can repay the graciousness of one's host that are not based in monetary standards. Not all guests know how to repay their hosts in this way, but the gracious host will be repaid, sooner or later, in one form or another.

I have done a great deal of traveling over the years, and have discovered several things that are clear gestures of honor and respect toward one's host. These gestures include eating gratefully and graciously whatever is served, offering to participate in work that needs to be done if the host allows, taking only what is offered with real gratitude and making no demands (unless absolutely necessary, such as in the case of illness), cultivating a keen sensitivity to the culture and needs and wishes of the host and then adhering to the standards of that culture, or aligning to the host's needs and wishes. For example, if the host seems tired at 9:00 P.M., then one might offer to retire early as a basic gesture of sensitivity and regard for the other.

Joli On Hospitality

Cooking for people is an offering of hospitality. The idea of hospitality often centers around food or drink, because you are offering the Earth—the waters, the plants, the rocks, what the Earth gives of itself freely—so that one is hooking up heaven and earth. The one offering hospitality enters into the archetypal role—the emissary, the messenger, or in some cases, guardian angel—between Mother Earth and Father Sky.

For me, the core symbol of hospitality is the person offering the cool drink of water; it's not the fancy, gourmet meal, the expensive wine, the Belgian chocolate—although these things can also be offered in this spirit. We need to go back to the basics to grasp what the principle of true hospitality really is, so that we are not fooled by glamorous imposters. Another important aspect of true hospitality is that one has no attachment to how it is received, so it is given purely for the sake of giving. There is no need for accolades and acknowledgement, or even thanks—even though the reciprocity in hospitality, from a practical standpoint, makes it equally important to be a good guest, in which case saying "Thank you" is quite welcomed.

Most of the great spiritual traditions contain this idea of what in Sufism and Judaism is called "the Guest," or "the Stranger." By serving the guest we have the opportunity to offer refreshment in the most profound sense of the word, to the Guest of God. Every occasion for hosting or for offering hospitality has this as an ultimate possibility. It happens anytime you have the chance to give: a comfortable pillow, a cool drink of water, a chair when someone is standing, a shady spot when you are standing talking in the sun and you see that your friend is squinting. In the religious traditions that speak of the Stranger or the Guest, the person you are offering the shade to is none other than the Divine. That is the essence and the inspiration underlying our acts of hospitality to others.

Being a good host means that we think of doing or giving things that our guests would like, not what we ourselves would like or find convenient to give. A good example of this occurred years ago when the restaurant where I worked was hosting a group of scientists from Japan who were traveling around the U.S. studying atmospheric research. This group had been hosted all over the country, and had even dined at the White House. Our city was the last stop on their tour. We decided to give them a real American meal, even though we could have provided a lovely traditional Japanese meal. The menu we chose for this event was baked and fried chicken with mashed potatoes and gravy, vegetables and pecan pie à la mode for dessert. At the end of the meal the group expressed their gratitude, saying, "Everywhere we have gone in America, friends have fed us sushi and Japanese food, when we were craving real American food! Thank you so much for this delightful meal!" We found out that their American translators had been unclear about what the guests really wanted to eat, and had been mistakenly telling their hosts to serve Japanese food.

When they realized their mistake, it was too far into their visit to make a difference, but somehow we had intuited what would be most appreciated—and it was! The evening was a celebratory feast that became also an event of good will and mutual respect among strangers of very different cultures.

Guests provide an important element in the ongoing cross-pollination that can occur as we open up to new experiences and share of our own bounty, both physically and spiritually. Even providing hospitality to a stranger or a friend overnight or for a weekend can lead to undiscovered possibilities in human relationship: a new friendship, an exchange of ideas and values, an opportunity to simply serve another person a meal.

The world needs more neighborhood barbecues and fish fries, weekend picnics and bake sales. Like the expanding ripples that circle out from the center of a pond when a stone is thrown in, such events spark many other cooperative and community-oriented efforts. What would happen if neighborhoods all over the country began to can and preserve food together during the harvest times of August and September? What would happen if we went back to baking cookies and bread and cakes for each other, for no reason, or to celebrate the season, a holiday, or the long-forgotten birthday of the elderly shut-in down the street? And what if this was done *en masse?* How would this change the direction our Western culture is heading in? These old fashioned ways of sharing food and hospitality lead us back to the true spirit of community. What if instead of using the impersonal atmosphere of a restaurant as a way to relieve stress and be entertained, we spent that time sharing food with others outside of our family or household, forging new friendships and simply enjoying each other's company? What if we were expansive and flexible enough to encompass and embrace many new people, to feed whomever came to our door, both literally and figuratively?

Creating Sacred Spaces

Consciously caring for spaces is an essential part of building a real community culture. A garden is obviously a space that is alive, but any room or place can become sacred depending on what kind of intention the community has for that space. In my community we consider all spaces to be sacred. To create and sustain that, we have to give respect, care and attention to those spaces. This includes paying attention to the protocol based on the purpose of the space. Sometimes this protocol is written down and talked about among everyone; or it may never even be spoken, but it's still there. In many instances it takes some sensitivity to "sense out" protocol.

Protocol in spaces usually comes out of a general community agreement, but that agreement evolves out of and is informed by the space itself. For instance, when people enter a meditation hall they generally know it's not a place to carry on a casual conversation—although there will always be those few who do have to be told. The protocol of other spaces may be less obvious, however. Many people who are new to community don't know that it isn't a great idea to barge into the kitchen and start doing their own thing when the cook is preparing the communal meal. That is true of any space where people are working—in the woodworking shop or in the greenhouse or pottery shed. Everyone appreciates it when someone walks into a place where others are working and asks, "Can I use this bench? Can I use this tool? Can I chop veggies over here?"

The responsibility of the steward or caretaker of any space is that he or she is taking care of all the functional dimensions of the space—to clean, beautify and so on. But the steward of a space is also responsible for the space on other levels as well, just as the gardeners are responsible for the subtle dynamics of the garden and what it produces. Ideally, the caretaker would be an example of the context for the space, which involves being sensitive and attentive to what the space is asking for, and then responding accordingly. During our yearly celebrations, for example, a team of attendants keep vigil in our meditation hall, maintaining this room with special care so that is it is available for those who wish to use it, as well as assuring, by their own meditation and silence, that it remains a contemplative hub in the midst of all the activity that a celebration affords.

Spaces evolve, or have an evolution of their own. In the beginning of my community the kitchen was a free-flowing space, with people going in and out and making sandwiches for themselves. Every person decided what they would have for breakfast and then made it, just like back at home in the family they grew up in. Only one meal a day was eaten communally. Our casual relationship to the kitchen and to food was reinforcing a habitual way of doing things—in the kitchen and everywhere else. Now we have a cook who plans, manages and cooks our meals, and who takes responsibility for the kitchen and what happens there: how food is served and how the clean-up goes, and so on. Everyone eats together at the same time every day, breakfast, lunch and dinner. We no longer go into the kitchen casually. This transition was gradual and took some real willingness on the part of individuals to change. The effort and attention involved in this change has made us all more conscious of the sacred nature of food preparation and eating.

Some people in community are advocates of the free-flowing style we had in those early years. Some have a real aversion to any kind of formality. My experience is that having people in positions of responsibility and authority with regard to certain functions and spaces is a good thing. It's important in building community to be willing to cooperate with the parameters that are set up so that daily life can have an elegance and order that is beneficial to the group, as well as to one's personal growth and development.

Sometimes it is the internal "heat" that is generated when one is willing to cooperate for the good of the whole—when doing so goes against one's psychological tendencies, as in the case of a more formal kitchen management and relationship to food—that makes personal transformation in community possible. Thus, instead of making our own breakfast, we eat what has been prepared for everyone. This daily exercise has the potential to make us more flexible, more resilient, more giving and thoughtful of others, and more expansive.

Attention to detail in a space takes things out of the domain of being casual. In community, as in most situations, being carelessly casual ends up as sloppiness, which leads to poor time management and energy management, which leads to breakdowns of all kinds in the systems that manage daily life. So the more we pay attention to detail, the less sloppy, disorganized and scattered both spaces and people will be. Attention and focus is also necessary to bringing a space to life. The more attention we pay to details, the more "alive" the room or space is, whether it's a kitchen or a living room.

Attention to detail revolves around really ordinary stuff. For example, candles in a meditation space should always be long enough to get through the meditation period without burning out. A small detail, but important. Or, when setting the space for a communal meal, it is a good policy to set a few extra places just in case last minute guests arrive. In that way, the space is always prepared to welcome people and provide hospitality.

Then there is the whole science of geomancy—dealing with such details as where the windows and doors are; what the natural flow of the traffic is; where plants are placed; the direction in which the furniture is arranged and so on. While the subject of geomancy goes far beyond the scope of this book, it is fascinating and worth studying, especially if we are in the midst of creating or building entirely new spaces.

A community space is a reflection of the state of the community simply because everybody is responsible for that space. Private spaces like bedrooms are also reflections of their inhabitants. For example, most people's bedrooms demonstrate their inner state—their state of consciousness. A bedroom that is clean and orderly usually bespeaks a person with some degree of self-discipline and clarity. I have a friend who is in charge of a woodshop. The space is a mess that is always in the process of getting organized or cleaned up, but somehow always remains a mess. It is full of stuff that he will never use. It's interesting that he listens to the radio all the time—to talk shows, news, whatever. He fills up his mind with useless stuff, and his work-space reflects that perfectly.

Through trial and error I have found out that I can't control what people do in and to spaces that I consider sacred. Trying to control others only creates more friction. That doesn't mean there aren't boundaries around what can be done in a space, but to try and manipulate people because I may have a more developed or sophisticated view of what needs to be done in a space is just going to create more dissonance and inelegance in the space. If someone does something in a space that is really out of line, the person can be provided with information or guidance at a later time. But it is also important to allow people to feel comfortable in their own way in the space as a principle of hospitality, which applies not just to guests, but to those who are residents in community.

When people are breaching unspoken protocol and are not reprimanded in some way for it, they are given the opportunity come to the realization for themselves of what is appropriate behavior. Most of us have the sensitivity and conscience to come to an awareness of what is right behavior in any situation. When we discover something essential about being elegant or tasteful in relationship with others and with spaces in this way, it has a completely different impact. The realization belongs to us personally

43

when we come to it on our own. In addition, when we notice that, "Nobody said anything!" that too makes a communication.

One of my jobs has been to serve food in my community. In the beginning I was of the opinion that people were making pigs of themselves, so I used to try to limit the food. As a result, I became very stingy. Eventually, I realized that dictating to others how much to eat was in direct conflict with the mood of the space, which was about generosity, abundance and hospitality. What I really needed to do—rather than police everybody else—was to serve with magnanimity, and that meant putting myself aside.

Speech provides a similar example. Conversation in spaces cannot be dictated to people. The rigidity with which we try to dictate behavior to others—in an attempt to serve the protocol of a space—inevitably backfires, and we are suddenly acting in the same way that we were so righteous about in others. When we "listen" to what is organically true of a space, then the intention of the space itself calls us to be in a way that is in harmony, whether it is a kitchen, library, play area for children or formal meeting room.

Entertainment

Living together in community replaces restaurants, television, and shopping malls (the entertainment choices of isolation and alienation) with group games, storytelling, skits, or just sitting around a fire with a cup of tea and talking or reading—old-fashioned fun that requires that we relate with others. When we stop running from relationship, we suddenly find that there is time for inspiration and creativity as well—for arts and crafts, for weaving, pottery, woodworking, painting, music, song, for writing, for poetry and reading. In this way what was fragmented and separate in our lives becomes coherent and linked in community. Life then has a continuity and becomes a circle that expands to encompass one set of experiences after another, with relationship at the center, rather than a series of separate lines laid out in a linear or rigid order. This continuity has a calming effect on the human nervous system. As we stop running around frantically seeking more stimulation, we quiet down, center ourselves and soften the hardened shell of modern life that has grown around us. We begin to *feel* more deeply. We begin to realize our place in the community of the world and we live more lightly on the Earth—consuming, taking and demanding less.

Entertainment should be recreational—that is, it should re-create us. We should feel rejuvenated by the pleasure we experience through entertainment. Too often entertainment is draining; for example, movies that depict unconscionable violence and degradation of the human spirit abound in mainstream Western culture. Addictions come into play in any consideration of entertainment, because for the vast majority of Americans, entertainment revolves around our compulsions. Getting drunk or eating until we are sick at a party certainly is not rejuvenating; neither is the compulsive buying of consumer goods a way to bolster our personal energy resources. On the other hand, simple enjoyment with friends leaves one feeling good.

Music and dance are two of my favorite forms of entertainment and recreation, and community lends itself to these. In my community we have a rock band and a blues band that provide great entertainment, shared enjoyment and even exercise. Traditional communities have always had their musicians, poets, dancers and storytellers. These art forms need to be encouraged in community, as they are necessary to the transformational impulse—a part of human life that naturally brings people together. I have been in communal kitchens during clean-up when one person took a large pot and made it into a drum. Suddenly someone else had a couple of spoons clacking away in rhythm, and another shook a large jar of beans like a huge maraca, until a rhythmic communion filled the kitchen while the dishes were washed. These spontaneous events are great fun and tremendously enlivening; they seem to naturally spring out of the bond that is created when people in community share music together on a regular basis.

Storytelling is an art form that lends itself to community evenings around the fire. In tribal cultures it has been the primary mode of passing down information, tradition, spiritual principles and tribal, ancestral wisdom for thousands of years. Every community should begin to develop an "oral tradition" whereby the history, ideals and humanity of the community is cherished and preserved. Storytelling brings all ages together, and can take a central place in the scheme of communal entertainment.

Singing and dancing together is one of the great joys of life. Living in community today we have the great privilege of choosing from many different traditions in this regard, from the Beatles to Beethoven, to Navajo or Hindu songs, to old Christmas favorites or spontaneous creations of our own on a couple of guitars and some hand drums. Sometimes we have no idea about the hidden talents of our friends in community, when with a little encouragement we could delight and surprise each other and even ourselves. It might mean that we have to be silly or lose face a little in the process, but that too is part of the fun.

Laughing together over anything and everything is some of the best entertainment and medicine available. The camaraderie of bonded community makes laughing together easy because we share so many intimacies over time. We come to know each other so well that we might burst out laughing with each other over something as silly as our stumbling around to get our boots pulled on when there is six inches of snow outside. These nonsensical moments are rejuvenating; they will help to re-create us on a daily basis if we relax our seriousness and allow them to surface.

We must redefine entertainment to get past the passive approach, as in "I should sit back and do nothing and be entertained." That which entertains us should be that which engages us fully—body, mind, spirit—and makes us think and feel. Entertainment should provoke positive change as well, moving our actions in new and evolving ways. Going to see a great play or concert can be fully engaging and inspiring in this way, if we go in the right frame of mind; but walking and bicycle riding are equally great forms of entertainment, especially when done in pairs or small groups so that our activity involves relationship. Chopping wood with a friend or building a new bike shed for the community can be great fun and rejuvenating at the same time. Who can say when a conversation over baking cakes or building cabins in the woods will spark an element of a long awaited and much needed change within us?

When relationship is a key ingredient in entertainment, our individual possibility to grow and evolve is enhanced. If we sit alone in front of the TV with a bowl of popcorn and a quart of soda we simply do not generate the kind of energy or life force that is possible when we gather human resources in the warm glow of community to sing, dance, laugh, talk, or sit in silence together.

Practical Breakdowns are Part of the Play

We can free one another to worship and to recreate when the physical and practical needs of the individuals are served in the midst of our focus on community and the needs of the group. In certain Sufi orders the community must ask three questions before beginning the collective worship or *zhikr:* 1) Is there anyone in this group who has been wronged by another and wishes to bring this before us? 2) Is there any married person here who is having difficulties that he or she would like to put before this group for counsel and support? 3) Is there anyone who has any need, material or otherwise, that he or she would like us to be aware of?

Most practical breakdowns that occur in community can be resolved with relative ease, or circumvented if we keep a close eye on the legitimate needs—physical, financial, psychological, spiritual—of the individuals of the community and make sure that the administrative and management systems that we have set up are working for those individuals who must maintain them.

It is also important to be realistic about what is possible—from ourselves and others—so that we are not expecting more than we are humanly capable of. There will always be those areas in which we must learn, the hard way, what our true needs are, rather than what we psychologically perceive our needs to be. For community to be viable, the individuals of the group must be able to make this distinction, know when to ask for certain physical needs to be met, and when to make the decision to live more simply or to cut back. A good example of this dynamic at play in my community is in the area of health and healing. In addition to vegetarianism and organic gardening, we are committed to preventive measures and to self-healing by natural methods whenever possible. Each person is expected to make wise personal decisions in these areas. At one point, however, we found that community members were spending a shocking amount of commonly-held money on vitamins and other health-related supplements. When a concerted effort was made to educate the community about excesses and inappropriate use of vitamins and supplements, the bills were cut in half in no time. But this also involved a high degree of responsibility and integrity on the part of the individuals. As our finance person, Shannon, pointed out to us: "People had to really examine their own habits and psychological need systems. In other words, we had to ask if we were buying extra vitamins not because we really needed them, but because doing so made us feel safer, or more loved somehow? Only after we had answered some basic questions could we individually determine what was realistic, appropriate and actually useful in relationship to vitamins and health-care supplements."

48

In another community, children were taking oranges on the sly from the pantry. This was not happening because food was unavailable, or because the community could not afford oranges for the children, but because the food was not being made accessible for those who needed it. Somewhere along the line the communication system broke down and wasn't responding to the needs of individuals, in this case the children.

Clear systems of communication are necessary in every dimension of community. For example, when the food buyer does not know that the squash and green beans in the garden are ready for picking, he or she may buy squash and green beans at the market or grocery store. The cook is upset because now there is an overload of vegetables that may not stay fresh long enough to be eaten, and the bookkeeper is upset because resources have been used unwisely. In the meantime, the community-at-large has to eat green beans and squash for two weeks. Everyone feels the impact, when all it would take is for the gardeners to stay in communication with the food buyers and the cooks.

Established communities often have a system for making sure everyone's real needs are met. In a Zen Buddhist *sesshin* (meditation retreat) there are specific roles defined for this purpose. The *jikijitsu,* or elder monk, is charged with the supervision of the *zendo* and holds the sacredness of the space and the vision intact. The *jisharyo* has the specific job of looking out for people in the ordinary domain. If you aren't able to sit on the floor and need a chair, if you are sick, if many emotions come up that you cannot process, if you forget where the bathroom is or have another basic question, then the *jisharyo* takes care of you. *Jisharyo* literally means "to serve Manjushri" or the Bodhisattva of Wisdom, so the *jisharyo* views everyone as emanations of the Bodhisattva of Wisdom. Keeping in mind the limitations of human nature, we can imagine that without these two individuals and other members of the Zen community, the system would surely not work smoothly at all.

In a Zen community I visited a few years ago, the depth of commitment to serving the needs of others with compassion—as an outpouring of their own spiritual process—was evident. At the end of the introduction on the first afternoon I had been delayed in changing into the proper robes. As I arrived outside the dining hall, people all around me were walking to dinner in formal silence in a ritualized order while gongs rang out as a call to the meal. I had no idea how to participate in the protocol of the dining hall and the meal, and silence was maintained. No one was talking, and as the last person filed into the hall and took his seat I realized that I was lost. The monk at the end of the entrance hall continued to ring the bells, which seemed to me to be getting louder and louder. Feeling alone and confused and not wanting to breech protocol, I decided to skip dinner. As I started down the hallway one of the senior monks walked up to me. He had obviously noticed that I was going in the wrong direction, and that I was nervous and unsure of what to do. He reached out and touched my shoulder, indicating the way to the dining room. I don't remember if he spoke or not, but his communication was so full of kindness and compassion that I felt immediately embraced by this community of people. His help was framed within a mood of acceptance for me as a newcomer, a relative "stranger" to the Zen community. I was touched by this small act of kindness. This gesture of human connectedness, of simple communication and hospitality carried within it the essence of what community is about.

CHAPTER THREE

Working Together

The first peace, which is the most important, is that which comes within the souls of people when they realize their relationship, their oneness, with the universe and all its powers, and when they realize that at the center of the universe dwells the great spirit, and that this center is really everywhere, it is within each of us.

—Black Elk, Sioux elder

Traditional native cultures from the world over have believed that all life is sacred and ensouled; in that belief system, the Earth and the physical, material world is no less imbued with that all-pervading spirit or soul than any other part of life. Because of this, most of these original native cultures held that land, spaces and objects could not be territorialized or individually owned. Instead, they should be used with great respect and shared for the good of the whole.

A great benefit of community is that it can return our living and working situation to the most basic blueprint of tribal cultures, and to the more organic systems of sustaining life. This does not mean we have to eat grubs and berries, but that our arrangement of work and social life can be integrated in a way that has been lost in "advanced" civilizations. Instead of living many splintered "lives"our professional life, our private life, our public life, all parts of ourselves disconnected from each other— we can work together in a new way, predicated on a culture in which our basic wholeness and unity is understood and accepted.

Territory and Boundaries

> We must delight in each other. We must labor together, suffer together, rejoice and mourn together, keeping always before our eyes our condition as members of one body.
> —John Winthop

The issues related to property, ownership and territory are immense considerations within community. For the most part, we have been raised on competition, separative individualism and domination; we have not been taught the value of cooperation, partnership and sharing. So, this is a crucial area in which we must begin to reconsider and revision how we will relate with one another.

Community gives us an opportunity to confront—in the spirit of personal growth and self-improvement—those issues that for us are constellated around personal territory and boundaries. Becoming more conscious of these issues is a great way to find fuel for self-awareness, in which we may observe ourselves. We will get to see either our lack of boundaries and integrated sense of self, or our rigid self-containment and constant staking out of territory, which for most of us translates into power and control. The term "co-dependency" has become a familiar word that refers to the psychic enmeshment that often happens in relationships between people. When friends, partners, parents and children and co-workers do not know when or how to make healthy distinctions between themselves as individuals and the other person or persons in their lives, they become neurotically dependent, instead of interdependent. On the other hand, we can be so separated and isolated from others, and even pathologically detached, that we do not take others into consideration, but barge or float through life thinking only of our own immediate purposes, needs and designs. Most of us deal with a combination of these two tendencies and seesaw back and forth between them. Others are psychologically disposed toward one extreme or the other—being either obsessively territorial and prone to "power-tripping" others, or being very wishy-washy and feeling victimized by everyone else's needs, desires and dictates.

By "territoriality" I mean a possessive and dictatorial relationship to physical places, spaces, objects and even certain functions that properly belong to the group, the cooperative or the community. Claiming such things as our own, we maintain isolation through a subtle or dramatic desire to claim control or ownership. Territoriality, the way we are using the term, is fueled by the impulse to maintain dominance over others. On the other hand, by "boundaries" I mean knowing when to set appropriate personal limits, including a sense of when to assert our ideas and beliefs and when to be flexible—in other words, when to say yes and when to say no.

Sometimes the answers to our questions about territory and personal boundaries are clear; sometimes they are not. We may become territorially polarized with another in intentional community around how and when a particular communally-shared room gets cleaned and used; around who will arrange the flowers for a special event; around where to put the garden, when to plant it and how it should be cared for—even down to the details of where the carrots, peas and lettuce will be planted. I may feel certain—based on my experience—that the tomatoes must go on the north end of the garden and the green peppers go on the south end, while my friend who is working the garden with me is absolutely sure that the tomatoes and peppers make good companion plants and should be planted together on the east side, where there is plenty of room for the tomatoes to sprawl. If the two of us get polarized in a power struggle over the garden, then we are being territorial and have lost touch with our desire to communicate and share the garden with each other, and to experience communion and enjoyment in the pleasure of growing food. We have lost touch with the spirit of community.

We can get polarized with another about any small or large aspect of managing our environment and our physical well-being: what food to eat, when to eat, how to cook, how often the bathrooms should be cleaned, whether or not the cats and dogs can come in the house, how many visitors to our community we will allow at any given time, whether or not we will allocate $150,000 to build a new dining room or meditation hall. These issues that concern our basic life and well being are, after all, charged with the survival instinct. As a result, we have a tremendous emotional investment at stake when we square off with each other. In the moment when we are arguing territorially over whether the money is being spent correctly, or over who makes decisions about the menus for a special event, we do not consciously realize that our bodies are in "fight or flight" mode. At a physiological, chemical level, we are primed for survival—adrenaline begins to flow, the heart rate picks up and breathing becomes accelerated and shallow. It takes consciousness to face this reactivity and then to bring ourselves back into alignment with the values we are attempting to embody—values having to do with trust, cooperation, generosity, mutual concern and the goodness of community. When we are "in survival" we have forgotten the point. The point is not where the tomatoes get planted, but the commitment to live and work together in the spirit of unity.

Living closely with others in a residential community of about one hundred people, I have found that each person comes up against these issues of territoriality, and yet we search for common ground on which to meet and break through our separative conditioning. When I can really surrender my claims to territory, I find, paradoxically, that all territory is mine. The whole world becomes the space and place where I belong when my attention is no longer fixed on me but on an all-inclusive totality that has a greater purpose, and of which I am an integral part. When we are no longer caught up in separating ourselves from others by competing over territory—and if we are turned in the direction of unity with others, or non-separation—then generosity and respect permeates our interactions.

Our respect for one another, for objects and for spaces lays the foundation in considerations of boundaries and territory. This means respecting one's self as well as others. It means respecting someone else's expertise, being willing to take advice from others, honoring and abiding by clearly defined roles and lines of responsibility, authority and leadership when those have been decided upon by the group or governing body of the community. Too often we rebel out of habit, or out of lack of respect for ourselves and others. The more self-respect we have, the more respect we are naturally willing to give to others. This kind of mutual respect, along with self-honesty, a sensitivity to the needs of the whole and plain common sense, allows the community to function easily, efficiently and creatively, and guides our responses to situations. When we have a common agreement about the use of spaces and the treatment of community property this helps us care for those things. We learn to respect and honor them as life forms in their own right. If we learn from the ancient tradition of the native peoples of North America, for example, we can shift our perspective and see that we human beings are, after all, only caretakers or stewards of the natural world.

Many of the communities that arose in the early 1970s held this concept of stewardship of the land as an ideal. They formed land trusts to administer the care of the land based on incorporated principles. In this way, no one individual or group of individuals would own the land; instead, the land would own itself, managed and governed by the principles set forth in the legal contract. My friend Rhiannon lived for six years in such a community. The members wished to have the land held in perpetuity, protected from logging, pollution, over-grazing or agribusiness of any kind, hunting, poaching and the general encroachment of Western civilization, including electricity and city or county water systems. This group of young idealists and spiritual revolutionaries had come out of the social upheaval of the '60s wanting to live on the land in harmony with the Earth. They wanted to be self-sufficient. They wanted to find out what it was like to live without electricity, to live close to the Earth, and to come into resonance with the natural cycles. Their context for community was based on the sacredness of the land and many practical ways to protect and steward it, but it extended to include a desire for personal spiritual transformation, and the creation of an alternative culture that would be self-sustaining through organic gardening and cottage industries. The idea was to build a culture that would foster healing, retreat and sanctuary—not only for human beings but also for the indigenous plant and animal life.

To create intentional spaces or cooperative endeavors we must have agreement about spaces, personal boundaries and territory issues. As we will examine in the coming chapters, conflicts about territory are primarily resolved by referring back to the context of the group's identity; in other words, to the ideals, principles and goals that are the foundation of the community. In this way we can usually find some kind of objectivity in the midst of our varied opinions. To come to that agreement can be an active, enlivening process of give and take in which we find what best serves the group. When we make boundaries with one another as they are needed, they become a natural matter of course, not hard and fast lines we must fight about.

Sometimes we find we cannot sacrifice personal boundaries without losing our sense of ourselves, but this too may be a natural part of the process of growth and development, for both individual and community. Both "breakdown" and "breakthrough" are necessary phases in the life of community, important ideas that we will return to in the next chapter of this book.

Changing Habits

When we share common resources we have the opportunity to radically change old habits that become crystallized around control and territory issues. While this may seem mundane, changing deeply ingrained habits is what transformation is about. We transform ourselves through daily choices to be different—from being selfish and domineering to being generous and expansive to others.

Changing habits is hard to do. When we are locked into issues of control with others, panic and survival angst set in. Nonetheless, when we are most up against the wall is when we most have the opportunity for something different—some new possibility in relationship—to arise in us. I have found that typically I have two options in these situations: I can "muscle" my way through, with the strongest force coming out on top; or I can make space inside myself for a cooperative solution, which usually means that I must be willing to see the other person's point of view. I have to be willing to be flexible. When I do this, things always work out in the end—not necessarily exactly the way I planned, but perfectly well. I have also found that when one person in a stand-off steps back, relaxes and is willing to be flexible, then the other person will often follow suit. This can be a quite wonderful moment that can lead to some shared laughter or a bit of trust-building. When we see each other being willing to get off of our individual "positions" and really cooperate, it both inspires and encourages our commitment to community.

Not too long ago Georgia and I made an enormous birthday cake. After the hard work of mixing the cake and making the icing, I looked forward to putting the icing on, since that job is the most creative and fun, in my opinion—certainly more fun than the huge pile of dishes awaiting us at the sink! Georgia naturally wanted to put the icing on too, in her own style, which was of course very different from mine. I started to tense up, snapping at her about how she was doing it, when I realized that I had lost all perspective of the joy of our work together. I felt sad that I had spoken to her brusquely, but I also realized that I could change the direction things were going in—which was toward hurt feelings and possibly an argument over the food. Sometimes if we just admit, in the moment, that we have caught ourselves in the act of being territorial, it can totally de-fuse the situation. When I realized that I was claiming the cake as my territory, and in fact was completely taking over rather than sharing my ideas in a flexible manner, I apologized. "Here I am just being controlling and territorial again!" I told her. "Let's start over and talk about how we want to go about doing this together!" Georgia responded with warmth and understanding, and we came to an agreement about the job to be done, while sharing other stories of different ways we individually were working on ourselves to reframe the tendency toward being territorial.

In the sharing of common resources and territory we must realize what is simply our wanting to have personal control and what objectively serves the group. This is a process of discernment and self-honesty learned through diligent actions that spring from our sincere wish to be in healthy, loving relationships with others. For example, one woman I know has a fantastic sensitivity to spaces, logistics, hospitality and caring for the physical needs of others. She is also a fierce warrior who has a fiery nature mixed up with strong opinions, many fears about material scarcity and the drive to control others. Her particular insight into community is invaluable; she is a critical piece of her community's "body." But in order to communicate what she has to offer, she has had to work extremely hard to become more receptive and flexible, refining her motivations through self-examination.

Living in community does not mean we blindly surrender control and territory while ignoring our sense of rightful boundaries. Instead, we reorient our motivation for boundaries from a sense of defense and separation to a context of wisdom, maturity and wholeness.

Work Is Love Made Manifest

This is the true joy of life: The being used for a purpose recognized by yourself as a Mighty one; The being a force of nature instead of a feverish, selfish little clod of ailments and grievances, complaining that the world will not devote itself to making you happy.

I am of the opinion that my life belongs to the whole community and as long as I live it is my privilege to do for it whatever I can. I want to be thoroughly used up when I die, for the harder I work, the more I love. I rejoice in life for it's own sake.

Life is no "Brief Candle" to me. It is a sort of splendid torch which I have got hold of for the moment, and I want to make it burn as brightly as possible before handing it on to future generations.

—George Bernard Shaw

The mood in which we work at our physical tasks directly affects the mood of the community we are creating. We Westerners typically view work from a linear perspective, which often induces us to jump right into the job in hot pursuit of the goal, disregarding the humanity of the situation. We can become relentless taskmasters, wielding an invisible whip over ourselves and others in a way that quells any possibility of creativity, cooperation and communion. Community brings this issue to the forefront as we wrestle with the dynamics of territoriality. Swami Satchidananda, a contemporary spiritual teacher, once said, "Equality comes in realizing that we are all doing different jobs for a common purpose. That is the aim behind any community.

The very name community means let's come together to recognize the unity. Come . . . unity."

Using the metaphor of the human body, we see how a viable community is made out of many different systems, each completely dependent upon the interrelated working of other systems to sustain the whole. The health of the whole requires knowing where our personal boundaries are, and discerning how we must walk the fine line of both throwing ourselves into our work with complete passion, and knowing when it is time to rest, play and re-create ourselves. This interplay, of course, must be guided by the practical needs of the group or organization—particularly the financial obligations, so that we are not naive or wasteful of resources.

Whenever we are able to create community in a way that frees individual members to explore their creativity and imagination, it is a wonderful gift not only for individuals but for the well-being of the whole. Still, we must look toward shared responsibility so that a few are not carrying the great majority of the workload, while others only float and drift. This requires some conscious consideration of the labyrinths of human potentials, governing systems and political and/or spiritual ideals. While shared responsibility is naturally one of the common goals, every community, tribe or clan has had to, at times, adjust its workload to accommodate the varying needs of individuals. For example, an elder is not expected to carry the workload of a thirty-five-year-old. Elders are "carried" by the workforce with an innate appreciation for the immeasurable contributions that they make to the life of the group, whether as storytellers and holders of tradition, or as the physical embodiments of wisdom. In her groundbreaking book, *The Continuum Concept,* Jean Liedloff tells a story that illustrates this point.[1]

Two Indian families lived near the Caroni and Arepuchi Falls in the jungles of South America, overlooking a beautiful white-sand beach and lagoon. The male head of one family was

Pepe, and the other, Cesar. One day Pepe told Ms. Liedloff about Cesar's aversion to work.

Cesar, a Tauripan Indian, had been raised by Venezuelans, gone to a Venezuelan school, learned to read and write, and when grown had decided to try his hand at diamond hunting. He was working with some Venezuelans when another Tauripan Indian recognized him and urged him to return to his own people. Cesar decided that indeed he would be better off living as an Indian than as a Venezuelan, and so came to Arepuchi where Pepe lived. For five years Cesar lived with Pepe's family, and he married a Tauripan woman with whom he had a little girl. But Cesar did not like to work, and so he and his wife and daughter simply ate the food that Pepe grew. Cesar was very happy to find out that Pepe didn't expect him to grow a garden of his own, or even help in the work that had to be done in Pepe's garden. Pepe enjoyed working, Cesar did not, and the arrangement was fine with everyone.

Cesar's wife worked with the other women, but Cesar himself only liked to hunt wild game. After a few years, he started fishing, which he enjoyed, and so his catch was added to the food supply. After five years, and with assurance that no one was pressuring him to work, Cesar decided that he wanted to clear ground for a garden of his own. With Pepe's help, he chose a site and felled the trees. Pepe enjoyed this project all the more because Cesar laughed and joked the whole time. Pepe said that everyone at Arepuchi was glad because Cesar had been growing discontented and irritable. "He wanted to make a garden of his own," Pepe laughed, "but he didn't know it himself!" Pepe obviously thought it was very funny that a person should not know that he wanted to work!

Just as we offer individuals the opportunity to share responsibility in community, there must also be the space for individuals to come to their own sense of responsibility so they can respond to their innate movements to contribute to the group. This may be through a process of trial and error that involves some irresponsibility and lack of self-discipline, particularly on the part of the younger or newer members of the community.

I have learned to consider it a sign of maturity when people do not constantly remind and nag or shame each other about responsibilities and commitments that have apparently been forgotten. There is wisdom behind giving someone quite a lot of space to make mistakes and even to pull on group resources while learning the hard way—up to a point. The situation itself must determine where the line needs to be drawn, and when more responsibility should be demanded of the individual by the group. Furthermore, what works and is right for one community or one situation is not necessarily what works and is right for another. However, the principle applies across the board: once an individual has truly realized through personal experience the value of work and self-discipline, the value of making a contribution to the community, then the impact of that realization can last a lifetime and be built upon to deepen in further maturity. Knowing first-hand what the personal rewards of work, service, commitment and responsibility really are is unquestionably the best motivational therapy.

Working as a community, each person can fulfill his or her role or function in a way that best serves the group, and most directly utilizes the qualities that they have to offer. Some people can be gardeners, artists, storytellers or cooks. Some may "tend the hearth," so to speak, by raising children, cleaning spaces, caring for the grounds of the community or keeping the kitchen and bathroom stocked. Those who are best with the children can provide childcare; those who like to build can build; those who want to write can write, and those who are adept at administration and management can participate in those kinds of functions, while those who want to work at jobs in the community business or cottage industry can do that.

In Hinduism, there are several approaches to yoga, or spiritual endeavors. Three of these approaches are the *jnana* path, the *bhakti* path and *karma* path. The *karma* yogis have a natural inclination toward work or family life; they are learning to walk the spiritual path through their relationship to the world and through their innate abilities to manage concrete realities, including children, families, jobs and concrete service to others. The *jnana* yogi is disposed toward knowledge and wisdom and tends to take the more philosophical path of the intellect toward spiritual realization through study and contemplation. On the other hand, the *bhakti* yogi is focused more in the realm of the heart, feeling and emotion, and leans toward devotional activities, singing, dancing, service and love of humanity. In Hinduism, all of these co-exist within spiritual communities that are making efforts toward a common goal: self-realization or union with the Divine.

Even when there is not a job that we immediately like or to which we feel drawn, community offers a much more fertile arena in which to find, explore and develop our passions and to contribute in the way that most enhances our natural inclinations and essential talents. When people are given permission and empowered to do what they have a real passion for, then creativity is tapped that fertilizes the whole community. In such a direct and small system as an intentional community, we see the immediate effects of each person's work and service on the body politic. Each job is necessary in the workings of the system, and each job is important to the life of the community.

In Western culture we still live by hierarchical and patriarchal ideas about what is a meaningful and therefore fulfilling job. We often want to have jobs that carry a lot of status, that bring the spotlight on us as individuals, jobs that bring in lots of praise and recognition, without realizing that we sometimes pay a heavy price for that kind of "star" status. When we start to really appreciate community and what the joy of work and service is all about, we find that the person who is often found doing those jobs that no one else wants, and who works tirelessly to serve others, is often the happiest and most fulfilled one of the group. This may mean that someone has found that making and serving tea or coffee to the whole group, baking banana bread and cookies for the children's afternoon snack, watering the garden, washing the vehicles, keeping the library orderly and beautiful, placing fresh flowers in the living room every day and taking out the compost are the most rewarding jobs. These are the small, often unseen and unacknowledged actions that bring elegance and harmony into our lives, and we cannot underestimate their value.

It takes a lot of courage to live and work with simplicity in Western culture. Yet it can be one of the sure ways of discovering that "work is love made manifest," or that, "work itself is sacred and noble and an inherently worthwhile thing." [2] Our tasks may be thankless, and the rewards of our work may at times be intangible, as in the case of the endless details of daily life—sweeping, washing, cleaning—but if we discover the secret pay-off of working for the sake of the work itself, we are enriched.

My friend Bernadette, who spent eight years as a nun living in a monastic community before moving on to many other adventures in community, spoke about the ethics and conflicts we encounter around work within a group.

Bernadette Comments on Work

To count hours of work in the religious community [of Catholic nuns] didn't really do it, because the whole thrust of one's vows was to just serve as much as possible; we were always working! There were lots of nuns who did as little as they possibly could, and lots of nuns who burned themselves out, and everything in between. So the structure was such that you weren't going to be thrown out because you did less than what was desirable. In any group there are always a small number of people who are doing most of the work (or it looks that way to some people). Sometimes we don't see the kinds of work some people are doing, and they can't see what we are doing. And that's a core tension inside of community, because most of us have a work ethic that things must be fair—that everybody should do an equal portion. Sometimes that happens— in emergencies, everybody's there. But on a day-to-day basis it just doesn't come out that way. On the interior level, you just don't know what other people are working through or working on at different times, so to be judging people for what they are doing or not doing is risky. The more refined our work becomes, we could be doing ten times the work without it being particularly obvious or visible.

People go into community with very high ideals but they're going to see a microcosm of the world. Welcome to reality! Work, and who does how much and what, is going to be a constant source of tension, so we have to make our peace and even our joy within that. You have to know who and what you are doing this for— whatever it is—and then use that as your inspiration, even when things don't seem fair. When you are clear about what you're doing, then you can enroll other people who really want to help make the vision happen. If you are doing it for the sake of ecology, the survival of the planet, then you do it for that reason and you wisely get on your side the people who know how to get the job done. You band together in a subculture with those who have the skills to get the job done. And you do as much as you can to be kind and caring and tolerant toward those who don't lift a finger.

The Balance of Work and Play

There will always be plenty of work to do in community; the greater task for most of us is to learn to balance work with play. Remembering to celebrate our lives together helps to revitalize our commitment to the vision. This goes not only for play, but for other dimensions of life that are usually ignored in our driven rush to accomplish, achieve and do. A friend of mine was fond of saying, "We are human beings, not human doings!"

How many of us are comfortable just *being?* The art of being is something that we actually have to re-learn, although we do have some memory from early childhood, when being was the mode of life and we were permitted time to lie in the grass and look at the clouds passing in the sky.

At the Spiritual Life Institute, a group of contemporary Carmelite nuns and monks founded by Father William McNamara and Mother Tessa Bielecki, the balance of being and doing is clearly stated: "Our monastic life is a rhythm of work and play, solitude and togetherness, fast and feast, discipline and wildness, sacrifice and celebration, contemplation and action. Centered in Christ, we pray Lauds communally every morning at six and Vespers every evening at five except on days of solitude. Sunday is a holy day of leisure when we break our ordinary pattern of existence and waste the day by praying and playing." [3]

Our ability to work effectively depends on our ability to re-create ourselves—in play, in moments of quiet and in simple beingness that brings presence into our lives. These are qualities of life that most adults have lost touch with and even denied to a great degree, and so we feel a need to emphasize them here. My friend Joanne told the following story of what she learned about work and play in building community.

Joanne Speaks on Work/Play

One of my early experiences of community was during the summers that I helped to run a Youth Conservation Corps Camp. It was a federally funded work/education program for teenagers in which the students were paid to do conservation work thirty hours a week, and spent ten hours a week studying environmental education. Every Monday morning the staff would pick the students up and take them to our camp up in the mountains located an hour from the nearest town, then down a long and winding dirt road. Once we arrived at our camp, we spent the week building trails or constructing erosion control dams or repairing fences on nearby national forest lands. We also cooked, ate and played together. The program was fun, educational and work productive, and provided many of the students with their first work experiences. Since the students broke up into different crews that worked separately, the bonding among the students was primarily within their own work crew; unquestionably they became very good friends. But the strongest experience of community and bonding happened among the staff.

A dozen people were completely responsible for feeding and housing the students, leading the crews, driving the vans, teaching the students about the environment, coordinating recreational activities for the evenings after work hours, and handling all of the required paperwork. In short, our work never stopped until we hit our bunks at midnight each night, then we were up again at the crack of dawn. We really believed in what we were doing—teaching these kids good work habits and skills, to understand and preserve the environment, and more importantly, how to live and work together in a cooperative way. We all worked hard and we also played hard. On the weekends the staff had the camp to ourselves, and we could go for hikes, play tennis, swim in the lake, eat huge brunches and prepare elegant dinners that we shared. In the evenings we played cards or danced to favorite oldies, or just sat around talking and enjoying each other's company. My experience that summer was a tremendous time of learning, and it convinced me that we are missing some key ingredients if we think that playing together is enough to build community and bond people together. To me, it was clear that a combination of factors made these experiences so rewarding: working hard together, having a shared goal and sense of purpose, and then after the work was done, playing and relaxing. But I would never underestimate the value of working hard as the most basic building block of community.

If community is to succeed at the physical, bodily level, it must rest on the foundation of the shared context that is the thread that weaves all levels of community together—body, mind, heart and soul. Many intentional communities of the 1970s and '80s found themselves sliding into a state of disintegration, chaos and extreme discord in which members of the group experienced a level of psychological upheaval that they had never encountered before. Lack of cohesive leadership, becoming closed and insular, and being unable to hold the context of the original vision of the community while staying open to necessary changes are often the causes of failed experiments in community. In the next chapter we will take a closer look at some of these issues that are so vital to life in community.

Context and Culture

[I]n social groups, synergy represents the extent to which the activities of the individual support the group as a whole. Anthropologists studying primitive tribal systems have found that groups high in synergy tend to be low in conflict and aggression, both between individuals and between the individual and the group. This does not mean that such societies are full of "do-gooders" desperately trying to help each other; rather, they are societies in which the social and psychological structures are such that the activity of the individual is naturally in tune with the needs of others and the needs of the group.

—Peter Russell

Vision and Context

Community without context will simply not hold together; the form may continue to function and exist for awhile, but if the lifeblood of the community is not present, sooner or later it will become an empty shell, blown apart by the first strong wind. Creating a context means that we create a background milieu, or a foundation, woven from the fabric of the fundamental philosophy, attitudes, agreements and goals that have brought us together for a shared purpose. The environment, specific situation and overall culture of our community is then molded, sustained and evolved based on this context.

Defining context may seem like a mere exercise in conceptualizing for many people, but a cohesive context is the glue or

69

matrix that holds things together and the ultimate factor in the resolve of conflict. This is true for any organism or organization; context is everything.

Joanne, whom we quoted in the last chapter on the mix of work and play, had the opportunity to see firsthand—in the mini-community of a college experiential class—the difference that a deeper shared context makes in the building and bonding that occurs in real community. Many aspects of what she observed—interest in human potential and growth, willingness to communicate, to work through problems, to gain greater interpersonal skills and the desire for real and lasting relationships that widen our personal circle in significant ways—are fundamental components of a basic context and vision for community life.

Joanne Speaks on Context and Vision

Over the years that I taught a number of field courses, I experienced quite a variation in the degree to which a sense of community and bonding between students happened or didn't happen. My understanding of community grew and deepened as I worked for many years at a small alternative college that offered one-month and three-month field courses that were highly experiential. Being together twenty-four hours a day and eating, working and studying together provides a great medium for developing the relationship skills and sensitivity for community life. Some of these courses were designed to train outdoor leaders, but many others were for studying native cultures or for learning about natural environments—how to preserve them and live in harmony with them. Still other courses combined aspects of human growth and development in an outdoor setting, which enhanced the effects of bonding among students.

Community was strongest in the courses in which there was a human growth and development component—a subject which of course lends itself more to human relationships, communications and other interpersonal skills, including intimacy. In those courses the group usually had a desire for connection and cohesion and a predisposition to working through the conflicts that invariably arise when living and working so closely together. Without that desire for connection, the possibility for community is very limited.

I taught several courses that were focused on learning about a particular geographical area and its indigenous people. Even though some of these classes lasted for two months, and we lived, ate, studied and traveled together, the participants kept to themselves or in pairs much of the time, and had little or no interest in processing problems that arose. There was very little sense of community. What cohesion there was disappeared as soon as the course was over. In contrast, a three-week intensive course which explored transpersonal psychology in the wilderness and which included group or individual processing of conflicts—while also spending most waking hours in very close proximity—lent itself to building a sense of community and extended family. The group developed into something that felt more like a family, with close-knit bonds and friendships. After the course ended, the group still gathered together frequently. There was a feeling that everyone had been so positively changed by their experience together that they all wanted more. My conclusion was that the circumstances of living, working and playing together are important ingredients in developing community, but that a desire for real and lasting community and a willingness to work through the ensuing difficulties that will naturally arise is a prerequisite to the possibility.

Just recently I attended a reunion for the college where I taught for so many years. I sat at a table with several of my former students who had left the college fifteen years earlier. The major topic of discussion was how much everyone missed the feeling of community they had experienced during their years in these unconventional classes. They spoke about how difficult it is to find community out in the world, and about their longing for it. And I thought, "Yes, once we've had a taste of the richness of community we are never quite the same afterwards."

We are the products of our times. Certainly we no longer approach any format of community with the simplicity and innocence of someone who has grown up in an Earth-based, tribal culture. Many psychological walls have been erected in the Western psyche during the past fifty or seventy-five years that were not there previously, and which must be taken down to live optimally in community. As we have noted, a lot of the foundation work that must be done to live in community is done internally— through self-observation, acknowledging and coming to know our own inner "walls" and slowly letting them come down. As we relearn how to live in community with each other, we do well to appreciate and consider that building a culture of wholeness within community in modern times is going to be a more complex undertaking than it has ever been before in the known history of humanity. Getting the "big picture" like this is a function of having *vision.*

Establishing a clear context starts with vision. By vision I mean that which lifts us beyond our narrow concerns for personal survival, comfort and success into a much more vast field of play, in which the good of the whole becomes the motivating force. Vision takes us from a very small muddy pond out into the wide ocean itself, so that we are dealing with ideas, concepts and possibilities that encompass Life with a capital "L." Vision is, in and of itself, quite transformative, because once we are infected with the ability to see that which is far away with such clarity that it seems as if it is very near, we are moved to do something about it. We become eager to change, to live differently, based on the truth of our own vision. We are no longer satisfied with anything less.

Vision is that which invents from scratch, that which imagines what is possible and then compels us to go for it. Vision spins out of radical insight, faith, creativity, resourcefulness, originality, the innate instinct for life and the urge to evolve. Vision is our willingness to dream and to believe in the power of our dreams.

Mainstream Western culture typically considers visionaries to be quacks, romantic idealists—Don Quixotes of the worst kind. Anyone who is choosing a non-traditional or alternative lifestyle in our society based on his or her vision—or who chooses not to buy into the norms of our society—will more than likely be confronted with misunderstanding, confusion, and the persistent, unconscious pull of the collective psyche to conform to the norm. We are then forced to question the cultural directives that are also inside of us.

It is always healthy to question; it serves the evolution of the human race. But in order to stand clear in our purpose in the midst of a culture that may not understand our vision, we need the support of others. In a system of mutual support—a community—we share with one another the questioning, the spark, the ideas that feed a vision. We are going against much of what we have been trained to know and believe, and so we come together in community with those who share in the excitement and passion of our vision so that we may take what is in the mind and make it real in the body and soul.

In the book *Grey is the Color of Hope,* author Irina Ratushinskaya has much to say about vision, commitment and context in community. Irina was one of a group of female political prisoners in a Russian prison during the 1970s, and her book describes their lives together. Harshly sentenced, these women had no idea when, if ever, they would be released. They were kept separate from the larger prison population, which meant sharing living quarters, work space and eating facility (which was the same as their living quarters). In the miserable circumstances of imminent torture and death, the urgent need for solidarity quickly became apparent for these courageous women. They could not afford to reveal any weakness to the guards and prison authorities. Therefore, when one member was vulnerable in some way, the group had to cover for her. In situations where the tension was unbearable and their lives were at stake, they knew that any dissonance among them would be used against them.

Irina and her companions created community out of the utter necessity to survive. They often spoke about the hardest times as occurring when they were isolated from each other, thrown into a separate cellblock as a further punishment.

Their goal to survive was fueled by their vision of what it means to be truly human, and informed by some fundamental questions: What ethic is at the core of a life well-lived, regardless of circumstances—a life of selflessness, kindness, generosity, mercy, loyalty and compassion? How does one embody one's beliefs for the ultimate liberation of the human spirit within a circumstance that attempts the ultimate degradation and destruction of the same?

One poignant example of solidarity occurred on the occasion of a prospective family visitation. Every year or so each woman was allowed one visit from a relative, if the right had not been revoked for some reason created by the prison authorities. These visits were a lifeline for all the women, keeping them connected to friends and family on the outside. Whenever one of them had a visitation turn coming up, the group worked together to pool whatever resources they had to prepare the woman for the visit, especially psychologically, since their physical resources were severely limited. At a time when one such visit was scheduled to occur, the group had been dealing with a very big problem—a female guard who had been particularly inhuman to many prisoners. Knowing that any small interaction could catalyze some cruelty from the guard, the group made a commitment not to acknowledge the words or presence of this guard at any time. When the guard entered the room to announce the arrival of the visitor, the women stood unified in the strength of their commitment not to acknowledge the guard, even though a loved one awaited just in the other room. They would have pursued their commitment to the point of sacrificing the visit if necessary. Luckily, another guard who was somewhat more sympathetic to the plight of prisoners and their situation also came to announce the visit, and so the loved ones were united.[1]

A Sense of Purpose

> It is true that we are created to be individually unique. Yet the reality is that we are inevitably social creatures who desperately need each other not merely for sustenance, not merely for company, but for any meaning to our lives whatsoever. These, then, are the paradoxical seeds from which community can grow.
>
> —M. Scott Peck

When we have a sense of purpose, then we can draw meaning from each of our experiences no matter how seemingly insignificant. Before we have uncovered the knowledge of what our purpose is, many of us experience confusion and the ache of meaninglessness. In my teenage years I had to confront an inner emptiness that drove me to look for something different from the dominant culture and the beliefs I had inherited from my family, but I didn't know what it was. I talked for hours with friends about alternatives, but still felt locked into a limited life. At the same time that I was seeking something meaningful I was also running from the feeling of being lost. In retrospect, I was seeking for the spark that would ignite my innate vision. I didn't always have the exact words for that vision, but I could feel it, alive, deep inside, calling me on.

As I explored many avenues of purpose, I knew instinctively when I had encountered one that resonated. I had this sense of "rightness"of coming home, in a way. That is the moment when a sense of purpose begins to dawn for most of us; when our

75

vision begins to focus, to solidify. Piece by piece the vision came together for me: I wanted a lifestyle that was not self-destructive in any way; one that included deeply bonded relationships; a lifestyle aimed toward serving a higher purpose. As the years passed, my vision matured and grew through experience, gaining depth, clarity and sophistication.

Whatever compels us toward community sooner or later reveals itself as a greater sense of purpose. That purpose may be as simple as relating to others with kindness, generosity and compassion, or treating others with honor and respect. For some people it may be to take a more active role in the ecological well being of the Earth, to become an educator or advocate for the world's children. Purpose may be to communicate a concept worldwide that will serve the well being of all humankind, or it may be simply to live with absolute integrity, or to create and communicate through the mediums of art, music, poetry or writing. For someone else the purpose of life may be relationship with the Divine or to live in constant prayer. It may take a lifetime to find the right means for expressing that purpose which is unique to us, but once we have acknowledged that yearning that says, "I must have a higher purpose, a reason to be here," we cannot leave it alone without great cost to our own wholeness.

Malidoma Somé is an African tribal shaman who as a child was taken from his tribe by French Jesuits to be educated in another part of Africa. Upon returning to his tribe at age nineteen, he found that his Western education in the hands of the Jesuits had changed him, and in order to re-integrate, the elders insisted that he undergo the initiation process with the boys of his tribe. This ordeal changed his life, and he later immigrated—on the instructions of the elders—to the U.S. to teach the West about his people, their culture, religion and society. Somé's books are wonderful sources of inspiration and practical information about community. On the subject of having a personal vision or mission, he playfully writes about how each person has been sent to the

Earth with a purpose—a "dossier" so to speak—but has lost the dossier along the way. In his own case, the name he was given as a child—Malidoma—means "be friends with the stranger/ enemy." His people, the Dagara, believe that every person is born with a destiny, and his was foreseen in the name given long before his encounters with Western culture and academia.

Somé now is a medicine man and diviner in West African culture and holds three master's degrees and two doctorates from the Sorbonne and Brandeis University. He has dedicated his life to bridging the cultural gap between his people and Western cul- ture—a living example of one who is willing and able to "befriend the stranger."

Aristotelian philosophy contains the idea of an "entelechy" in each individual, which is the seed of potential for the true actualization of existence based on what is essential and core to the organism. It is similar to a blueprint for the individuation process. For example, it is the entelechy of a seed to become a tomato or an eggplant, or an apple or banana tree; it is the ent- elechy of a caterpillar to become a butterfly. It is the entelechy of the tiny two-celled organism called a *zygote* to become a human being. The entelechy of the human being is much more complex, because each one is unique, and the unfolding of entelechy has its own timing and catalysts in each case. Coming together in community gives us an arena in which to live out our entelechy, to manifest the ideas in reality, in the action of our moment to moment life. It is easy to keep the sense of purpose pure when it stays only in the domain of concept and thought. For purpose to become real and embodied, it has to be evolved through ordinary daily life. Our vision must be tested out through action; commu- nity gives us a place to do this, and is in fact an immediate feed- back mechanism as to how deeply we are committed to making our vision a reality. There is an often-told story of the Hindu yogi who reached enlightenment—the culmination of his vision— after meditating in solitude for many years in a cave. After he became enlightened, he wandered back down from the mountains and into the frenzy of the marketplace. While walking along, someone jostled up against him, throwing him off balance; his immediate response was to throw back his hand in a flash of anger as if to hit the person who had stumbled against him. He realized in that instant that he had not attained enlightenment, and he knew that he would have to gain the equanimity and clarity of the enlightened state while living in the world.

The sense of purpose, a shared vision, gives us something to focus on beyond the mundane details that can sometimes seem so overwhelmingly important in community—like, "How come Carmen is on the dishwashing schedule only once a week when I am on four times, and why does Ed always leave his stuff lying around when the rest of us abide by the agreed upon rules?" Many people may find that a shared vision in community has drawn them together with their partner or spouse, but that without this mutual purpose, they would never have been drawn together or connected beyond a casual acquaintance. Of course community is not always enough to hold couples together, yet the vision draws us beyond our common frame of reference. Vision gives us the inspiration to go on in the face of difficulty and hardship, and especially in the face of interpersonal conflicts, chaos and change.

Most communities have a written statement of purpose. Groups that are legally incorporated may have this written into the articles of incorporation, while others that are more informal may simply decide to write up a mission statement for the use of the members. The San Francisco Zen Center, which has been in existence since 1962, has a document called "Ethical Principles of the San Francisco Zen Center." It begins with the reference to "Three Refuges of Buddhism": 1) "To take refuge in the Buddha," which acknowledges the Buddha Nature of all beings. In this way, the organization recognizes that while there are various levels of responsibility and authority within the Zen Center, everyone is equally an expression of Buddha Nature. 2) "To take refuge in the Dharma," in which the community seeks to make accessible the wisdom and compassion of the Bodhisattva way of life and the teachings of the Buddha, as conveyed through the lineage by the Zen Center's founder, Shunryu Suzuki Roshi and others. 3) "To take refuge in the *sangha*," which recognizes the value of the community of practitioners. A supportive and inclusive environment is created for everyone's participation in the Bodhisattva way. The community strives to encourage open, ongoing communication at all levels among residential and non-residential members of the community or *sangha*. This document goes on to elucidate decision-making policies, how the welfare of children should be supported and fostered, and how parents should sustain a balance between family practice and zendo practice, thereby maintaining healthy families.[2]

The Rochester Zen Center Code of Conduct statement (revised in August 2000) offers both general resolutions and Ten Cardinal Precepts to which "the Director and other staff members, as well as Trustees, Officers, Instructors and Affiliate Leaders" subscribe, stating that they are "striving to incorporate the Thirteen Items of Good Conduct into their daily lives." "The Three General Resolutions" are: "1) I resolve to avoid evil; 2) I resolve to do good; 3) I resolve to liberate all sentient beings." The "Ten Cardinal Precepts" are: 1) I resolve not to kill, but to cherish all life; 2) I resolve not to take what is not given, but to respect the things of others; 3) I resolve not to misuse sexuality but to be caring and responsible; 4) I resolve not to lie but to speak the truth; 5) I resolve not to cause others to abuse alcohol or drugs, not to do so myself, but to keep the mind clear; 6) I resolve not to speak of the faults of others, but to be understanding and sympathetic; 7) I resolve not to praise myself and disparage others, but to overcome my own shortcomings; 8) I resolve not to withhold spiritual or material aid, but to give them freely where needed; 9) I resolve not to indulge in anger, but to practice forbearance; 10) I resolve not to revile the Three Treasures [Buddha, Dharma, and Sangha], but to cherish and uphold them."[3]

Not all organizations will chose to delineate their context and purpose in such concrete terms, but many do find value in such an exercise. Writing a mission statement together as a group can be a tremendously clarifying and bonding process. When the vision is clarified, disagreements and confusion can be dispelled and contextual agreement can be reached. In the natural foods cooperative where Mary worked, the managerial staff and board of directors went into a week-long retreat to rewrite the mission statement and articles of incorporation when the business underwent radical changes in form. In this case, the creation of a mission statement marked a definite turning point in the company's evolution.

The Context of Chaos

> In all chaos there is a cosmos, in all disorder a secret order.
> —Carl Jung

As we envision a context for community and culture we must realize from the outset that a great deal of difficulty is involved in creating anything worthwhile. Our parents and grandparents might call this the "ups and downs" of life—good times and bad times. As all ancient cultures and wisdom traditions teach, this is the way of life. One must have the resilience to weather such storms.

In community, group synergy often intensifies the "ups and downs" of life in the same way that synergy will intensify creativity and possibility. We can find ourselves, very early on, enmeshed in some difficult interpersonal and group situations. If we have a basis of wisdom upon which to rest when we are beset with chaos and conflict, we will find that through perseverance and the willingness to give and take, we will not only weather the storm, but come out on the other side stronger, wiser and even more ready to carry on with renewed inspiration. Anyone who has spent years in a committed relationship knows this principle to be true. Such times of chaos and even loss are actually necessary to our growth because these are our opportunities to embrace change—and therefore to evolve as human beings.

No matter how sophisticated and educated we are, at a fundamental and even primal level change often seems like death. Indeed, there will be times when it seems like our community or relationship will perish—or *does* perish. If we have a context within which to understand the natural processes of change, we will be able to hold on in the roughest of times and wait to see what evolves. Jody, a long-time co-op activist, spoke of the hard times his group went through.

Jody's Comments on Chaos

When I first came to work at a wholesale natural foods warehouse in 1978, it was collectively run. That meant that the workers made all decisions by consensus, and no one had more authority or responsibility than any other. We rotated tasks so that everyone would have opportunities to do both manual labor and managerial tasks, and everyone was paid the same hourly rate. Seniority of years working at the co-op was the only differentiation in benefits, which meant that the longer one worked there, the more paid vacation time you got every year. The Board of Directors was elected every year at the annual membership meeting, and the warehouse staff had to report to them quarterly.

After almost a decade of struggling along, the business had evolved to over $3 million a year in sales and a trucking operation that delivered a wide range of natural foods and personal care products to co-op storefronts, health food stores and buying clubs over a seven state area. We also did our own long-distance *trucking to pick up goods in California and the northern Midwest. The business was growing by leaps and bounds, but it was completely out of control financially. We were on the verge of bankruptcy—a ridiculous proposition for a business that had a sound customer base and was standing on the brink of tremendous potential.*

Our collective decision-making process was killing us; it took hours to make even the smallest decisions, and rotating tasks meant that there were lots of mistakes on every order that went out, since nobody could build any momentum toward mastering their particular job. There were no clear lines of authority or responsibility, so there was no system for accountability on the part of the workers. The Board of Directors was frustrated and concerned, even alarmed. The workers were divided into two camps: 1) maintain the egalitarian ideals and "freedoms" of the workers' collective at any cost, or 2) make whatever changes are necessary to ensure the survival of the business, including instituting a management hierarchy. Most of the "old-timers" on the staff fell into the first camp, while the newer staff members fell into the second camp—a complicated situation indeed.

The members finally took charge through their elected Board of Directors. A management consultant was hired who specialized in turning around dying co-operatives. He recommended that we dissolve the workers' collective and institute a managerial hierarchy. Along with this, we attempted to weave in as many of our egalitarian and humanistic principles as possible—like profit-sharing, avenues for empowerment and incentives for those who would not be in management positions. After three years of helping to develop the distribution arm of the business and driving trucks, I ended up on the three-person management team for the co-op, and became the manager of the marketing department. I developed a performance evaluation based on measurable objectives, instituted many changes that would upgrade systems and place quality controls on various tasks within departments, and in order to save the business I had the unpleasant job of having to fire many people who were unwilling to cooperate with this approach. These people seemed to hold the position that the business could go down as long as their political idealism got to be naively and selfishly lived out. What was demanded was a sacrifice that many were unwilling to make—the life of the co-op for our own personal needs! A couple of years later, one of the three of us was hired as general manager, and the business had to make even greater changes in order to stay alive, but it did.

Today it is a successful business that has received acclaim, one of the few wholesale natural foods cooperatives that has not only survived but thrived since the early 1970s.

Embracing Chaos

Most of us were indoctrinated as children in a paradigm that is flat and dualistic—everything is either black or white, good or bad . . . with no other possibilities. We were also raised in a culture that is terrified of change of any kind, and that typically sees the chaos, conflict and disruption that usually accompanies change to be bad and fearful. We think that we have failed because what was ordered and under control is now out of control.

If we have a different context for change, then we can trust in the process of what is occurring. We find that we have the patience to wait, to endure, to feel our way along until insight comes, or until we suddenly know instinctually what to do next. Miracles can happen, or something new can be invented. It takes a lifetime for most people to really change the way they think about things. It takes much more than an intellectual grasp of a concept to effect change. The concept has to be integrated at the level of the body for real transformation to take place.

Years ago I read Fritjof Capra's, *The Turning Point,* and other books written by some of the visionary scientists of our day.

83

These scientists have been attempting to educate society about the need for new ways of thinking—a new paradigm that is clearly necessary if we hope to survive as a species on this planet. Ilya Prigogine's discovery of the theory of dissipative structures was a breakthrough in scientific understanding for which he won the 1977 Nobel Prize in chemistry. Since then, his theory has been applied to biological systems such as the growth of plants, the regeneration of limbs in simple organisms, the excitation pattern of nerve cells and many other biochemical processes. It applies equally well to social groupings like bee swarms and slime molds as it does to human economic interactions, human society, ecosystems and the Earth as a total organism.[4] Put in general terms, Prigogine's theory gives a blueprint for how any organization, individual or organism is self-ordering as it goes through various stages of recurring patterns that involve "creation through destruction," as the Hindu *Upanishads* might phrase it. The organism grows to the point that it must manage so much burgeoning energy that it falls into entropy and chaos. On the other side of chaos a self-ordering factor appears, in which the organism re-orders at a higher level of efficiency or possibility. These transitions of transformation involve considerable chaos because of the maximum flow of energy and matter that is moving through the system, creating a maximum dissipation of entropy into the environment. The system may collapse, but if it survives this period of chaos, it is capable of evolving.[5]

Prigogine notes that one of the particular elements that must be present to define a dissipative structure is that the organism must freely interact with its environment. If it does, we have an "open system," as opposed to a "closed system." In a closed system, the organism is cut off from receiving energy or input from its environment, whereas in an open system the organism is involved in a reciprocity of relationship with its environment. In communities, as in human relationships, we can easily see why an "open system" is so important. The downfall of many communities over the years was that they became too insular and cultic to allow for healthy exchange of energy, time, ideas and experience.

If we consciously choose to bring a new context for change—or growth and evolution—to our experience of community and of human relationships in general, our troubled times can be valuable. We can begin to embrace the breakdown, knowing that breakthrough is possible. If we become too literal and materialistic in our thinking, we will find that times of chaos are extremely threatening, rather than understanding them to be a natural part of the process. We can see that this process of breakdown and breakthrough shows up across the board: in developing new finance systems, in group process when decisions must be made, in hashing out the childcare schedule, in working through the cycles of intimate relationships and in evolving our vision and refining the culture of community.

Having a vision that acknowledges the nature of change or transformation is basic to our desire for ongoing personal growth and development. Tribal people do not need to articulate these intentions for community life because they are connected to the primal pulse of life. As Westerners we have been so cut off from this pulse—which is toward growth and evolution—that we must bring conscious remembrance and a conscious intention to it.

Humor in Chaos

A sense of humor is absolutely essential in the face of chaos. When community becomes rigidly fixated about context and vision, we can become righteous and insensitive to when it is more important to overlook something or make exceptions in order to maintain the true spirit of our vision. The organic friction created in the company of one another can help us to maintain humor and perspective about ourselves and our sense of purpose or vision so that we can be alert to the tendency to become dogmatic.

We have to be able to laugh when the community's large, one-room office has twenty people in it—all of whom are talking at the same time as five phone lines ring incessantly and children run through yelling and laughing—while our important project is one day away from deadline and we've hit a major snag in getting it completed in time. (This may sound preposterous, but I am describing the current moment as I write!) Having a sense of humor is equally necessary to avoid becoming self-important about how significant our vision is; how portentous are our efforts! This is especially true for spiritual or religious communities and organizations. Serious, fundamentalist doctrine has been the source of untold suffering and misery in human history.

Healthy communities make a point of satirizing themselves—in skits or in the community newsletter, for example. Such exercises can generate lots of laughter, and also help keep us on our toes, remembering that even though we should take our context seriously, self-importance and rigidity are not what is called for. We can also make fun of ourselves on the spot. One day, a friend of mine who runs a small publishing company for his community caught himself hovering over a co-worker in a serious, authoritarian posture. As soon as he realized what he was doing he jumped up on the desk, pantomiming himself. Everyone in the office started howling with laughter as he joked about his tendency to be controlling, exaggerating it with gestures and making ridiculous faces. When we are willing to just admit our human foibles, a sense of humor can go a long way toward alleviating tensions that build between people and within the community as a whole.

Tending the Fire of Our Vision

We all experience times where we question or even forget our vision, or feel apathetic or confused. We may fall into thinking that community is only about fitting as many people into as small a space as possible, or about sharing the bathroom or being annoyed by twenty people in one day. I have found that the vision must be fed to keep it alive; those of us who live and work in intentional community are very busy people, and so the time must be set aside for this kind of tending of the fire.

Many communities have regular times when they gather specifically to talk about the vision, separate from logistical and managerial meetings. Otherwise we neglect our need to remind ourselves of our vision and purpose in the demand to address the pressing details of daily business. Perhaps we simply share what we are reading about or working on that would inspire one another. In my own community, a weekly educational meeting facilitated by different people helps us to further elucidate the community's purpose. In addition, three times a year the community holds a four-day celebration, during which we play and feast together, give talks and seminars, speak about our mutual work— the failures and triumphs in the life we have chosen to live. We often invite guest speakers to present formal seminars that are both educational and inspirational for the extended community. This gives us the opportunity to interface with a network of peers, keeping the system open and free-flowing.

Each community will find its own way of maintaining and evolving its vision and context. But only through commitment will the vision be made real, and each member of the community must take responsibility for that.

Commitment

The hope lies in the longing we have to be adults.
—Robert Bly

The Baby Boom generation that spearheaded the back-to-community movement of the past four decades is a generation that finds commitment difficult—an attitude that has continued in succeeding generations as well. As poet and author Robert Bly pointed out in his book, *The Sibling Society,* mainstream American society has refused to grow up, and has lost touch with the values that commit us intentionally to participate in the profundities of life. We want to eat the icing before the cake is finished baking. Is Bly right? Are we as a society dealing with a high degree of arrested psychological development, which has cost us our ability to live fully, to commit, to take responsibility and to serve others? And what does this have to do with whether any given community can make it or not?

Growing up in the U.S. many of us were raised in an atmosphere that never allowed us to fully be children, with all of the accompanying phases of childhood. We were not allowed our anger or rage, our sadness and sorrow, our boisterous, joyful exuberance or the complete selfishness that is so natural at age three, for example. We were forced to share our toys and to express remorse—"Say you're sorry that you took Susan's toy away"—long before we were developmentally able to do these things. We are still acting out a great deal of childhood behavior because it was thwarted as a natural and necessary part of our psychological development. By contrast, certain tribal cultures, like the Australian aborigines, allow childhood to be a time of free expression and exploration. They do not repress the natural survival instinct, which often shows up as a kind of self-centeredness and selfishness in a child. When aboriginal children become adults, they no longer need to act out this kind of selfishness, and are able and ready to take up their commitment to serve the tribe with a steady heart.

Arrested psychological development may show up in our adult lives and relationships as an unwillingness to commit and take responsibility—elements that are necessary to the creation of any culture, society or community. Carolyn, who has lived in several intentional communities over the past thirty years, and in her current community for sixteen of those years, commented:

"Baby boomers are sad and disillusioned because their attempts at living in community and actualizing their other ideals and dreams over the years since the idealistic 60s have failed. But they have failed because we baby boomers have typically been unwilling to lose ourselves for something larger." It seems like Robert Bly's assessment may be right.

Commitment has been the vital factor that has sustained successful community life, even though the stereotypes still found in the media portray the more than five hundred communities that are alive and well in America today as somewhat flaky hippie communes, where women wear long skirts and men smoke dope and hang out in baggy blue jeans that fall off their skinny hips while they stir the tofu pot. An article about community in the *Philadelphia Inquirer* (September 1996) depicted some of that stereotype, and yet it was also heartening to see that intentional, alternative community has survived to the point that the mainstream press is moved to give it some recognition.

Commitment is not a static thing—like once we get it, it is written in stone. Commitment is not about a rigid position in life; commitment ebbs and flows, like all things, and we are constantly faced with the need to renew our commitment. Commitment is something we do on a day-by-day basis. There are natural evolutionary stages that we pass through as we mature as human beings—at times we are more drawn to community, at other times we may want to pull back; times when we want to settle down, and times when we legitimately need to move on. So, when we realize that we need to commit, the wise perspective is to know that we will need to re-commit over and over again.

We go through cycles: initial passion or even infatuation, indifference, boredom or dissatisfaction, and then a rekindling of excitement again. Sometimes the cycles move us to different places. Sometimes, if we stay in the same place doing the same thing, we are also moved in imperceptible ways. Paradoxically, we move more deeply into where we already are. Practicing the art of staying still with attention while everything about us moves—our emotions, our cycles, people and events—allows us to see that which is unchanging. It takes time and commitment to stay still and stay committed through our own ups and downs. After going through the same cycles again and again for ten or fifteen years in community, we can sometimes finally say, "Oh it's just *that* again," instead of feeling like we have failed or have to get away. We build the wisdom to recognize these cycles for what they are—a natural part of life. For many of us it will take years to really settle down in community, as commitment grows. It takes time for commitment to permeate our lives.

As with any intimate relationship, there are peak experiences of knowing we are loved and then there are valleys of not feeling loved, or not feeling very loving. In the arena of community we have the opportunity to create a force that sustains itself through ups and downs, and remains steady in either situation. We can realize that who we are at the essential core of being is no different whether we are in a good mood or a bad mood. Moods and states of mind come and go, as does success and failure, but underneath that there is something constant. Our commitment to endure over time with steady, consistent attention to our lives is what can help us realize this kind of equanimity.

For the first ten years that I lived in community, the degree of commitment that my heart wanted to make was in conflict with what my head wanted. My mind kept saying, "You're losing your individuality! What about all those great things you could be doing out there in the ordinary world, outside of community? You could be traveling, going back to school, creating a fabulous career! You could be free to do whatever you want to do, instead of being weighed down by all these people in community." If anyone described me as being an integral part of the community—and many did from the very beginning—I found it terrifying because of my tendency to be rebellious out of a fear of being controlled by others. Another factor for me was a fear of intimacy, the basic intimacy that real relationship is based on, which we are called to engage in community. At one point I moved away from my community for more than a year while staying in close contact and coming to visit regularly. I traveled to Europe for awhile. But as beautiful as it was in Greece and in my ancestral land, Italy, nothing could replace the bonds and the friendship that I had in community back in the U.S. I began to realize that I was more committed than I thought! And that my commitment did not make me a prisoner; instead it was freeing up my life to experience greater and greater wholeness. I moved back into the community residence and threw myself into the fray with renewed enthusiasm. Eventually, I stopped wanting to bolt every time I thought about a deeper commitment to community, and today my commitment to community is firm. I must say that my vacillation was a valuable part of the process of committing to community. In the end, what bonds us together in community is our shared vision, and that became more important to me that anything else.

Unquestionably community is a difficult and challenging process. As Buddhist practitioner, writer and social activist Joanna Macy said, "Community means dealing with some of the people you least want to be with." [6] Many of us want to run at the first sign of conflict, forgetting that conflict is inevitable when we attempt to live with others. This is especially true when we live with the diversity of others that we usually find in community, where different psychological types from different backgrounds and even racial or ethic groups come together.

It is important to think of commitment as being about something we choose to build in our lives, rather than something we are forced to do by some pressure we feel from outside ourselves—our peers, our parents, and other societal authorities.

If we maintain a rebellious adolescent stand against commitment throughout our adult lives ("Nobody's gonna tell *me* what to do!"), we will find it very difficult if not impossible to ever build anything of real value—long-time commitments of marriage, friendships, relationship with family and children, a rewarding business or career. Actualizing artistic talent requires commitment. Raising children requires commitment. Excelling at sports or business management requires commitment. Friendship requires commitment. Something as simple as growing a garden requires commitment; if we don't stick with it, the weeds will take over, the garden will wither in a dry spell and there will be no harvest.

Anything we can endeavor that is worthwhile requires our commitment—to give of ourselves, our time, energy, resources, care and love. What a difference it makes in a friendship to take regular walks together, or to cook together, or make opportunities to talk more intimately than our busy work schedules will usually allow. The same is true in a marriage or committed partner relationship: quality time and attention is necessary for the relationship to flourish. But giving time and attention on a regular basis requires that we be committed, so that we are not easily knocked off course. "Sorry, I can't make our date together because something came up!" The more we break our commitments in relationship, the more our sense of trust and faith in each other is wounded or dissipated. The same is true in community.

Love does not appear out of nowhere requiring nothing from us, but is built through our attention and commitment. Beginning with a foundation of mutual regard (or even in some cases animosity), our actions contribute to the creation of that love. Our modern society sadly lacks the concept of building consistency in almost anything. We have been trained to search for instant gratification and to fear uncertainty. We run from uncertainty rather than turning to face it. Building love takes time, but the payback is more than worth it.

Community is built brick by brick as we slowly come to appreciate each other's differences and discover a different kind of love than the romantic Hollywood version. By acknowledging our responsibility and commitment to each other we allow a space of vulnerability to arise. We begin to understand another person in ways that we never could before as we see that at fundamental human levels we are all the same. We see each other go through breakdown and breakthrough, we see each other laugh and grieve, play and rage, and we can relate with those basic experiences. Because there is understanding, there is generosity, kindness and compassion. We realize that what we do affects others because we are connected on many levels—emotionally, physically and beyond. This principle is certainly true on the grandest level in our connection to all human beings, but community can be the perfect place to begin to practice that in ordinary life—the place where we can *really* make a difference.

Not everyone's commitment will look the same. Some people need the space to come and go within community. Others are always there, the stable backbone of the community—the steadying factor. There are people who are committed to generating lots of ideas and energy, but try to get them on the dishwashing schedule and you are bucking against a wall of resistance! Everyone who has experienced community or group efforts of any kind can relate to this: there is always someone who just never shows up as we want or expect them to, and in fact it seems truly impossible for them to do so. There are also others who prefer to offer their support occasionally, who are ready for a taste of community but not the whole commitment. Flexibility in not expecting the same level of commitment from everyone can keep a community strong.

CHAPTER FIVE

Power and Participation

Every community has to struggle with how to put its vision into systems for governing, and when and how to empower and participate in leadership. Some kind of leadership is necessary to any community or organization, because practical decisions *do* have to be made. In the same way that vision and context are basic to community, so is leadership fundamental.

Many forms of leadership exist: from one person at the head of a hierarchical organization in which the leader then empowers others in positions of authority, to radical styles of shared leadership based on egalitarianism and consensus decision-making. A community may also have a combination of leadership styles: a centralized authority or leader for the community at large, but a consensus-style for smaller sub-groups within the community, or the other way around. No one leadership style or decision-making style is right for every community or group effort, and what worked for the first six months or ten years of a community may not be what will work later as the community grows and changes. Sunrise Ranch, an intentional community in Colorado, provides such an example. Founded in 1945 as headquarters for the International Emissary network, Sunrise is a non-sectarian spiritual community of friends. In 1988, the group's second spiritual leader, Martin Exeter, died and the community decided to reformat their leadership by shifting from a hierarchical system to management by consensus-based governance with elected councils and rotating leadership.[1]

Whatever the style, there is the need for a larger perspective for leadership—a foundation for participation that makes the details work in a way that best serves the community as a whole. Too often, unconscious and unresolved issues around power and powerlessness sabotage our attempts to to fully participate in the approach that our community may have chosen.

Clearing the Way—From Politics to Purpose

Control creates bondage. —Stephen Levine

Whether we are in formal leadership roles or not, control—and whether or not we feel that we have it—is a big issue that every person faces each day. In community we get lots of chances to work on "control issues": from giving up control, to exercising it with others in ways that are either creative or destructive, to exercising control in and over our own life. The strange thing about control is that to be really healthy and fully functioning human beings, we must maintain a delicate balance, knowing when to relinquish control, and knowing when to exercise it judiciously. This is tremendously difficult in a society based on a structure of power and powerlessness, and the deeply embedded fear of change; a culture in which we have not been taught to act based on the greater good of the whole, as in a tribal society.

The fear of losing control is primal. We are most afraid of losing control in our lives because most of us have never had it. True control and empowerment comes from confidence and self-knowledge: the knowledge that we are organically good, complete individuals, and that we have the ability to make appropriate distinctions for ourselves—as in the case of being able to discern whether a charismatic leader is an authentic guide or mentor for us or not. When our sense of self is integrated rather than fragmented and shrouded with shame, doubt and confusion, we have the ability to make these distinctions. But this clarity and conscious sense of wholeness is a rare or hard-won condition for most

Westerners. The great majority of us were forced by the dictates of the dysfunctional family system at a very young age to relinquish our core selves. In his book, *Healing the Shame That Binds You,* John Bradshaw states that psychological dysfunction in family systems is rampant in the West, and that virtually no family is free of this dynamic, which is a function of toxic shame. Feelings of toxic shame are intricately intertwined with feelings of powerlessness and loss of control. Instead of the toxic shame that lies at the core of the basic sense of self, there should be what Tibetan Buddhist Chögyam Trungpa Rinpoche called "basic goodness":

> When we speak of basic goodness, we are not talking about having allegiance to good and rejecting bad. Basic goodness is good because it is unconditional, or fundamental. It is there already, in the same way that heaven and earth are there already. We don't reject our atmosphere. We don't reject the sun and the moon, the clouds and the sky. We accept them. We accept that the sky is blue; we accept the landscape and the sea. We accept highways and buildings and cities. Basic goodness is that basic, that unconditional . . .
>
> The four seasons occur free from anyone's demand or vote. Hope and fear cannot alter the seasons. There is day; there is night. There is darkness at night and light during the day, and no one has to turn a switch on and off. There is a natural law and order that allows us to survive and that is basically good, good in that it is there and it works and it is efficient . . .
>
> So basic goodness is good because it is so basic, so fundamental. It is natural and it works, and therefore it is good . . . The same principle applies to our makeup as human beings . . . Our being is good because it is not a fundamental source of aggression or complaint. Basic

goodness is what we have, what we are provided with. It is the natural situation that we have inherited from birth onwards . . .

Basic goodness is very closely connected to the idea of bodhicitta in the Buddhist tradition. Bodhi means "awake" or "wakeful" and citta means "heart," so bodhicitta is "awakened heart." [2]

This idea of "basic goodness" is not part of traditional Judeo-Christian culture and patterns of thought. The lack of a sense of basic goodness results in the feelings of inadequacy, insecurity and powerlessness that are so pervasive in Western culture, and that are easily activated by the politics of leadership and authority issues. Our lack of a deeply felt sense of basic goodness clouds our perception of what real leadership is about.

Basic goodness is the fundamental empowerment of our humanness. Without it, we are bound to feel disempowered at a core level, which can either show up as rebelliousness, ruthless competition and self-aggrandizement, or feelings of unworthiness, shame, victimization and powerlessness. While each person may have an intellectual relationship to these psychological impulses, we also have an unconscious relationship to them which is typically fraught with unresolved feelings of aggression and anxiety. We are anxious and even panicked about our survival, self-respect and self-image. These unresolved and quite complex feelings make up the emotional tone of our personal "underworld"—a realm that lies beneath the rational dimension of our thought patterns. The only way we can become clear about the difference between these levels is through stringent self-examination and a clear understanding of the familial relationships that contributed to neurotic patterns in adult life. Without this self-knowledge we are like Persephone walking unaware through the fields of flowers—at any moment Pluto may reach up from the underworld to drag us down into Hades.

The work of Alice Miller provides one of the best sources for clarifying dynamics around control, power and authority. Miller is a psychologist whose writings on the "poisonous pedagogy" of the authoritarian family system echo the earlier writings of psychologist Wilhelm Reich. She points out how we are conditioned and adapted to behaviors, perpetrated by authority figures, that belie our deepest instinct for what is right:

> An enormous amount can be done to a child in the first two years [of life]: he or she can be molded, dominated, taught good habits, scolded, and punished—without any repercussions for the person raising the child and without the child taking revenge. The child will overcome the serious consequences of the injustice he has suffered only if he succeeds in defending himself, i.e., if he is allowed to express his pain and anger. If he is prevented from reacting in his own way because the parents cannot tolerate his reactions (crying, sadness, rage) and forbid them by means of looks or other pedagogical methods, then the child will learn to be silent. This silence is a sign of the effectiveness of the pedagogical principles applied, but at the same time it is a danger signal pointing to future pathological development. If there is absolutely no possibility of reacting appropriately to hurt, humiliation, and coercion, then these experiences cannot be integrated into the personality; the feelings they evoke are repressed, and the need to articulate them remains unsatisfied, without any hope of being fulfilled. It is this lack of hope of ever being able to express repressed traumata by means of relevant feelings that most often causes severe psychological problems. We already know that neuroses are a result of repression, not of events themselves." [3]

When the basic sense of self has not been supported and acknowledged, one is prone to easily give control over to others—who are more than willing to take it, and often take advantage of it. This is one part of the psychological tangle in people who give themselves away to charismatic leaders who are psychopathic.

The other common control issue is to fight "tooth and nail" not to lose control, and in the process become so rigidly controlled that there is no flow of relationship with other people or the environment. When we have grown up with self-confidence and self-esteem, or if we have developed this, then we are not so afraid of losing control in ways that are a healthy part of a mature life; it is then that we have an inner strength that cannot be taken away no matter how much it appears on the surface that we have lost control. For example, the bereaved who have watched their intimate loved ones go through a process of completely losing control to illness and death are then faced with their own loss of control and feelings of powerlessness. "I wasn't able to prevent my child's death," or "I couldn't stop my wife's pain," or "This loss came out of nowhere and completely wrecked my life, and I had no way to stop it," they frequently say. Now, in the state of grief, they must let go and surrender to the fact of loss, and allow themselves to mourn naturally, which is the only way to heal and go on with life. But initially, or even for a long period, such grief may feel too threatening. The fear of loss of control and powerlessness stops many people. As a result, the bereaved are not released to love and remember with happiness and joy the person or marriage or situation that has been lost. Stephen Levine, who writes extensively on the subject of grief and loss, has said, "Control is our attempt to make the world align with our personal desires. To let go of control is to go beyond the personal and merge with the universal," [4] and, "Because of our long encouragement to be something special, we have lost trust in the universal. We would rather polish the bars in our cage than become free." [5] In order to become free—in a way that allows us to deal with the politics of power from a position of equanimity and purpose—we must have a strong sense of self.

Feelings of powerlessness are tied into control issues, because we mistakenly feel powerful when we are in control, and feel powerless when we feel out of control. This dynamic can show up in something as ordinary as a card game or a round of backyard basketball. We may find that we experience feelings of powerlessness and shame when we have passionately argued a point at a community meeting and the group has voted in favor of the opposing view. We feel powerless and ashamed when someone gives us feedback that cuts to the bone, as if what they are saying is the whole picture of who we are. While it is a psychological habit for many people to feel shame when feedback is given, no matter what the feedback is about or how it is given, even these situations that carry the seeds of disappointment or which tarnish our self-image or self-esteem can be of tremendous benefit to our growth. The paradox here is that when we release our drive to control in those situations in life that call for some degree of healthy surrender of control, we find that we are empowered and enlivened in sometimes subtle and intangible ways. Embracing change—which involves loss of control as we enter into chaos and uncertainty as to what will arise after the old form is broken down—is necessary to discovering this paradoxical truth.

The only way we can learn the wisdom of releasing control is to do it, but it helps to look to those who have put these idealistic principles into action. The females prisoners in *Grey is the Color of Hope* who went through much suffering yet still maintained their vision are good examples of individuals who were able to live in a situation in which they had no control or ostensible power, and yet their humanity was empowered. The many monks, nuns and lay people of Tibet who have kept their vision intact by practicing compassion and kindness toward their enemies in the face of unimaginable pain, hardship and powerlessness—as they watched their homeland and thousand-year-old

100

religious traditions destroyed—are another profound example. Stories of these courageous human beings compel us to honestly question ourselves and what motivates us, and to ask ourselves if we guided by principles of right living, real humanity, compassion and kindness, or driven by our own woundedness to maintain power over others, or powerlessness with others, no matter what the cost.

Issues of power and control in community are ripe with transformational possibility as we are challenged to let go of control over people and situations. For many people, the simple act of cooperation feels like an immense loss of control because they are so rigidly defined by the need to dominate. Fritz Perls used the terms "top dog" and "underdog" to describe the neurotic dance of power and powerlessness that we play out again and again. Most of us experience both of these unpleasant positions in life, but are usually more stuck in one, unconsciously looking for others to play the opposite role. In this "dance" we give control and power away when the situation matches our patterns; we interact with someone who—like pieces in a puzzle—is the perfect fit for our own neurosis, and we either take the role of top dog or underdog quite unconsciously. We may consciously detest whatever position we are in, but we perpetuate the behavior because it is tied to an unconscious payoff. If we are in the powerless position, we get to feel safe—our neurotic view of the world as the persecutor and ourselves as the victims has been affirmed and, once again, justified. If we are in the so-called powerful position, we continue to feel safe through domination and the illusion that we are, in fact, in control.

Usually the person who finds herself in the victim position will, sooner or later, switch into the persecutor, since we all have the drive to control other people. Living in community will force us to face our desire to control others, as a friend's T-shirt facetiously yet insightfully suggests, "If you can't control yourself, control others." Out of a sense of helplessness within ourselves we often try to control others: our children, our partners or spouses, the other members of community, the person on the other end of the phone, the clerk in the store—you name it.

A friend of mine tells a humorous story about her own drive to control. She loves milkshakes, but only when they are thick and lumpy, not thin and soupy. When she asks the counter person at the ice cream store to make them that way and they don't comply with her wishes, it causes her so much angst because of her lack of control that she has stopped ordering milkshakes and just sticks to ice cream cones. This is a mundane and even silly example, but she uses it as a way of pointing out how deeply embedded the desire to control life really is. If we can't have our milkshake the way we want it, we experience anxiety. Of course this applies even more so to those areas of our lives that are more primally connected to our survival than ice cream. (Although for some of us, ice cream is about as primal as it gets!) At this point, we must be able to laugh at ourselves. Through humor, honest self-reflection and the support of other members, community begs and demands that we empty ourselves of our need to control.

If our control issues are not honestly faced, and as a result we do not relax our grip on life, letting go of the belief that we should be in control because we are right and "they" are wrong, we will not enjoy the communion and companionship of real community. Instead, we will find that our life in community replicates our life before we entered into community—alienated, angst-ridden, full of unnecessary and uncreative conflict, panic and bitterness.

One of my dear friends has tremendous wisdom to offer her community, but it has been obscured for years by her unresolved and unmanaged obsession around power and control. Her life in community has forced these issues to the surface in strong and relentless ways, and she has had to listen to a great deal of feedback and criticism over time about her aggressive, domineering interactions with others. For example, she has attempted to control one of the communal kitchens because it happens to be

102

in the household in which she lives, even though the cook is the designated manager in this space. This has been an almost constant source of pain for her and for others living with her. After years of inner work on the underlying dynamics that fuel her need to control—having to do with feelings of powerlessness, victimization, betrayal and abandonment experienced early in her life—she finds that each time she speaks to the group she must go through a process of refinement and inner questioning. She must take her raw insights and communicate them in a way that can be used by the community at large. Sometimes this is just about the practical skills of communication and sometimes this requires that she let go, once again, of all the reasons why she wants to control this situation right now. One by one she works with each situation until her essential wisdom can come through.

We cannot wait until we are free of all confusion and ulterior motives around power, control and authority to enter into community life, and so we go on with living and working on refinements while we are interacting with others. When we have reached the clarity of really seeing our own habits, we then have new choices other than just reacting. We can begin to give up our fear of losing control, or our habit of giving away our control to authority figures, or our ferocious attachment to maintaining power over others and the outcome of situations. Finally, we can question, challenge and be a positive force for change in community with an energy and a power that is clean, confident and effective while at the same time cooperative and honoring of others as well as honoring of the group process. This is not an easy transformation.

Unraveling our individual relationship to issues of leadership, authority and power is a difficult journey to make, and sometimes we are simply unwilling to undertake such a healing. Instead, we go along with the status quo. Too often, however, the stance of denial leads to apathy about our individual responsibility within community, family or social group. We can

103

give our own power away all too easily in this case, which leads to the rebelliousness, suspicion, distrust, competition and the adversarial mood that so characterizes the way many modern adults relate to authority figures. When apathy and passivity masquerade as cooperation or being a team player, for example, they obscure the view that we are all responsible. In effect, we are all leaders whether we are in a position of recognized and formally empowered leadership or in a position of participation, in which we are called to support the formal leaders.

We need to connect to the view of community as being "one body" in which each individual has a different role to play—a role that may change from time to time. This vision should encompass serving the larger body in whatever way will most benefit the whole, which means a new appreciation for the meaning of work, participation and individual responsibility. We recognize that what each part contributes is invaluable to the functioning of the entire group. We can embrace these principles whether we have a group that functions strictly from a shared leadership or consensus model, or from a model in which there is a more hierarchical structure.

Sharing Leadership

A working community is a community of all leaders.
—M. Scott Peck

Many people are drawn to the ideals of shared leadership. In my experience, consensus decision making, for example, works best if the group remains small—five to ten people—although some communities have made this system work with much larger numbers. Working toward consensus can encourage bonding, and may benefit a type of group process that is intimate in character, particularly for healing or therapeutic work. It may also be helpful in projects undertaken by smaller subsets of the community. In this case, informally shared leadership and rotation of tasks can be tremendously inspiring and dynamic.

Some basic principles to apply in any consensus group situation include the following:

- Honesty is the best policy. This principle applies to self-honesty first and foremost, but equally to relating with others members in the group, or to the group as a whole. For example, consensus decision making lends itself to filibustering or grandstanding, and a lot of energy and momentum are lost by giving too much time and attention to this kind of activity. Usually a person who does this needs attention and gets it by creating emotional dramas, characterized by an unwillingness to cooperate in a system that depends on cooperation. Honesty here means being willing to confront the person, perhaps asking him or her how the group can best serve their needs. This kind of honesty may also mean confronting the whole group, like when a covert agreement not to talk about certain issues has crept in.

- Prioritize. Without the discernment to prioritize issues, a group can get extremely scattered and caught up in the personal domain of psychological "processing," thus forgetting or ignoring the big picture. Place time limits for every item on the agenda, including personal issues.

- Allow each other to be different. It's okay to disagree in the midst of discussion; through cooperative negotiation and the willingness to be flexible and hear each other out, we can usually come to some agreement that is satisfactory to everyone.

- Appoint a facilitator for every meeting and respect his or her authority. For example, when the facilitator says, "We've

105

spent too much time on this," or "Dan, you're not hearing what Susan is saying. You need to put your projections aside and listen as objectively as possible," we need to abide their direction. Allow each other to take turns in facilitating group process. Also, be willing to allow leadership to spontaneously arise as necessary. In certain moments, one person will automatically be the voice of wisdom, while at another time someone else may have their finger on the pulse of how group vision and context needs to be applied to a situation.

• Trust the process. Allow yourselves to come into an organic, instinctual relationship to your lives together. When we are in touch with the wisdom inherent in every human being we can trust the greater intelligence of life itself to guide unerringly.

"Consensus minus one" is another variation of group decision making. In this case, if the group as a whole is willing to come to agreement, but one person still disagrees, he or she can, in the spirit of cooperation, decide not to vote.

One of the dangers of consensus decision making in larger groups is that one or two persons, or a small sub-group may decide they are no longer willing to cooperate, and can begin to dominate over the majority. Without the strength and vision of a leader or authorized decision-making body of leaders, a group can fall to the lowest common denominator, and dissent, resentment, anger and even violence can break out as members get locked in a vicious power struggle. Rhiannon's story testifies to such a situation.

Rhiannon Speaks About Power

At Beech Creek Community decisions were made in a circle. Whenever a conflict arose or a major decision had to be made, the group would gather together out under the big walnut trees in good weather, or in the living room of the old main house around the huge cast iron stove in the winter. There we would spend hours hashing out the issues, giving everyone an equal voice and vote, and attempting to come to consensus. Sometimes we handed a stick or a gourd around to designate who had the floor as we took turns talking. We wanted everyone to be equally empowered, and our belief in shared leadership bordered on religious fanaticism. So much so, that after six years, when our community was in a state of extreme fluctuation and some of our original number had drifted away to live in cities and pursue careers, we made the decision to become exclusively a women's community. It was 1976, and radical feminist politics and spirituality were strong, vital undercurrents in the alternative communities that could be found all across the U.S.

As a women's community, we took our radical politics and ideals even further. We attacked anything and everything that we considered patriarchal in ourselves and others; we shunned hierarchies of any kind, and charged headlong into the morass of classism, racism and prejudice that we saw in each other. It was like advancing full speed through a swamp; many areas remained murky for each of us, but we pursued them aggressively anyway.

We tried valiantly to have shared leadership, yet just under the surface of this idealism, some of us wielded a kind of unacknowledged and therefore unconscious (to the group) authority. There were those who naturally rose to the need for leadership at different times, and served in these positions no matter how much the group wanted to avoid centralized authority of any kind. In later years I found in other communities that this is quite common.

We chose to live, so that we had as little interaction with the world at large as possible. We were busy gardening, building cottages and cabins on our land, and psychologically "processing" with each other. We were fascinated with our own life stories and with building mythologies around them; we were shamans, we thought—politico-spiritual warriors dancing out on the edge of our

107

times. We discovered the Goddess and created many rituals long before they were a popular New Age pastime. We made beautiful jewelry with seeds and feathers and played drums and danced around the fire at night. We invoked a tremendous tribal spirit amongst ourselves. We chanted in the sweat lodge. We made our land and our resources and energies available to women in crisis, women who were just out of prison, women dying of cancer, women who were seriously ill and needed twenty-four-hour care. We provided some degree of sanctuary for them and for each other.

But we were also wallowing in our own unconsciousness and selfishness—split between our conscious idealism and our denial about our own shadows. Alcohol and drugs began to spring up among us; we became more and more abusive of substances and each other. While we were exploring territory in human relationship and attempting to build an alternative culture inspired by our vision, we had no idea how far we really were from being able to wisely embody the spiritual or political principles we so righteously articulated. We advocated the free expression of individual liberty, total equality for each person, freedom from racism, classism, sexism, agism and prejudice against sexual preferences, an environment that supported the individual's spiritual growth and self-actualization, living in harmony with the Earth and so on. But we hadn't done the basic housekeeping necessary to deal with the indoctrinated conventional world that each of us carried deep inside. We hadn't faced our own greed, drive to power, vanity, pride and avarice. We also hadn't really faced the ways in which we lacked self-respect and self-esteem. We began to tap into forces in our own psyches that we had no idea how to handle. We were wounded healers, lost in the underworld of our own arrogant lack of true self-knowledge. And, we had no structure for real leadership.

When a group of women who called themselves "gypsies" approached our community in 1977 asking to live there, we assumed that their intention was the same as ours. We wanted to make the opportunity to live on this beautiful, immense piece of land available to other. With some reservations, we opened the doors to the land and the community. It was the right thing to do, based on our beliefs.

Within weeks, these newcomers to our community were suddenly different. They became controlling, defining what was politically or spiritually correct based on motives that were clearly self-serving. They quite masterfully divided us amongst ourselves, and soon they were dominant forces within the community. We struggled with them in an effort to maintain some unity around our original vision, but at the same time we wanted to be flexible to change and "do the right thing." Because of our deep lack of self-respect as women, we were easily swayed by guilt or by someone who touted themselves as a greater authority than ourselves.

A year later, another group of women came who also wanted to live on the land. Again we said yes. Soon there was a distinct split between two factions—one made up of the newer members, women of color and "gypsy" women, and the other of white women who had lived on the land and been in the community from its early years. This latter group desperately struggled to maintain some semblance of the original vision, yet also succumbed to a self-destructive impulse in themselves. The two groups became consumed by their differences, and the shadow side of our group unconscious—those parts of ourselves that we wanted to deny and avoid looking at—took over.

At the end we were locked into a war of domination, a power struggle over the land itself. Someone was going to dominate and rule, and we women had become the very thing we denied and rejected in mainstream patriarchal American culture—authoritarian bigots corrupted by power and by the very empowerment that we had given to each other, or else scared, powerless victims of a tyrannical oppressor.

For me the last straw came when I was away for a week and the women on the land made a new "rule"—no male children were allowed on the land. My son had been living and later visiting regularly on the land for six years, since he was two years old. I was shocked and betrayed, but I also realized that I could no longer live with the "ideals" that were being embraced and even enforced.

I left the land and did not return. In fact, all those whose names were on the deed to the property and who had been in the community since the beginning also left the land. We were broken hearted and deeply disillusioned that we had been unable to transcend our racial and political and even spiritual differences (a contradiction in terms) to bond into a greater possibility and ultimately, to steward the sacred land that was entrusted into our care. What we saw in each other was our own shadow, including all the injustices we had perpetrated on others, on our brothers in community, on our parents and friends. We too had participated in a kind of fascism disguised as left-wing politics. We saw our own unwillingness to be kind and understanding to those who differed from us in any way. What had happened to our vision, our spiritual quest, to the magic and freedom of the early years in community? What had happened to those years of loving the Earth and learning so deeply from the land itself? What had happened to caring more about the land than our own petty drive for personal power? What had happened to our bond as human beings? How could we have gotten so lost? The shadow exists in any group or any individual, but we were, for the most part, young and inexperienced, and those members of the original community who were older and more experienced, and who tried to talk some sense into us, were just crying in the wind. In retrospect I wonder, if we had had wise elders to guide us, would we have listened?

Today Beech Creek Community is an empty piece of land. The ownership is reverting back to the woman who originally purchased the land in 1970. Its former inhabitants are scattered in all directions, and many have gone on to live in other communities, as I have. The lessons I learned there were invaluable to me. I've found that one either grows in wisdom and character from these kinds of broken dreams, or one becomes bitter and hardened. It took many years to integrate the experience I had at Beech Creek, because it was my home for six years, and I was deeply identified with its ideals and vision. To see those hopes and dreams smashed on the hard rocks of reality was a shocking lesson, but it became fuel for a fire that wouldn't die—my belief in community, in the basic goodness of all human beings no matter how confused or wounded, and the possibility of living a life dedicated to a higher purpose.

The Beech Creek experiment was a good example of the theory of dissipative structures at work. The community was dealing with a level of energy, or chaos, that forced change every two years or so. For the first six years, it was able to re-order itself on the other side of chaos, but the more closed and insular the system became, the less it was able to ride through the high energy of change to survive. And, without the rudder of solid leadership to hold steady the vision and context, the entire community fell apart. This kind of "death" can be the most natural and appropriate next step in the evolution of the community. As an organism that should benefit its members; there are times when a community must disband, releasing individuals to carry on with their lives in completely new directions or circumstances in order to grow and evolve.

The intention held by the active leaders of a group—whether they are formally recognized or informal, unrecognized leaders who arise out of a consensus-type group—makes a large difference in the results of any decision-making process. Educator A. S. Neill and the Summerhill school he ran in England is a good example of this. At Summerhill, each person had an equal vote in all decisions—each child, each staff member, Neill himself—and the majority ruled. After Neill's death it became clear that it was not so much the democratic system itself that worked so much magic at Summerhill as it was the context he had created through his vision—his passion for the school and his respect for the children. Because he held the context for that

111

vision so strongly, his work was an inspiration to many parents and educators for years to come.

Another great example of the egalitarian, shared leadership vision working within community is seen at Twin Oaks, a thriving intentional community founded in 1967, and based on the principles set forth in the book *Walden II*, by behaviorist B.F. Skinner. Impressively, for over thirty years, Twin Oaks has survived the tests of time. Deborah Slavin, one of the founding members of Twin Oaks and its sister community, East Wind, commented on their system of shared leadership: "Most of the people here have been managers, and they don't like it. If they wanted to be managers, they'd be out working for IBM." [6]

East Wind Community, founded in 1974 in the Ozark Mountains of southern Missouri, is another very successful, non-hierarchical egalitarian community. East Wind members boast that they have no bosses in their three community businesses which gross more than $2 million a year. Within their system, which has worked for a quarter of a century, they make decisions democratically and promote nonviolence and equality among members. Writing about their management system, Anna Young notes:

> As an egalitarian community, we try to ensure that all members are equal in status. Of course, some tasks are hard to accomplish unless someone is nominally in charge. For this reason, we elect or appoint managers for different work areas; these managers control community-set budgets and approve the hours labor workers have claimed. Managers get no extra financial rewards; however, they gain satisfaction from seeing their work areas run smoothly and from reaching valued community goals. They don't have special or formal rank, but earn the informal respect of their peers through their contributions and accomplishments.[7]

Bernice Reagan is the originator and informal leader of the four-woman African-American gospel group, Sweet Honey in the Rock. In a workshop she made a fierce point about shared leadership, saying "You've got to let go your part, if you want to sing the way we do." She and the other women of the group have to be willing to step down from center stage and give each other space to weave in and out in a dance. This is true in community; in order to "sing" or work in one unified voice that flows, and inspires whoever listens, we've got to be willing to "let go our part" and allow leadership to arise as it is invoked within individuals. Furthermore, in order to become part of the greater whole, we must at times surrender our part, whether our part is a leadership role or a support position.

Leader as Servant

A new moral principle is emerging which holds that the only authority deserving one's allegiance is that which is freely and knowingly granted by the led to the leader in response to, and in proportion to, the clearly evident servant status of the leader. Those who choose to follow this principle will not casually accept the authority of existing institutions. Rather, they will freely respond only to individuals who are chosen as leaders because they are proven and trusted as servants.[8]

—Robert K. Greenleaf

Hierarchies have a bad name. Historically, they have been based on domination, competition and abuse of power, and kept in place by force. Typically, the wealth was owned by a few, and the power was wielded by a few, while everyone else suffered. Our European ancestors suffered from the oppression of hierarchies—from the priesthood of the church, to the royal and aristocratic families of Europe who bound their own people in

113

feudal servitude. For African-Americans and Native Americans, the wound of slavery, genocide and oppression has always been painfully in the forefront.

Yet, *Webster's Dictionary* defines "hierarch" as "a steward or keeper of sacred things." Undoubtedly, that definition has its roots in something ancient and forgotten in our culture. In her ground-breaking books, *The Chalice and the Blade* and *The Partnership Way*, Riane Eisler begins to revision the principles that a life-serving or "actualization hierarchy" might be based upon. Such a hierarchy would be exemplified in the molecules, cells and organs in the body, which represent a progression toward a higher and more complex level of functioning *for the good of the whole.*[9]

In my experience, at any level of community functioning a leader who has integrity is motivated by service rather than a hunger for power or the drive to control others. The leadership of any group will put in more hours, have more worries, and shoulder a greater part of the burden than others. In some groups, particular in Polynesian tribes, the shaman or spiritual leader of the community is expected to prove his leadership by his ability to feed the entire tribe at regular feasts. Not only does the shaman have to have the resources or wealth for this service, but he must also be able to orchestrate such a gathering—draw everyone together and even cook the meal.

Those of us who have worked in the business world know that a really good manager is one who empowers those working under his or her direction to grow and become all that they can become. Most of us have had at least one empathic boss who was able to inspire our loyalty and who motivated us to work hard with enthusiasm and even joy. The authoritarian boss, on the other hand, wielded power with a heavy hand, was shaming and repressive, acted superior and used threats to motivate. His or her communication was, "If you don't do what I tell you to do and suffer whatever emotional abuse (or other kinds) I dish out, you'll lose this job." On the other hand, a boss who is a real leader is an advocate for her employees, is willing to roll up her sleeves and pitch in to help whenever necessary. Such a leader does not find any task "beneath" her, is willing to listen openly to feedback and grievances, helps with problem-solving and freely gives of her support, time and assistance. A leader who serves others will also give needed criticism or corrections in a timely manner and then make every possible opportunity available to help others make those changes that are necessary. Leadership is about service to others.

Bernadette Speaks About Leadership

In the late 1960s, two years before I left the convent, I wanted to protest the Vietnam War. When my Mother Superior learned of this, she called me into her office. "I am against this," she said, "the other nuns are all against this, but I must tell you that I cannot ask you to go against your conscience. If this is what you must do . . ." She could have threatened me, forbidden me to do it, but she had too much integrity. She could have used her power and she knew that I would have obeyed, but she followed the spirit of the law rather than the letter.

Her willingness to have a personal relationship with each of the twenty-five or thirty nuns in our convent was a phenomenal expression of her commitment and her leadership skills. She was in her late thirties, and she had nuns under her care from elders in their early seventies to young nuns in their early twenties. She had to be extremely flexible. She was warm, motherly, intelligent, and a tremendous listener. She was willing to hear out many sides of an issue. She wasn't afraid to call something that she didn't approve of, or to say no, or to make a difficult decision. At the same time, she wasn't willing to use her authority to provoke a crisis of conscience. Even though she personally did not agree with what I wanted to do—and the position of the Catholic Church was that

115

they did not want nuns and priests taking political stands against Vietnam or marching in Selma, Alabama (one of the first times American nuns and priests had made a physical political presence)—she was willing to bend the rules for what she considered a higher law.

The following chart from *The Partnership Way* by Riane Eisler gives us a quick view of the differences between a social order that is based on domination, fear, force and competition, and one based on mutual respect, peaceful cooperation and creativity: [10]

Dominator Model	Partnership Model
fear	trust
win/lose orientation	win/win orientation
power over	power to/with
male dominance	gender partnership
sadomasochism	mutual pleasure
control	nurture
ranking	linking
one-sided benefit	mutual benefit
manipulation	open communication
destruction	actualization
hoarding	sharing
codependency	interdependency
left-brain thinking	whole-brain thinking
negative conditioning	positive conditioning
violence against others	empathy with others
taking orders	working in teams
alienation	integration
nuclear arms race	international partnership
war	peace
secrecy	openness/accountability
coercion	participation

indoctrination	education
conquest of nature	respect for nature
conformity	creativity

Eisler's model can be helpful in articulating something that we have all tasted in relationship—a sustenance for the soul that is deeply healing. Leadership is about relationship; in fact, we find that everything seems to boil down to relationship. Who doesn't want their relationships to be based on support, mutual respect and appreciation, creativity, peace, empathy, a sense of partnership? Regardless of how desensitized we may be to the politics of domination and conquest that run our world, we have been deeply wounded by the same within our family systems, our schools, our jobs, our churches. We are starved for real communion, for relationships that encourage us to be our very best. We are starved for trust, for someone to recognize and acknowledge our being, and to take a stand for that being. We long for the sanctuary of real partnership—for a message that says, "We are in this together, and you can count on me. I recognize and honor and celebrate that which is noble and essential and good in you. I will gladly stand beside you and be the beacon that calls forth that which is possible in you." A real leader communicates this to others.

The following reflections on leadership, service and transformation in community are taken from an interview with Craig, a longtime resident of a spiritual community, who has held many leadership roles.

Craig Speaks About Leadership

I was headed toward community since before I even knew it. In 1975 I put up signs that said, "There's got to be something more than what happens in college. Can we come together and figure out what it is?" I thought just a few people would respond, but

117

seventy-six people showed up! I had no experience in speaking to groups. In fact, I had no experience of being in groups at all. Suddenly there I was sitting in front of a room of people—that's where it started for me.

The group met once a week and we called ourselves the Thursday Night Group. We met for a year and a half and it soon came down to fifteen people. I think the group got smaller when people realized that we were serious—we were not just going to "talk about it," we were going to "do" it. And so we did.

We did a lot of crazy kinds of things that college kids do to go against the norm. But it got to the point for me where it wasn't authentic or deep enough because we were only together for three hours on a Thursday night and sometimes on the weekends. I wanted community, but I didn't use that word because I didn't really have any clear concept of what that was, or what it was that I really wanted. I wanted people who were willing to live at the level that I wanted to live, and I knew that level of intensity didn't come from what we learned in school. I wanted life at a higher level of meaning, intensity, clarity . . . all of that and more.

I started talking about "Aliveness" to my friends in the Thursday Night Group, and they said, "What are you talking about?" I said, "Let's make a temporary community; let's set up a three-month time period in which we will basically live together. We'll have our own school where we will live together and work together."

We borrowed a piece of land, which turned out to be at the very tip of Baja, California, on the beach. That added a whole new dimension to the experiment. We just packed all of our stuff into two cars and headed out to live on the beach for three months— together.

It was an fantastic experience and I learned a lot! For one thing, I learned the "Last Guy" principle, which is that in a group of people, no matter how big—even in a group of two or three— there is going to be a "Last Guy," the person who is farthest away *from the group norm. The Last Guy is someone who's always got a problem, who always has a different opinion, who never agrees with anybody else. The typical human psychology says, "If we could just get rid of this guy then we would be fine," and so you get rid of this guy and then somebody else becomes the Last Guy. That's the principle: there is always a Last Guy.*

Community is about living and being in a way that includes everyone, so I use that principle now on the ashram in France where I live with eleven other people. There is clearly always a Last Guy there too: somebody who is older than everybody else, or who is more stuck in his or her neurosis, or who is less enthusiastic. But that's not what community is about. It is about including those people, and so leadership is about creating a place where the Last Guys are all included.

You can't create inclusion by forcing other people to say, "Hey, this is the way it is," or "Hey, just get off it and line up with everybody else around this," whatever it may be. You can't force the group to accept someone's differences. But a group leader can and must create the space to include the last person.

Community can be hell, because you will always have individual psychologies or chemistries that don't fit together well, and serious clashes and craziness can happen. When you get a diverse number of psychological types and chemistries trying to blend together to create a coherent group, the only way to live together under those circumstances is if the group is really committed to serving something—a vision of something—that is bigger than themselves. The leader's job is to serve that vision.

Creating community with all those diversity of types means you will have to invest a lot of time and energy in being together— besides working and maybe playing some too. This means having meetings: decision-making meetings, teaching or educational meetings, household meetings, meetings about special projects, meetings to work out interpersonal differences. This is what it takes to feed the vision of what your community is about. Many people don't see these meetings as feeding the vision together, they see it as solving problems. But there are two ways you can look at all this time and energy being channeled into meetings: one is the fun way, the inspired way, and the other is the way of complaint and problems and the impossibility of it all. Of course, from one point of view it is impossible to create community, given the human psychological condition that we all must deal with in ourselves and each other. So the vision that fuels this whole thing has to come from outside of the domain of human psychology, which brings us back to serving something greater than ourselves. Anyone in a leadership position has to make that vision of something bigger the center of what we do as leaders, rather than putting "me" as leader in the center. The vision is what makes it all work, that which makes it inspired and meaningful and worthwhile.

There are two kinds of leaders. One is purely a facilitator, which is what I tried to be for a long time. I was willing to organize and be responsible in ways, but not to be a real leader. So I might be willing to organize a meeting and ask if anyone wanted to talk about anything, but I wouldn't bring the vital issues to the forefront, and take on the role of inspiring and educating others. I was willing to listen and nurture others, but not to take a stand for what I knew to be critically important to the fundamental vision and purpose of our group. That worked okay for awhile, but we didn't really go anywhere with it. I learned that I kept waiting for somebody else to be the leader, because that's what I wanted to be involved in—a dynamic, forward moving group led by someone with creative insight. But there was nobody else willing to be the leader, so it ended up that if I wanted this ashram to happen, then I had to be the leader.

To create something that moves toward and beyond the edge of what human beings are capable of is my vision of community as a transformational vehicle. It doesn't have to happen in some dramatic way. It can happen just in terms of raising children or in simply living together.

We can move beyond the limits of what's normally possible for humanity in any area of life, in something as basic as embodying real kindness. But nothing extraordinary will happen until there is an individual or individuals who are willing to sacrifice or surrender their personal agendas and private, personal life to fully serve the good of the group.

Being a leader is like being a conduit for the group so that something can become possible that wasn't possible before. Who I seek to be in a leadership capacity at our ashram is the space through which transformation occurs. When you sign up for a leadership position, then you have signed up for responsibility in spades; you become responsible for serving the higher purpose or vision of the group. What I'm talking about is like signing up for something much bigger than you are—like IBM Corporation, for example. Once you sign the contract, you might make yourself useful to IBM, but you have just hooked yourself into $50 billion and tens of thousands of people and computers, and enormous resources. Good people are attracted to you because of what you represent. Suddenly you have a secretary and staff and lots of people helping you, but that is because you represent something that is much, much greater than you.

In the same way, a person in a spiritual community, like the one I am part of, can sign his or her name on the dotted line and become the opening, the conduit, that someone in a leadership role is, because he or she is representing a much higher possibility.

Just like an IBM representative, a real leader should be accountable to a higher authority. In my community I am accountable to our spiritual teacher, who also has a living spiritual teacher in India, who had a spiritual teacher in his own time. The higher authority or power is a whole lineage of individuals who surrendered their lives to the Divine. Even in the leadership role of spiritual teacher, if the teacher is a real teacher, is authentic, then he or she is also accountable to a higher authority.

For me, all this boils down in incredibly simple actions. Washing dishes is an incredible space for communicating, for relationship, and even for transformation of your psychological habits into something organically natural and radiant and appropriate to the needs of the moment. What you are doing is washing the dishes, but what is happening is alchemical. Therefore, you might consider, in any space like that, how fast or slowly you are moving, or what you are talking about. For example, in order for a space to be transformational, one can only speak the truth. There is no room for playing psychological games of one-upmanship or victim/persecutor. There are a zillion things you can do in the action of washing dishes, and a leader demonstrates this to others by exemplifying it, so that when you ask who wants to wash dishes, twelve peoples' hands go up! That is because washing dishes has an infinite possibility now. As a space holder or group leader, at whatever level, you can create that! This is part of how a leader opens up the possibility that people are something other than just a mechanical, psychological being. That's what facilitates the group staying together: it is guided by something that is greater than their psychology.

A so-called "normal" Western psychology will not sustain community because community confronts our illusions of who we are; of reality versus our opinions, projections and preferences. Without a guiding source that has some transformational power in the face of that kind of psychological bias, community cannot happen. This guiding source must have an influence that is big enough, with enough force, to make the energy available to produce love in a psychological domain that can be hell. So community produces love in hell—that's magic, and that's impossible! It doesn't happen in a linear way.

How my spiritual teacher guides me to be in a leadership role is not a linear process for him. It's not like he says to me, "Here's an outline for a procedure for the meeting you are about to have."

I have to be receptive to organically and instinctively know that we need to have a meeting at our ashram, and then organize and facilitate and bring inspiration and guidance that represents his teaching to that meeting.

What I am looking for is feedback from my teacher. The ideal way to work with feedback from my teacher, or mentor, is conveyed in two words: one is yes, and the other one is okay. If my teacher comes in with a suggestion, saying, "Craig, why don't you do this or that, how about it?" then the answer is yes. In order to learn from him, I need to approach our relationship in the spirit of agreement and receptivity in such a way that he can work with me and facilitate my own education. If he gives me feedback—praise, for example—then the answer is okay. If my teacher gives me feedback that is critical and I have to "lose face," so to speak, the answer is also okay. That kind of willingness to learn, to fail, to succeed, to be steady in the face of positive or negative feedback, facilitates my ability to serve something greater than myself.

I'm willing to take direction and without hesitation to say yes. The thing is, I have to know that I need guidance from someone who has gone farther down the path than I have. I have to want that guidance, to really desire it. I have to want my own growth and transformation, and I have to be willing to sacrifice and work hard for it.

Anyone who wants to be a leader has to commit one hundred percent, and anyone who wants community to work has to commit one hundred percent. Community is not designed for efficiency. It's more like hiking overland barefoot with as much weight on your back as you can carry and sore feet.

In my experience, community has to have trustworthy leadership, which means that the leaders are accountable to a higher authority, and are working on themselves—relentlessly! There is no end to that process.

The Charismatic Leader

Sometimes there is one individual in community in whom the vision burns so brightly that we choose to empower him or her as a leader. This "bright burning" is true of charismatic leaders—those visionaries who embody a context and vision to such a degree that, in some instances, they are a living representation of it. Because they have embodied a vision, they are able to inspire others to live that vision.

Many religious communities are founded by a charismatic leader, but secular communities will find that this is an issue as well. Psychotherapeutic communities are usually founded by one charismatic leader or couple; sometimes one individual will stand out over time in a community and slowly take up a position of charismatic leadership. This too can happen unconsciously within a group. Rhiannon of Beech Creek Community remembered a visitor who came to her community, who later reported to friends, "Don't believe what you hear; that community is controlled by one powerful and charismatic woman." This was the visitor's perception of the underlying dynamics of a group committed to a shared leadership and consensus structure.

The shadow side of charismatic leadership has caused a great deal of fear. As soon as we see a charismatic leader emerge—a guru, for example—we are prone to yell, "Cult!" And yet there have been many examples of charismatic leadership— both religious and political—who have inspired our allegiance, called forth a vision for positive change and had a transformative impact on the human race: Gandhi, Martin Luther King, Ramana Maharshi, Lech Walesea, John Kennedy, Sojourner Truth, Golda Meir, Nelson Mandela, Teresa of Avila, Anwar Sadat, Anandamayi Ma and Jesus of Nazareth, to name a few. I would include extraordinary artists who draw world attention with their message, like John Lennon or Bob Dylan, in this category as well, because the artists and actors of today are certainly in positions of acting leadership in our culture. The contribution of these charismatic leaders is untold. On the other hand, we have Adolf Hitler, Jim Jones, Imelda Marcos, Jim and Tammy Baker, Jimmy Swaggart, Ayatollah Khoumani as representatives of destructive charismatic leadership.

If we as an entire culture, or we in the microcosm of our respective communities, try to suppress or legislate against all avenues of charismatic leadership, we are cutting ourselves off from a basic creative impulse in human nature. Where would the world be without these extraordinary individuals who have taken on the yoke of inspired leadership, often at great personal sacrifice, even the cost of their own lives? We will find that certain individuals carry the community vision in a fiery and passionate way, and have the ability to articulate our cause, to mobilize and move us, even around a simple project. For example, if our community is restructuring its legal incorporation, one person in the community might have the charisma—that is, the clarity, vision and passion—for getting this job done for everybody's sake. On a larger scale, someone in the community may become nationally known as an impassioned spokesperson for the principles of community in general. If our group is generally biased against charismatic leadership, these individuals may come under fire of criticism from their peers, rather than being supported to be as creative and forward leading as they may be. We need to keep an open mind with regard to the "stars" that arise within community, and the "comets" as well. We need to give individuals the space to be brilliant in a way that can serve the good of the whole, rather than repressing that brilliance out of fear. That very brilliance that can bring the transformational impulse to life in community, and within the individuals of the community. When any one of us catches fire in a way that is transformational, that fire can then be passed on to others. A culture of wholeness and relatedness has no need to fear and every reason to embrace this kind of creative fire because this too is part of the totality of life.

Charismatic leaders may arise when there is a great need for change within our group or community, when a new insight or direction is needed. Some charismatic leaders take the form of a mentor, as in many academic or therapeutic situations, because they have the skill, insight and knowledge that others want and seek to learn from.

Although every community needs to allow and even encourage creativity on the part of its members, when it comes to the activities of leaders, especially the charismatic kind, we as individuals cannot afford to forego our personal responsibility. To follow blindly is a dangerous thing. Any charismatic leader with integrity will make it abundantly clear that they do not welcome blind followers, but are interested in fostering psychologically healthy individuals who choose to engage the particular relationship with a teacher, mentor or leader from a place of clarity and maturity.

The pitfalls of blind following are tangled up in our projections on others, and no one is free of unconscious projections. Father-figures, mother-figures, authority-figures, you-name-it-figures, are the perfect foils for our own unconscious psychological complexes. Most people are still attempting to "work it out" with their mothers and fathers through current adult relationships, even beyond the middle age of life. So, when a charismatic leader comes along, we may find ourselves doing things because we want Mommy's or Daddy's approval and love, rather than because we really agree, as adults, with the direction the leader wants to take. It requires a clear and confident individual to respond wisely to the guidance and impetus of a compelling leader or strong mentor.

We must question ourselves, our ideals and vision, and the leader; and then question again. This questioning process does not have an end point, but is an ongoing inquiry into the truth. Such personal inquiry is transformational for the individual who takes it to heart.

Of the many alternative communities that arose in the 1970s, the Jesus People's Shiloh Youth Revival Centers were the largest communal network of the Jesus People movement. It has been estimated that over 100,000 people participated in the Shiloh experiment during its twenty-year history. Shiloh eventually dissolved in a crisis over tax-exempt status, scandals related to money and a $1.7 million claim made by the IRS. But, one of the biggest blows came in 1978, when members asked charismatic leader and founder John Higgins to step down. From that time on, leadership was shaky at best. It seems that it was difficult, if not impossible, to recapture the earlier spirit of the community.

In spite of all these problems, many former Shiloh members today consider their time with the community to have been "the best experience of my life." [11] As *Communities Magazine* reported, "Most faulted their leadership's inability to process the conflicts maturely, as well as the squabbling of people hungry for power and control . . . [But despite] the problems, hundreds, if not thousands, of lives were changed for the better through the efforts of Shiloh and its people." [12]

Another example of charismatic leadership gone astray was the case of Graham Pulkingham, "a significant 'mover and shaker' among Christian communities in the 70s and 80s." Pulkingham headed the Community of Celebration in Scotland, and was later affiliated with the Community of Celebration in Colorado and the Church of the Redeemer in Texas.[13] A highly charismatic leader, Pulkingham was the religious mentor for thousands of people attempting to live in community. He founded a movement of discipleship or "shepherding" in which each Christian submitted to his or her spiritual authority. People who mentored directly under Graham Pulkingham and his wife Betty, submitted to them. These disciples, in turn, had others who submitted to their authority, and so a hierarchical structure of "shepherding" was created that spread throughout the U.S. Christian communities.

As this hierarchical system spread, all issues of life were put before one's spiritual mentor. This may not sound particularly problematical, but it unfortunately degenerated into an authoritarianism in which people's lives were controlled far beyond the basic Christian credo as put forth in the New Testament. In the Word of God community, for instance, men wore white cloth vests or "mantles" at community meetings to symbolize headship, while women wore white veils symbolizing submission. Husbands were encouraged to make up a weekly schedule for their wives to follow at home. Strict and highly repressive gender roles were insisted upon for religious reasons, and it was because of these kinds of authoritarian rulings that the Word of God community broke up in 1990.

Pulkingham's system within the Church of the Redeemer seemed to be maintaining its momentum until a series of sex scandals broke out in the early 90s. But the most shocking news to church members was that their charismatic leader had been involved in homosexual relations with several men during their community's "golden era."

Before his death from heart failure in 1993, Graham Pulkingham was asked what he would have done differently in his three decades of leadership within the religious community. He responded that he would have made himself accountable to an outside spiritual director or confessor.[14]

This issue of accountability is a recurring theme that becomes particularly urgent when one is dealing with charismatic leadership. Issues around gurus abound in Western culture today, and indeed there are many horror stories of sexual, physical and emotional abuse perpetrated by so-called gurus. But again, we must look to ourselves as the responsible parties: each person has to do his or her "homework" internally. The following story from Carolyn is a strong example of a hard-earned lesson in personal responsibility around a charismatic spiritual teacher.

Carolyn Speaks About A Charismatic Leader

After four experimental and wild years—one in India and the others in the U.S.—as a devotee of the Indian guru Osho Rajneesh, I planned to move to his ranch in Oregon. I had been committed to the spiritual path for many years, and had spent a great deal of time engaged in spiritual practices, and now was anxious to find the next step in my spiritual evolution. In that state of transition, I was not only vulnerable but also very susceptible to the charms of a man I will call Bill—a maverick American spiritual teacher, or guru, who had recently popped up on the scene in California. I was immediately drawn to his charisma, his brilliance and something strangely undefinable about him that I found very alluring but couldn't quite put my finger on. When I first met Bill, he questioned why I was going to the Oregon ranch, and he implied that I would be very influential and high up in his organization if I joined his small group instead. He found me mid-stream, so to speak, and offered security in a new path when I was unsure about what I was doing. He offered the promise of spiritual quest and enlightenment, but also the seduction of power, pure and simple. He appealed to my desire for power, saying that I would go right into his inner circle.

I had spent many years in what I thought was self-examination and spiritual disciplines, but this area around power was a whole area of my psyche that was unexamined and unconscious. Therefore, this power issue was ripe to be triggered and hooked into by someone as savvy and smooth at exploiting others for his own gain as Bill turned out to be.

He was, without question, a very charismatic leader with tremendously seductive powers, both sexually and energetically, who was so brilliant that people were fooled by his appearance.

129

There were so many different avenues along which he appealed to people; there was just enough idealism and raw reality that he was attempting to expose that it was incredibly desirable. His promise was "Liberation," a type of liberation and enlightenment power that would boost the individual to the status of an "Avatar"—a spiritual teacher in one's own right who would be redeeming humanity by one's very presence. One of the major flaws in his approach was that tremendous energy was being evoked in us, without any kind of training or practice to build a matrix, or an inner vessel, that would have the strength and maturity to work properly with this kind of force. The energy around him just over-amped your circuits until you blew out and burned up.

That is what happened to me. I had a nervous breakdown. When I was at my lowest point—feeling like I was the most worth-less piece of garbage on the face of the earth—he would be there, telling me that I hadn't "made it" because I was so willful and stu-pid, and that I was the reason his work wasn't progressing. He did not just do this with me; I saw clearly that this was his style with everyone in the group.

There are many legitimate spiritual paths that guide one toward shunyata (emptiness) or the realization of non-duality—most notably Vajrayana Buddhism—by undermining the tena-cious hold of ego, the mechanical personality and mind. But in this case, he was destroying our personalities without holding out a real possibility for transformation and without building a matrix of practice and context in us.

Even though I had years of discipline and prayer and years with Rajneesh, I still had never encountered this level of power. Bill was like a magician, casting veils of illusion over his disciples in the name of clarity, enlightenment, and even the Bodhisattva ideal. It is still difficult to talk about these things because so much of the pain and confusion was tied into my desperate wanting to have made this experiment work. But most of all, it's so embar-rassing to look back and see how seducible and crazy I was. Any

130

time I tried to figure out what he was doing, I would find myself just spiraling into more and more insanity. Even to this day it is difficult to see all the dynamics of what was going on.

Over time I have begun to see it wasn't just that he failed his disciples by not giving practices to build a matrix for spiritual life—he was a master manipulator, a charming psychopath who had to have the attention of all these people who worked with him at that time. He was a very sophisticated tyrant, he was a crazy-maker, he was deluded. A true tantric teacher might use what is called "crazy wisdom" in the Buddhist tradition, but he or she also gives you something that builds you and about which you can exercise discrimination. This man did neither. The language he used in describing what he wanted to do for the world was so close to the truth of the highest spiritual and humanitarian ideals that it was difficult to discern the twisted motives in it all, or the fact that he was kidding himself. It wasn't until you saw the results in his disciples that you knew there was something so wrong, so "off."

And that is precisely why these charismatic leaders are so profoundly dangerous—because what they say is so close to the truth, so misleading, so insidious that it twists the mind. You know that something is seriously wrong, but you end up thinking that you are what is seriously wrong. When you ask for help there is no way to get help because everyone else in the community is desperately trying to make this thing work. And you've been told that everyone outside of the community is a worm, deluded, or at best just plain ignorant.

Don't get me wrong; I was a well-educated thirty-five-year-old woman with a master's degree who had spent years teaching school and participating in many service organizations. I had been a social activist and a committed spiritual practitioner. I genuinely sought enlightenment because I wanted to serve in humility and clarity. But the raw facts of my experience with a charismatic leader who was doing it for all the wrong reasons is that he was able to hook into that in me which was unconscious and unworked, and to manipulate and control me from that place.

I am lucky because I got out, healed myself with the help of some very dear friends, went back to work teaching and eventually found another community and a remarkable teacher, with whom I have now worked for seventeen years. My teacher's integrity was well established over more than twenty-five years of teaching, and he is accountable to his own teacher in India, who is a revered saint and holy man.

One of the most valuable ways one determines whether a spiritual teacher is authentic or not is by looking at the results: if the students are generally clear-eyed, mature, strong, grounded, responsible, kind and compassionate with others, then the teacher is passing on something of value. If the students are scared, abusive, fragmented, scattered, nervous, spouting hysterical and adamant rhetoric, then one needs to think twice before getting involved in any way. I can think back on my time with Bill and see that was the case. Like I said, I count myself extremely fortunate; once hooked in, most people don't get out of these kinds of situations in time to really heal and go on; too often, these kinds of misguided, self-deluded charismatic leaders take their disciples down with them, in one way or another.

One of the great things about this story is that Carolyn was able to restabilize her life with the help of friends and then move on. She didn't let the experience make her bitter and distrustful, but stayed open and fluid in relationship with her environment, using it all for her maturation and growth. This is an example of gaining wisdom through perseverance. By staying committed to her original vision of finding an authentic spiritual teacher and path, Carolyn was eventually led there.

We will close this chapter about leadership with comments from Lee, a man who has led a spiritual community for more than twenty-five years.

Lee Reflects on Leadership

Essentially the reason someone should be chosen leader within a community or group, whether secular or spiritual, is because they have not just vision but also skills beyond the average skills in the members of the community. Leaders should be chosen not because of personality or because they've been around a long time. The skills the leader has helps the community run more smoothly, helps people find wisdom and clarity when they need it. Without that kind of "servant" at source—someone who can cut through the clouds of ignorance, fear and confusion and make decisions based on what is good for the community, based on the health and strength of the group—community must be essentially flawed.

Every community has to have a source individual. Often, a group of common individuals can't hold source together. By definition, the leader is servant, because without such a source any community must fail, or become totalitarian or fascist, or lose its sense of purpose, or become just a corporate entity. Sometimes the strongest visionaries can be neurotic or psychotic, so a visionary isn't always the best leader. The best leader must have the vision, but must also have a broad wisdom that can serve the complexity that any community is. In this day and age, one in a leadership role must understand the politics, decisions, legalities, and must have a foresight for the long-term implications of decisions. Without that kind of leadership function, the community is just guessing or working in the dark in terms of what is needed to be stable, ongoing and healthy.

The leader also has to stay contemporary in terms of education in the field in which the community is active, so that their decisions take into consideration current moods, fads, cultural trends, politics and so on.

Obviously every leader has to watch out for compulsions or obsessions with power. The leader has to make decisions based on the good of the whole, so he has to be mindful of and watchful for those personal decisions that he would certainly make differently were he not living in community. As for favoritism, certainly there is a human tendency to favor those with whom you have resonance or where there is an erotic attraction. The leader has got to make decisions absolutely based on what is just and right for the entire community at large. The leader has to be strong enough to resist those kinds of petty assaults on his or her integrity.

The leader must delegate authority to those who are reliable and trustworthy, and who will not fall into those same traps that are also dangerous for the leader. In the small picture, a person to whom the leader has delegated authority may take it as their purpose in life to make sure that other people "get the message," and that tendency toward authoritarianism or fanaticism is very dangerous. We have seen all too many examples of the delegation of authority getting out of hand in spiritual communities over the past twenty years, as well as examples of charismatic leadership running far off the track of serving the community.

Although the physical or practical functions of the leader may be very different from those of others in the community, the leader has to demonstrate a particular integrity, which is required of someone in a leadership position, so that all those who are in lesser positions of authority have that as a measure of rightness. I've known people who have fallen from charismatic leadership. I knew someone who, every time she gave a seminar, she took all the money from the seminar and went on a personal vacation with her husband, and nothing was put back into the community. It was as if she believed that the community should survive on her charisma alone, and no community can survive on charisma alone.

CHAPTER SIX

Diversity, Conflict and Communication

The most intense conflicts, if overcome, leave behind a sense of security and calm which is not easily disturbed, or else a brokenness that can hardly be healed. Conversely, it is just these intense conflicts and their conflagration which are needed in order to produce valuable and lasting results.

—Carl Jung

Community is anything but boring. According to Prigogene's theory of dissipative structures, mentioned earlier, an organism will either evolve—that is, change—or die. Like the yeast in bread, diversity can be the catalyst that gives life to community and keeps it expanding and evolving. Diversity is necessary for a truly creative synergy to happen within any group. If a community is stagnant then it is on it's way to degeneration.

Part of community's gift to its members is that it provides an arena for many different elements to coexist, so that an organic cross-pollination can happen among individuals. Thus we can learn and grow from each other, and discover that in spite of our differences, we are fundamentally much the same. Differences of opinion, of style, of beliefs and background actually can give us a tremendous pool of resources from which to draw enrichment for our common ground of community.

While many intentional communities attract only certain types of individuals, exaggerated efforts to create an ethnically, racial or socially diverse community can leave everyone feeling artificial. It may be more desirable to allow people to be drawn together naturally by the specific purpose and goals of the community, rather than attempting an "equal opportunity" situation. While still remaining open to diversity in *form*, we can definitely create diversity in *mood and context*.

We create a mood of diversity by allowing members room for self-expression, and by encouraging fluidity, new solutions and alternative ways of viewing present situations. To invite diversity means to open ourselves to considering anything, within reason, that might aid in the creation of our vision, even though such things may push up against our comfort level. It means to open our minds to endless possibilities, instead of thinking only in black or white.

We are creatures of habit, and while we may intellectually know the value of diversity, *living with it* is another matter. Spiritual teacher Andrew Cohen speaks of a sense of always "leaning forward, slightly off balance." Such a condition means living on the edge of infinite possibility, thus preventing complacency. The seduction of comfortable complacency and apathy are so common to our culture that if we want to stay creative, alive and growing, we must guard against these attitudes. Encouraging diversity is one way that we can keep things free-flowing. On our own, without community, we might not create situations that involve new ideas, different kinds of input and the stimulation that actually irritates and provokes our indifference and attachment to a sluggish status quo.

Another way to foster a mood of diversity is to encourage visitors and guests. The influx of new energies from outside of our own intimate milieu is invaluable to community. We are given the opportunity to welcome the "stranger," and to provide hospitality to others, which is a gift in itself. The tendency to become inbred and cultic exists in every community. After all, we all speak the same "language," know each other well, have spent years together weathering storms that have created deep bonds—all wonderful aspects of community. But if we become too smug and insular in the security of a familiar and safe world, we can become a closed system, which can lead to the community's downfall. Jargon, for example, can be a problem in any system. Even among ourselves we may think there is agreement in the particular words and phrases we commonly use, yet we each may have a different understanding of them. Imagine the confusion this intensifies when interacting with those outside of our circle.

Widening our circle by encouraging visitors might include having guest speakers at community events to inform members of new ideas; it can mean staying in contact through the mail, telephone, e-mail and by visits with like-minded communities that share a similar purpose and vision as our own; keeping an open policy regarding visits by family members of community participants; or taking on a project that gets us out into the world in a service capacity, such as hospice work, mobilizing the community to organize food drives, or working in a shelter for the homeless.

In keeping an open relationship with the rest of the world we create a fluid exchange between the greater environment and the immediate environment. Our ability to communicate becomes a function of immediate human relationship and empathy, our horizons broaden, and we are seeded by new ideas so that community prospers.

When we foster diversity we are taking an attitude of generosity toward our fellow human beings, and that in itself is tremendously enriching and satisfying. When we allow others the freedom to exist in their diversity—and even in their idiosyncrasies and neuroses—we allow ourselves some of this same freedom.

In the spectrum of community we get to see, firsthand, how quickly and habitually we criticize and police one another and ourselves, and our aversion or fear of differences and diversity can really add fuel to this fire. This is often the case in the earlier stages of community, when we are still young as a group, and these super-critical tendencies have not yet been tempered in the fire of living together. When our goal is the creation of a community vision, however, we need to accept that even eccentric manifestations in ourselves and others often serve the creation of that vision. Pure creativity seems to hold no prejudices—it takes all the raw materials and uses them to its advantage. At some point within most communities, members reach a point where they stop constantly telling one another what they have done wrong, or complaining about the differences of others that rub them the wrong way. Others are left to discover their own mistakes and profit from them as they will. In this kind of culture, based on wholeness and acceptance of diversity, if someone has forgotten a responsibility they are not criticized or shamed for it; instead, that which was forgotten is just taken care of by another person. In most cases, when the original responsible party realizes his or her mistake, they are very capable of using that to firm up their commitment to be responsible in the future.

Different . . . But the Same

Many psychological and/or esoteric systems classify human beings within a limited number of psychological types—such as those identified in the Enneatype system, or in Carl Jung's psychology of types, or in the archetypal patterns of astrology. The fact that certain people remind you of others you have known in your life, as you remind others of people they have known, testifies to the viability of typology. Within community, therefore, you can be sure there will be someone who is, for you, the perfect projection of your mother, and someone you relate to as your father or big brother. As a result, life in community can and will put our unresolved and sometimes painful familial relationships in our faces over and over again. When we see these dynamics played out in ourselves and others, we are often

138

dismayed and shocked. Over time, however, such confrontation can help us to realize that our conflicts and irritations with others are not usually personal. In fact, such conflicts are more likely a function of the habits of a lifetime, crystallized in our individual psychological types, as we interact mechanically with other types.

If we are wise about human nature and have honestly examined ourselves, we find that the personality is only the surface level of who we are. Human beings are much deeper and more mysterious than this. Such acknowledgement helps create the imperative to push past the form of personality, and to know the other at the essential level of our common humanity. At the same time, knowledge of personality systems can be of tremendous value as we seek to transform ourselves through greater self-knowledge and understanding of the other.

In an earlier chapter, Bernadette's story affirmed that we may not always be able to tell, from the surface, how someone's work is serving the larger community, or the world for that matter, especially if their work is not predictable or preapproved. Accepting diversity forces us to search on a more instinctual level for the truth about ourselves and each other. Sometimes it may appear that something is disintegrating the community. In the Christian tradition, Judas might be seen as the example of the force of disintegration, yet his actions have been interpreted by some as absolutely necessary to Jesus' mission. Things are not always what they seem to be, and we have to be willing to look beyond the letter of the law to see with the eyes of wisdom.

G. I. Gurdjieff, a Russian mystic and spiritual teacher who lived and worked in the early part of the twentieth century, described three universal forces or principles of life at work in any given situation: the affirming force, the denying force and the reconciling force. To Gurdjieff, these three forces represented inviolable universal laws that are necessary to the process of evolution. Applying his distinctions to our life in community, we might say that sometimes a person is expressing the denying force in a given situation. I experienced an example of this when Mark, a man in my community, decided that he was not interested in pursuing any of the already established jobs that were available—jobs that very much needed to be done. The only thing he was passionate about was compiling a book about sexual relationships and how they could be transformational. Mark spent almost all of his time working on this book, often to the chagrin of the rest of us who had a different idea of what he could or should be doing. Of course, he got a lot of criticism from his peers. People grumbled behind his back as well as to his face, and the fact that the group did not release him psychically to work on his project probably made it much harder for him to get the book done. My own attitude toward Mark's work was one of disapproval and resentment. "How can you be so selfish?" I said to him.

Mark's book was eventually published and has since become a source of tremendous benefit to our community—as well as to many other people—in many ways we could not have imagined during those two years when he worked on it. For me, the success of Mark's project was a stark reminder that sometimes it is the person who appears to be the most neurotic, the most irascible, the most uncooperative or seemingly unproductive member of the community who actually serves its long-term growth by forcing us to go beyond ourselves—to transform our feelings of scarcity and fear into generosity and understanding.

In the merging of work and energy that community fosters, we should strive for the balance of blending but not homogenizing. We need to keep the friction created by diversity conscious, rather than letting it stop us from coming together. In fact, we can actually use that friction-energy toward personal transformation. More often, for the sake of comfort, we push one another to convert to our opinions and beliefs, instead of taking all that comes as fuel for the process. Diversity that is allowed to thrive in

140

community creates a self-checking mechanism. When we allow and encourage questioning and differences we prevent rigidity from taking hold within the group; we discourage a cultic attitude or a "group mind" from forming.

Group Mind

"Group mind" refers to the herd mentality that can take over a community, in which we become blind followers instead of conscious, discerning individuals. It is one of many ways in which denial is propagated within groups. An unconscious community "head" easily arises—that is, a habitual pattern of thought which the members share in a covert way with one another without honest self-reflection or questioning.

Our unquestioned assumptions, opinions and general mindsets stem from our upbringing (or reaction to our upbringing), the present values of the culture we live in, or the habitual nature of the human mind. We tend to pick partners and friends who will maintain that structure with us, and then we raise our children to join us in maintaining that structure. For example, we may indoctrinate children in the commonly held spiritual beliefs of the community rather than giving them options and education about many different faiths and traditions, while also offering opportunities to participate in the spiritual tradition of the group. (It has been my experience in community that when children are given options and information, they will gravitate toward the spirituality that is most resonant for them, at the age that is organically right for them.)

Every group, therefore, has a number of shared mindsets, some of which are positive—a natural function of our mutual vision and purpose; an outgrowth of our bondedness. The downside, however, is that the peer pressures of group mind can fool us, encouraging us into actions that as individuals we would never do. We begin to feel that our group knows more, has the

141

inside line on how things should be. Our own individual insecurities and lack of self-worth are assuaged by believing that we are part of a group or movement that is superior. Religious communities are more susceptible to this seduction, but secular communities can polarize themselves against the larger world and human family as well.

Peer pressure within a bonded group can become very dangerous without a context that helps guard against the negative side of group mind. When we are creating our group vision, this is something that needs to be profoundly considered. Encouraging diversity within our group can also do a great deal to help alleviate the negative side of group mind.

Group mind is unavoidable, but if we have a conscious agreement to identify and break false assumptions, we can create a strong support system. Scott, who has lived in community since he was fourteen years old, talks about confronting group mind.

Scott on Group Mind

People in community sometimes think they are immune to the dynamics of group mind because they are in an intentional community, and that assumption is very dangerous in my experience. That very assumption is the nature of group mind—"It could never happen to us, it just happens to them." I have had experiences of pointing things out in my own community and seeing people react as if offended at having group dynamics pointed out. In spite of this kind of reaction, I have found that I have to speak the truth as I see it.

I think everyone has consciousness. But on the other hand, if people examine themselves, if they self-observe with honesty, then they have to acknowledge that primitive-mob-mind-stuff is part of their psyche. It's part of every human psyche. No one is exempt. Because of this, a continuous conscious struggle against group mind is necessary—it's an ongoing human battle, forever and ever.

The mob mentality is hard-wired into us as social animals. The dynamics of mob mentality are coded in our DNA, so a constant vigilance is required to become conscious about this biological tendency. People would like to think that they've considered it and can just move on, but that simply is not the nature of the problem.

When someone new walks into any crowd, everyone else turns and looks to check them out to see if they are a threat. Even within a community there is usually an "inner circle" and an "outer circle"—the "in" crowd and the "fringes." I have been in both positions, and I see that wherever I was, was what I identified with at the time. There was a tendency to feel that whichever group I was in seemed to hold the higher moral ground.

Communities can become tremendously exclusive and inbred, which also contributes to group mind. Getting honest with ourselves about these dynamics probably won't be a singular cosmic event. Really, the antidote is just to have a sense of humor, because group mind is humorless. Group mind takes itself very seriously.

Self-parody and skits can be a good thing for a group to do. If someone in the group notices the discussion going in a direction that is bureaucratic, or going in a direction that is really exclusive and righteous, or "us versus them," it can be very helpful to offer something that breaks the momentum in the conversation, or returns the group to a more balanced perspective. This might be done by making an absurd comment, or by exaggerating an obvious end to which the discussion is leading. Someone could also just interrupt and say, "Wait a minute—what are we doing here?"

It is tremendously important for group mind to be intentionally confronted in this way within community. It's a dirty job sometimes, because people can get really angry and defensive about it. But, the way I see it, somebody has to do it!

If we don't bring humor to the confrontation of group mind, the foibles and limitations of community as well as our limitations as human beings will make us despairing, bitter or self-hating.

143

In my community, we try to incorporate humor in our observations of self and others. (What else can one do in response to the absurdity of the human condition sometimes, but laugh or cry? I prefer to laugh as much as possible.) During times of celebration, we often spoof ourselves in skits and songs that have us all laughing hysterically at our own silliness. Once we published an entire issue of our community journal that was pure satire in the attempt to stop taking ourselves so seriously. In the creation of that piece we saw how difficult it can be to balance honest self-observation and humor without criticism or cynicism. That heartful balance is necessary for viable community.

Another way of disempowering a rigid group mind is to embrace the contribution of new members. It is all too easy to write off the insights and feedback of new people by relegating them to a "junior" status, when in fact their very newness can be used for the good of the group. New people bring new life to community with their innocence, enthusiasm and fresh perspective. They are often willing to confront those monuments to group mind—the "sacred cows" of community.

Every community has sacred cows—ideas, systems, or even individuals who have become so institutionalized (and thus crystallized) that no one dares to challenge them, even though they may have become inefficient and obsolete. Guests and visitors also make us aware of those things that the "group head" may be in denial about. For example, they may challenge a sacred cow quite innocently, unbeknownst to themselves, simply by an offhand remark. Such input is invaluable to community, however, because the tendency of human beings is toward inertia, to maintain the comfortable status quo.

A man who had been a long-term resident of my community moved to San Francisco to work for awhile. One day he sent us a letter entitled "Just Visiting," in which he charged his friends in community with having failed to call him to task on the principles to which he had dedicated his life. In other words, we did not

144

draw forth his essential being, but let him slide into old habit patterns that were not conducive to his growth. This was done by giving him a "senior member" status, and by not questioning his actions or calling him to accountability. In effect, he had become a sacred cow, as no one had been willing to risk giving him feedback. As a result, he felt he had missed a chance to take full advantage of the benefits of community while he lived with us. When leaders are romanticized and idealized to the point that community members are afraid to question their decisions or a direction that is being taken, then leaders too have become dangerous sacred cows.

As community grows we can easily fall into depersonalization, creating a system of rules and protocol that separate us from dynamic relationship with one another, thus creating a group mentality that goes unquestioned. Such tendencies can sneak up on us so that we are blind to them, sometimes until it is too late to make the necessary changes that will shatter the growing crystallization.

There are many other ways that we can work against an unconscious community "head." For instance, each individual can learn the difference between rhetoric and inspired speech—the first, a function of living in the mind as separate from the rest of the body; the other, an affair of the body/mind as an integrated whole. Through self-observation we catch ourselves when we are speaking the party line without really feeling and choosing the words and thoughts that make it up. Our power of choice must be kept alive, and community involvement is a choice we make over and over again. When we chose with consciousness, and admit the times when we are not choosing it also, we take full responsibility for life rather than falling victim to it. When we move away from our own raw and felt experience, and speak in intellectualized or blanket statements—as we all do at times—we separate ourselves from one another and from our own reality as well.

Children help us to confront group mind, if we let them. I have found that the children in my community—and children in general—serve to remind us to be real, immediate and ordinary with them, rather than mechanical and righteous. When adults consistently say, "That kind of energy dynamic is not appropriate in this space," or "Please calm your energy down," rather than just saying, very simply and directly, "You are being too rowdy in the house and I want you to stop," it is no wonder the children tune them out. In our community, the adolescents feel free to tell the adults when we are mechanically spouting our community lingo rather than speaking *with* them. Hopefully in a culture that encourages diversity and communication based on relationship rather than impersonal ideology, we can all remind one another when we have forgotten the human spirit.

Conflict Within Community

Many books are available on conflict resolution in community or groups. My intention is not to re-hash any of that well-covered ground, but rather to focus on the context of resolving conflict in human relationship.

A community can have all the processes, psychological formats, and one-two-three steps for conflict resolution in the world, but without heart, sincerity and most of all, context—the deep desire to resolve or let go of any conflict that comes between us as human beings—genuine resolution will not happen. We may be able to patch up minor skirmishes, but when we come head-on into serious conflict, we will be stopped. What often happens in such cases is that the issue has been resolved, but the roots of the conflict continue to fester under the surface as resentment and even rage. Sooner or later, the conflict will erupt again, and often in more unpleasant ways, and the power struggles will wage on. Unresolved power struggles—which is what almost all conflict between people is ultimately about—will escalate until the container of community either breaks from the force of tension, or one of the two conflicted parties or factions leaves.

Whether we are resolving conflict within a partnership, a marriage, a family, between friends or co-workers or between factions in a community, we must have relationship with others as the goal and guiding star. As we've discussed previously, to be in relationship means that we have to be willing to compromise, cooperate and put ourselves in the shoes of the other, to listen openly, to strive for objectivity, to be willing to ruthlessly examine ourselves and our motives. Relationship is based on empathy, which means that we tacitly know we are interdependent as members of the human family. As we live that interdependence, our artificial sense of separation begins to dissolve and we find that staying in a cooperative, mutually respectful relationship with the other is what is most beneficial to the community and to ourselves.

Conflict is inevitable and necessary. Out of chaos, conflict and destruction, an environment or organism can reorder or recreate itself at a higher level of functioning. The passion or even anger that characterizes a conflict situation in community may be the agent that initiates change, clarifies something of great importance, or simply clears the air so we can move on.

Timing is Everything

There are times to express our feelings, to bring conflict out into the open in a way that can serve the whole community, and times to internalize, to go within and resolve conflict in solitude. The wisdom to know the difference comes with experience and the sincere desire to live in a way that is consonant with higher principles—such as kindness, generosity and compassion. I have found that clarity and real power can come through allowing issues to "cook" for awhile without endlessly discussing them in an attempt to resolve what is just not going to be resolved right now. The factor of time itself cannot be under-estimated in its value in aiding communications. But, we can only try this out if we are willing to accept that it is okay to dis-agree. We can generally take up an issue again in another day or another week, to find out if there is more clarity about it.

Sometimes there will be no immediate or even short-term resolution to a situation and we must carry on amidst the tension. Most of us are very uncomfortable with such tension—we want to "fix" things and "make them better." To practice forbearance and prudence in our communications is not easy when we are hot and heavy into a communications tangle with someone, but it is well worth using the opportunity to discover the skillful means and self-mastery that can come from such practice. If you experiment with not trying to stop the feelings that these kinds of situations bring up, and instead let the tension and the feelings soften you, they will eventually spur a deeper compassion for the limitations of human beings, including yourself. For example, when you have a seemingly unresolvable conflict with someone with whom you are close, don't do what most of us typically do: go to our friend, partner or spouse and further argue our case; or follow them around trying to resolve the thing or somehow undo what has been done in an effort to recreate the openness that has been tem-porarily closed down. Instead, just let it be there; accept the sit-uation as it is and don't reject yourself or the other person in any way. Remember, you don't have to fix the situation; you can trust that the mutual caring and regard between the two of you, com-bined with a little time and space, will soften or completely melt the hurt or hardness.

This internal mode of conflict resolution with another, or others, has to be a conscious act or we run the danger of just shut-ting down—closing off to the other person, cutting them out of our lives and our hearts in a way. It is vitally important that we maintain openness even in the midst of disagreement. Along these lines, Bernadette shares some memories from her years in the community of the convent.

Bernadette Reflects on Conflict

From the early stages of our novitiate training, when we recognized a conflict with another nun or novice—like when we had raised our voice or been brusque toward them—we would go to that person and ask forgiveness. But after I left the novitiate, that form of resolving conflict began to dissipate. In a house with ten or twelve nuns it was really evident when there was conflict, but in a house with thirty nuns it was easy to avoid—just cut the person off and forget about it. I always had the option of shutting people out when there was interpersonal conflict, and then just gravitating to those with whom I had an easier relationship. I found that many nuns made a real effort to keep kindness and sisterly camaraderie alive. We were deeply connected in each other's lives, we were friends, and unless we were starting to establish relationships on the outside—which was one of the factors that moved me out of the convent—then we had to realize that these were the women that we were going to live our lives with. It was very important that we created and cared for those relationships as family.

When I started protesting the Vietnam War in the late sixties, Sister Anthony would always scream at me, "How could you do this, how could you say this? They are killing people; we have to fight back!" Two years later she came to me in tears saying, "I am so sorry that I made life so difficult for you; I see now what you were trying to say to me two years ago." Her brother was getting drafted, so it was now beginning to hit home for her as she began to realize that the war was a travesty of justice after all. This is the kind of act of conscience in relationship that builds bonds of trust.

Most longstanding communities have experience with a variety of methods to clear the air; processes that allow the group to work more deeply and freely with each other. All of these processes either begin with, or allow us to come around to a basic respect and regard for one another in community. The bibliography at the back of this book lists several good resources for specific conflict resolution techniques that may be used.

In the case of disagreements and conflicts that arise in hammering out policy decisions, the group's formally agreed upon leadership and decision-making systems may need to be used. At other times, conflict is only resolved when a dissenting party leaves the community, which is a natural part of every community's evolution, although not at times without its sorrow or anger.

When Violence Erupts

Community should act as a safeguard against violent speech and abusive language, or psychological abuse of any kind between adults and children or even between consenting adults. Any community is wise to make it clear, up front, in the written and spoken group aims and purpose, that ongoing abuse will not be tolerated. This is important not only to protect the physical and emotional well being of its members, but also to preserve the integrity of the community's context—the principles and purpose that have brought the community into existence in the first place. Lori told the following story, which describes how violence erupted at an otherwise peaceful Medicine Pipe Ranch, an intentional community in which she lived in 1975.

Lori Speaks About Violence in a Community

Janna had been living at Medicine Pipe for two years when she broke up with Jason, a very charismatic and fiery man. Distraught and highly volatile, he confronted Janna one day when she was outside, working alone with her four-year-old daughter. As Jason spoke to her, Janna quickly looked around for one of the women to be with her daughter Zephyr, so that the child wouldn't have to be involved in the drama that was clearly escalating. Another man, Peter, was the only person present at the moment, so Janna asked him to take Zephyr away to play for a few minutes while she tried to talk with a furious Jason.

Up at the house, Peter stood watching at the window holding Zephyr. The child witnessed the entire scene that ensued outside, as Jason lost all sense of appropriate relations with Janna and became physically violent towards her. Finally, Janna broke away and ran to the house only to find that Zephyr had seen the whole thing.

Peter really didn't understand that he had done anything inappropriate in this situation. His lack of consciousness was another factor in the shock that this event had upon the whole community, as Medicine Pipe Ranch had been formed on the principles of nonviolence and an egalitarian ideal between men and women. When Peter was asked later at a group meeting why he had let Zephyr observe the scene, or why he had even allowed such a thing to happen when he could have attempted to stop it early on, he said that "Jason wasn't really hurting Janna, and Zephyr wasn't crying or upset." If the child had been crying he would have taken her away, he said.

The women gathered around Janna in support, utterly dismayed and horrified at Peter's attitude. We called a meeting with all the members who were living on the land at that time. A heated discussion followed, in which the two men involved were given very strong criticism, but the damage was done. Even though the other men in the community didn't condone Jason's or Peter's behavior, there was a split in the community between the men and women that seemed irrevocable, as trust was seriously eroded. These unresolved resentments and bad feelings made Jason's violence and Peter's lack of action appear as an eruption of something that was brewing under the surface; something that had a much larger "root system" than any of us had suspected. This was one of

151

several catalysts for the changes that came about a year later, when community went through some times of great upheaval and change.

That was my first experience of violence in community, and I wish I could say it was my last, or that violence didn't arise again at Medicine Pipe Ranch. I came to realize that violence is not something we are necessarily free of because our intellectual ideology is against it. But, during those years at Medicine Pipe Ranch I did come to the resolve that violence and abuse were not going to be on my agenda for community life, and that these kinds of events represent human aberrations as the result of deep, unconscious psychological wounds. I came to the conclusion that acting out violence plays no creative or useful part in the life of people working, living and relating together.

As a result of my experience with Janna and Jason, and later with others who fell into violence, however briefly, my question became: How do we live in a way that brings us into conscious relationship with our own inner rage and violence, so that we can be responsible in community to manage these impulses so that they are never inflicted on those around us? And how can I support others to do the same?

Lori poses questions with many different facets and no easy answers. The answers that may be found are certainly beyond the scope of this book, but the question of violence must not be swept under the carpet in any consideration of community. In many cases, communities may be dealing with couples, for example, whose relationship has become psychologically and verbally abusive. In this case, counseling or professional help may be needed, but the community itself should provide a matrix of support to help the individuals move through and hopefully evolve beyond an abusive cycle in relationship.

The community must intervene in any instance where violence or child abuse is involved, regardless of the difficulty or complications involved. The bottom line is that we must each individually commit to live in a way that precludes the irreparable angry, violent and damaging outburst, no matter how justified we may feel that it is in the heat of the moment.

Communication

The art of conversation and communication is essential to community; it is the garden out of which the flowers of genuine communion may blossom. The fundamental context for communication is our desire for life-positive, creative, loving and compassionate human relationship. From this kind of relationship and communication, a transformational experience of communion between two or more human beings becomes possible.

The necessity of an open flow of communication among the parts of any system cannot be overemphasized and we can easily find many examples of this in our daily life. If we don't get the message that our teenager called home and has gotten a ride from school, we will stop our work, drive to the school and sit and wait for thirty minutes until we decide that she must have gotten home some other way. If we don't know that we have ten guests joining us for lunch in the community dining hall, we may come up short on food amounts so that people leave hungry. If for some reason our computer is not properly wired to the printer, we cannot get our manuscript printed out on time—a good metaphor for what happens when the lines of communication are not hooked up properly. One of the things that we have to learn from tribal cultures is a kind of communication that comes from being bonded with each other and tacitly focused on community aims, so that we cooperate in an instinctual, reciprocal, circular flow rather than from a rigid structure that is enforced from the top down.

Often good communication hinges on stopping the action long enough to really listen to what the other is saying, so that the need is fully heard and registered. Rabbi Zalman Schacter-Shalomi, an elder who leads seminars on aging and wisdom, talks in his workshops about the art of true listening. Through our receptivity and empathy, i.e., our listening, we actually "witness and bless" the other. He believes that that this openness to witness and bless through listening is one of the main functions of a wise elder, especially with adolescents and young adults. In order to do this, however, we must be receptive and still within ourselves, while at the same time listening actively, staying fully present to the other person.

This type of listening is much easier to do in a situation of caring and concern. We all know in our hearts that real communication can only happen when we are committed to fostering loving and creative relationships; when we are willing to meet the other person half way; when we are willing to compromise, cooperate and maintain an attitude of positive regard and respect for the other in the midst of disagreement. But, in the midst of a conflict it is often very difficult for most people to sustain these ideals.

Living together, our patterns of communication easily get sloppy. We habitually jump to conclusions while others are talking, rather than being internally still and actually listening. We automatically think we know who the other person is and what he or she will be saying, and we may even finish sentences for them. We are usually thinking about what our reply will be while the other person is talking. For listening to really work we must begin to practice the art of emptying ourselves and staying with the person *in the present moment* rather than jumping to our own conclusion—or theirs for them—and living in the future by planning our response.

In a small group meeting with some community women, I had just given some very strong criticism to a friend who was sitting right next to me. She turned red and said, "Could you repeat what you said?"

I snapped back, "You're angry with me now, aren't you?"

Another woman intervened and asked her, "What are you feeling right now?"

She responded, "I'm feeling scared."

I immediately realized that I hadn't actually heard what she said to me. All she asked of me was to repeat what I said, very simply, and I assumed that I knew what she was thinking and feeling, and then projected that onto her. When I listened to what she was saying, "I'm feeling scared," and took it to heart, it completely changed the direction in which our interaction was going.

Humanistic psychologist Carl Rogers said that the first obstacle to real listening during conflict is lack of courage. Instead of having the courage to simply listen to what may be threatening to us, we switch over to evaluating what is being said. He says that we must find the courage to listen with the other, the opponent, in order to get out of the "I am 100% right and you are 100% wrong" attitude. Once we are out of that attitude, once we have the maturity to agree to disagree in a friendly way and are truly listening, then we can come to a more objective truth about the situation.[1] However, this often requires the intervention of a third party. The third party can simply be present without saying anything, or may need to help the other hear what is being said, rather than hearing through the filters and the survival issues that have been activated. The book, *Carl Rogers on Encounter Groups,* is a classic guide to the psychology of group dynamics and both group and one-on-one communication.

Active listening is one of the most refined arts of relationship, and has the power to heal and transform both the listener and the one who is being listened to. Rogers used the term "mirroring" to talk about one aspect of this art. To "mirror" is to repeat, in our own words perhaps, what we have understood the other to say: "What I heard you say was . . ." Such a process not only clarifies our understanding of what was said, it also encourages and draws out the other person in their efforts to express more clearly. For many people mirroring is a natural way of conversation. Whether we do it automatically, or whether we deliberately practice it, mirroring increases the empathy between two people who are conversing.

When our complete, benign attention is focused on the person speaking to us, we are demonstrating another aspect of active listening. Attention is an amazing force—it calls forth the essence of the other person because it is freely given in the mood of respect and regard. Such attention brings things to life—we can see how our friend will blossom, becoming animated and articulate, even passionate, when we really pay attention to what they are saying.

One dramatic example of this occurred between myself and a coworker who talked incessantly. Jerry was constantly pulling on everyone around him for attention, and his chatter was so irritating that people tended to avoid or even shun him. I imagined that if I gave him my full attention he would talk forever, but I made the conscious decision to experiment with active listening anyway, putting aside the other things on my mind, without showing impatience. Amazingly it took Jerry only a few minutes to feel satisfied that he had been heard, and to move on to something else without requiring further attention from me.

The tremendous value of paying close attention and being present is obvious with children, who instinctively feel whether or not an adult is present with them. Children often act out to get attention until the adult stops being preoccupied about something else. One night I cared for a child whose mother was away. The little one was restless and upset for two hours; no matter how I tried to comfort her, she wouldn't go to sleep and would not rest in my arms. A friend who was with me, observing the interaction, asked, "Where are you? It feels like you aren't really here." This piece of honest feedback struck home at once, and I

156

acknowledged the tremendous sadness that I was trying to fight off—a sadness that was indeed keeping me preoccupied. I spontaneously started to cry. As soon as this happened, the child relaxed and snuggled up in my arms. She had been asking for her mother for over an hour, and suddenly she just fell asleep! As soon as I became present to her, she instinctively knew that she was safe and cared for.

Another challenge to bringing presence to the art of listening happens when someone is giving us feedback that is not easy to take. Here we need to listen past or beneath the form of what is being said. If we can sense that the other person has our best interest at heart and is trying to be compassionate, then it is easier to listen in spite of our desire to push away feedback that we don't want to hear. Such courage to listen is essential for building healthy relationships, where honesty and feedback are necessary elements in the give and take of everyday life.

There are times, however, when the other person does not have our best interests at heart, and their feedback may be motivated by selfish reasons. In this case it is also best to listen without defense. After all, they may be offering us a gift that our truest friends wouldn't. Later, we can sift through the feedback to glean what is true and of use to us, and what is not. Our integrity and desire for positive change and transformation will carry us through any murkiness or mixed motives on the other person's part. Their lack of clarity or integrity is something they will have to deal with in their own time and their own way.

Good listening requires that we make a distinction between the information we are receiving and the other person's particular style of communication. Sometimes we do not like what someone says to us, or do not agree with it, yet it is to our benefit to learn how to listen anyway, without taking everything personally. It is possible to "listen in disagreement" while staying receptive to hearing the grain of truth. At the same time, it is important to be able to discriminate between what is valid feedback and what is the other person's projection. Often, feedback—both positive and negative—is a combination of objective observations on the part of the other mingled with their projections and personal issues. It is easy to disregard another person's valuable feedback to us off by saying to ourselves, "She's just projecting." This, along with self-justification, are typical reaction to feedback that is threatening in any way.

A useful practice in listening and responding to feedback that could potentially create conflict is to say, "Okay, I'll consider that." And then leave it alone. Don't try to process the information with the other person right away. If we allow the feedback to settle within us, if we try to keep an open mind, what is valuable will clearly surface, while what is not will fall away.

As we discussed in the chapter on leadership styles, when a group comes together for discussions the process can be dragged down with endless questions and opinions. Individuals can tyrannize a space with their unexamined psychological needs to control, to create conflict, or to simply get the attention that they never got as children. Most adults attempt to consciously work with this kind of neediness in themselves, but some are constantly waving invisible red flags in the air that say, "I need to have and control everybody's attention, all the time, or I will make trouble!" With experience we become more savvy to these dynamics and more adept at being able to handle them with compassion and generosity. At the same time, we should not sacrifice the well being of the community under these circumstances. Sometimes real compassion is very tough. Allowing people to continue such negative life patterns is not loving or compassionate, whereas demanding that they break out of crystallized patterns that prevent them from becoming whole, happy and creative people may the best thing we can do for them and for the community in process. Firm, clear and steady leadership is important in these situations, as is communicating with clarity of purpose.

If we are afraid to bring up issues to certain community members or afraid to talk about things in a group setting, we must ask ourselves what we are building together. M. Scott Peck told the story of beginning his lectures to church groups by requesting that people not ask him questions during the break. Invariably they did. When he asked them to bring their questions back up during the lecture, he was chagrined to hear them say, "Oh no, we can't ask this question in front of the other members of the church!"

The health of the community calls for freedom for questions and directness with one another, without precluding elegance and regard for one another's privacy or personal process. At the same time, if the community has covert agreements—if there are things we unconsciously agree that we can't discuss or be honest about—that is a serious weakness in the fabric of the organism. John Bradshaw once said of the dysfunctional family system, "Families are as sick as their secrets." [2]

Some of the danger signs that destructive secrets may be harbored in community are: 1) A lot of "sacred cows"—subgroups, individuals, projects or dogma that are "untouchable" or held as sacrosanct. 2) When the individuals of the group as a whole cannot carry on a conversation with someone outside the community without using community jargon and idioms. 3) When a hierarchy develops that refuses to explain its actions and decisions, but that insists on special privileges. 4) When resources disappear and no one can be held accountable. 5) When visitors and relatives of members are not openly welcomed to visit and participate freely. 6) When children are unhappy, exhibiting signs of depression or stress, such as drawing foreboding pictures and having frequent, recurring nightmares. 7) When addictions are being covered up with the knowledge or direct help of non-addicts. 8) When the community has no active network of ongoing friendships and contacts with other communities.

In regard to covert communication and secrets, intentional communities and less organized, more informal groups suffer the same effects. That which is kept secret by design or withheld intentionally from others because there is shame or guilt tied up in it—either because of inherited toxic shame or because something is out of integrity—tends to gather a subversive, demoralizing and generally unhealthy quality. Personal privacy is another matter completely, and should be respected; I am talking about the kind of covert agreements and secretiveness that engenders distrust, falsehood and inauthenticity among people, and that can become a cover for even more dishonest and destructive behaviors. Honesty, goodwill, and the willingness to risk, are the hallmarks of open communications that foster healthy, creative and nurturing interpersonal interactions. And such interactions are among community's greatest gifts.

CHAPTER SEVEN

At the Heart of Community—
Good Company, Bonding and Intimacy

I am because we are.

—Xhosa people of southern Africa

When all the knots of the heart
have been released
Then truly a mortal becomes immortal
Thus is the teaching.

—Katha Upanishad VI. 15

The domain of the heart must be nourished to be enlivened. The types of "food" we feed the heart cause a response in our being as immediately and directly as that created in the physical body by ingesting physical food. Relationship with others, care and love of children, shared work, celebration and ritual—these are only a few of the necessities or "foods" of the heart. And these are some of the substances that may be found abundantly within community.

We humans are essentially social creatures who seek the company of our own kind, even though we may take time in solitude to enrich our sense of togetherness and unity. Good company, then, is a heart-food that is necessary to our individual well being, and an essential ingredient in creating a culture of the heart. Just the fact of living together, however, does not necessarily make us good company for each other. Like love, "good company" is built, or formed within community.

161

Good company generates an atmosphere or mood of camaraderie, but that is only part of it. Good will, honesty, clarity,
acceptance and generosity of spirit—these will also be present.
Good company is about having conscious unity within the diversity of the group; accepting those who are vastly different than
ourselves. In my community, for instance, there are many people
I would not have been drawn toward as friends outside of community. Nonetheless, I have found that our mutual concerns and
commitments, and our desires to widen our individual circle, has
made it possible to forge the bonds of good company.

Good company is about the acknowledgement, appreciation
and reinforcement of our essential nature and basic goodness. We
become trusting and trustworthy when we live with the certainty
that such basic goodness exists in us. I have found that this certainty comes not from aggressively proving myself worthy but
rather from stilling myself through meditation and contemplation
until I know, through experience, the goodness that exists in
human beings, myself and others. This is the respect that is the
medium within which relationship flourishes.

Creating good company is not in any way about formulating
strict moralistic codes or about building exclusive "clubs" with
one or two other people. Rather, it is about what the human heart
instinctively knows to be right in relationship. Good company is
expansive and embracing of others, naturally resonant with the
free flow of human exchange, and in the innate evolutionary urge
of the human spirit. It is uplifting, and calls forth the spark of life
from all those who are involved.

Good company is based in mutual respect and honor. If
genuine relationship is the heart of community, then one might
say that respect is the cells that make up the heart. A foundation
of respect for ourselves, for other human beings and for life in
general provides a place for intimacy and vulnerability to grow in
good company.

Marta, a mother and teacher, who has lived in community for over twenty-five years, talks about her experience of good company.

Marta Reflects on Good Company

People tend to think of good company as being made up of people of like minds, but my experience in community is that good company is not a result of like-mindedness, but like-heartedness. In our community people who dedicate themselves to this way of life need to have an affinity and a sense of being drawn to the ideals of a transformational way of life, and that is what gives everyone a natural bond. It's a bond of the heart, not a bond of the mind, because people have very different backgrounds and opinions and biases about things—from politics to movies—due to upbringing and conditioning. But there is a basic similarity in the quality of longing for personal transformation that we share, and that can melt a lot of the differences and frictions that naturally arise in community.

Going to visit my parents and siblings recently, the memory was sparked of what my life was like when they were my only family. Upon returning to my life in community, I was struck by how elated I felt being back with my chosen family and friends—the people with whom I share a basic contextual understanding and common aim. There is tremendous joy in this bond—in this big, sprawling, sometimes chaotic and bawdy, chosen family of mine.

For me, good company in a spiritual or transformational community includes a recognition of the illusions of the conventional world. Our bond in community is not based on the common niceties and superficial social games that people typically play—games we all learned to varying degrees in our blood families. Instead, we share a tacit recognition of the emptiness of many of those social norms. Our friendship, our bond, therefore, is prior to or underneath what it takes to interact with and "succeed" in the conventional world. In such a bonded community, you can often just look at someone and know there is a tacit understanding about what you are mutually perceiving in any given situation.

In good company, as I refer to it, there is vulnerability about the level of "brokenheartedness" that we all have in various ways. The underlying understanding between those who share this kind of heart bond can naturally inspire light-heartedness, and the remembrance to take things in stride, to be grateful, to enjoy life and to not take ourselves so seriously. Because of that shared broken heart we can laugh together at our foibles—after all, we're really not that different!

Like people who have been married for fifty years, when you live in good company you aren't trying to change and control each other anymore, so that the eccentricities of others become endearing to you. If you can relax and trust the people you live with, then that sense of humor is just natural; it arises spontaneously. This humor of the heart is a great gift that dispels the drive to distrust, protect and defend. It's a deadly serious affair when one is on-guard and uptight and suspicious—then there is no space for genuine humor. Laughing together in a relaxed way is good company.

The mood of good company was very strong on one particular night as about ten of us went to a restaurant after a movie. We were laughing, joking and exuding happiness together. Our group was very bright and free-flowing with this kind of carefree spirit as we ordered our food, doing our best not to totally overwhelm the waitress, who was obvious frazzled and in a hurry since it was late and time for the restaurant to close. Because she was so stressed, she spilled a full, large glass of milk on someone in our party. Anyone who has waited tables knows it's not uncommon for customers to get very angry when something like this happens. The waitress or waiter usually has to cow-tow to the offended person. But, instead of anger, what this waitress got from us was quite a surprise—we all burst out laughing! She looked confused for a moment, and then she smiled. She was drawn into our mood slowly as the meal went on, and by the end of the evening, she was laughing, relaxed and friendly, asking us to come back again.

I never get tired of good company. I find that the more I am with the people in my community, the more I want to be with them. If I don't see someone for several days or weeks because he or she is away on business, I realize that I am missing the particular "food" or quality that he or she brings to our group. There is never a mood of starvation because there are so many people. Our comings and goings are really felt with a kind of sweetness. People have grown to love one another in spite of their differences, in spite of being terrified of being alone yet terrified of being intimate . . . Good company is the antidote to all that.

Relationship and Intimacy

Love is saying yes to belonging.
—Brother David Steindl-Rast

Healthy, thriving relationships feed the entire community. When any two or more come together in the communion of mutual respect, the whole group prospers. I remember a day when I was taking care of one of the children in our community; we happened to walk by a couple who were obviously enjoying one another's company. After being near our friends for a moment I turned to the child and realized I was overflowing with that same love and appreciation for her. The couple's mood had spilled over onto us. If we are willing to become more deeply vulnerable with our mates, even if this may not feel very blissful, we set a positive pattern for that vulnerability throughout community.

Relationship and intimacy can be scary concepts to most of us raised in the modern world of isolationism. Yet, we spend our whole lives searching and longing for them. Many of us have a primal fear of intimacy; we are afraid to share our ecstasies or our tears. We carry the wounds of shame from childhood, when at our most vulnerable moments we heard, "Stop crying and be a big girl," or "Only sissies cry," or "I'll give you something to cry about!" We associate deep feelings with unpleasant memories—times when our deepest impulses were repressed and shamed—until we can only feel them as the briefest whispers of what they once were. In the place of real feeling, we have put up a façade that, based on experience, we believe others will find acceptable and non-threatening. We think that we have to keep this image of rigid perfectionism, or stoicism, or false gaiety, or forced enthusiasm intact for the world at all costs. Sadly, this "world" includes our best friends, our partners—lovers or spouses—our children and extended family. Meanwhile, we are starving for real intimacy, for a deep sharing of the heart with others. We are like people dying of thirst. Only the long cool draught of human kindness can relieve our pain and bring us back to life.

Our society has trained us to view relationship in a narrow focus—as a primary-pair bonding of a heterosexual couple within a church-sanctified legal union, or marriage. Such relationships for most Westerners very quickly become a closed system, as the individuals within the pair turn almost exclusively toward each other for all intimacy, affection and meaningful companionship.

I use the word *relationship* to include much more than this isolated coupling. I apply it to being related to all human beings, or the action of relating with all human beings. In its broader sense, relationship recognizes the interrelatedness of all creatures, and indeed all of life—our fundamental and healthy need of each other, and the gentle yet deep vulnerability that arises from acknowledging this. Such interrelatedness is easy to overlook, however. One day I bemoaned to a friend, "Oh, I don't have a relationship," meaning that I was not in a sexual relationship at the time. My friend stopped me short: "But you *are* in relationship." As she pointed out, I had many rich and rewarding close friendships with people whom I deeply appreciated, and with whom I shared affection, work, play, joy, humor and the deeper pathos and struggles of my life. That illusive, intimate relationship that I was searching for was already present, but in a slightly different form than the one I was somewhat fixated on. Over time, as I chewed on this new insight, I had to admit that my friend was right.

Just as there are many forms of relationship, so are there many forms of intimacy. Even after the sexual revolution and women's liberation movements of the 1960s and 70s, we as a culture in the U.S. still think "sex" whenever the term "intimacy" pops up in conversation. It is extremely important that we clarify the word "intimacy" for our purposes here, since we will use it frequently. While sex might be a part of it, intimacy actually encompasses a much broader range of relationship that includes friendship, open communication, affection, familial bonds, the vulnerability of dropping our masks with one another, sharing in triumph or disaster, in happiness or in sorrow together, and so on.

When intimacy is present, then communion—which is a function of heartful reciprocity between individuals—is possible. Communion and intimacy are exchanged in the language of the heart—a language that is often conversed in silence, or through simple touch. In moments of joy or shared humor, we experience intimacy through a glance, a smile, or hearty chuckles and even belly laughs. Yet, we tend not to think of these times as occasions of intimacy.

Sometimes in the process of breakdown, in the midst of pain, communion is made more possible. In fact, many of us first realize in moments of adversity and suffering that we are experiencing real intimacy outside of sex. To suffer together can create a deep bond between human beings as we are humbled through our dire need to seek the mirror of our own humanness in one another. Such mirroring, in turn, can draw forth deep compassion and care from our fellow human beings and from ourselves. Many people have known tremendous intimacy at the death of a loved

167

family member or friend—a moment of silence between grieving companions can carry a profound mood of intimacy; the simple gesture of holding a hand, or a feather-light touch on the arm can communicate tremendous reciprocity, compassion and intimacy.

One of the greatest examples of a community in the throes of profound suffering together today is the world-wide Tibetan Buddhist community, whether in diaspora—scattered into India, Europe or the U.S. or still living in Chinese-occupied Tibet. These people are the victims of an ongoing genocide perpetrated by the Chinese. Many Westerners have become aware of the suffering of the Tibetan people over the past four decades since the Chinese invasion in the early 1950s. Moved by the strong presence of compassion in the Tibetan people and their spiritual leader, the Dalai Lama, these supporters have joined together in their own communities to actively provide aid to Tibetans in the U.S., Europe, India and Tibet. Such group actions are good examples of how suffering and compassion can bring us together in some form of community when the heart is deeply troubled by the adversity of another.

Suffering takes down the walls of separation we have built. When we have nothing left to lose, or when we are called to an intimacy we wouldn't normally allow ourselves because of the serious need of another, we have a chance to drop the masks which isolate us. One such opportunity happened for my friend Shawn, who contracted a severe case of hepatitis while traveling in India with her closest community friends. She was forced to return to the States early and needed lots of practical help as well as tender loving care from other members of the community. Shawn was confined to bed for weeks, was extremely shaky, and needed a special diet because of her illness. The only person living in the same building with her at the time was Rafe, an introspective and often irascible man, who by nature tended to isolate himself. On the surface he was not inclined toward empathy or nurturing. In fact, Rafe claimed a dislike of others and tended

168

toward criticism and pessimism. His companions in community, however, often saw through this ruse, which was in fact a psychological protection for the extremely sensitive, caring person that lived deep inside, and they loved him in spite of his irritable demeanor.

With Shawn in such a fragile state, fighting for her very life, Rafe clearly saw what needed to be done and pulled himself out of his self-imposed exile from others. He extended himself by graciously nursing her through her illness—preparing food, carrying her if necessary, and generally serving her healing process. These acts of relationship were so against his usual psychological tendency, and so terrifying to him, that he was often trembling when he brought Shawn's tray to her at mealtimes.

Today, Shawn says that since she had the opportunity to see and interact with the hidden nurturer in Rafe, she now sees that quality in him first, even through his standoffish personality— which, although softened, is still dominant. For her, this tender and deeply caring part *is* who he really is, and Shawn holds that to be true for Rafe, even when he cannot hold that for himself.

M. Scott Peck has said, "Rugged individualism—it relentlessly demands that we keep up appearance, it isolates us from one another." And we Westerners are typically proud of our independence: "I don't need anybody, I can take care of myself!" we say, to the point of being prideful and harsh. We have been taught that we shouldn't need anything from others, because need makes us vulnerable to betrayal. After all, trust of the basic goodness of others is not commonly fostered.

"Don't wear out your welcome," we say, having so lost touch with our human bond that we no longer recognize and thus fail to honor the age-old unspoken laws of hospitality, which apply to the guest as much as to the host. Why wouldn't we want to host, to extend generously to others, to succor, nourish and honor anyone who comes to our home? Why wouldn't we see such hospitality as a gift, and graciously accept it without fear that we are really unwelcome after all? The answers are simple. We are so cut off from an appreciation of the treasures of relationship and intimacy; we deny the value of reciprocal giving and receiving that is inherent in hospitality; we want to stand alone. When a stranger or even a friend arrives at our door, therefore, we are frozen and unable to respond. Or maybe the stranger never comes, fearing the cold shoulder, and so the dance of relationship and the warmth of human hospitality never begins.

Bonding

> Until people know that their pain is heard and recognized, until they know that they are loved, it is much harder for them to let go of contraction and separation and to come into who they really are.
>
> —Kabir Helminski

The heroic, isolated stand of "me against the world" is one of the most insidious barriers against real relationship and intimacy. According to contemporary psychology, this stand has its roots in a lacking of bonding with mother, father and other primary figures in early childhood. Psychologists and cultural anthropologists today agree that bonding is a key element in creating community. But what is bonding?

To understand bonding between adult members of a community, family or couple, we need to examine the source of our ability to bond with another. Bonding begins in infancy and continues even throughout adult development as new elements and relationships come into play in our lives. But the foundation for bonding between individuals is established in the first year of life.

Babies who are held, cuddled, breast fed, and who receive freely-given affection and sensory touch will naturally and automatically bond to their primary care givers, usually mother and

170

father, but also with the extended family and close friends. Psychological research has shown that our ability to relax into intimacy, commitment and cohesive relationships, and to give and receive affection as adults—either with our own children or with other adults—typically depends on how well we bonded with people in our environment as children.

Bonding is an intuitive, extrasensory kind of relationship between two people, beginning with mother and child. It is a "felt experience," not perceived through rational, linear thought, language or intellect.[1] Joseph Chilton Pearce, whose books on childhood development are considered contemporary classics, writes that bonding occurs when an infant or child is met on both physical and subtle levels by his parent or primary caregiver. This meeting is rooted in the subtle heart system, and it is a process that roots the infant, and later the adult, in the core of his or her life and sense of self. According to Pearce, "[the child] is rooted within the great subtle intuitive energies that power physical life, no matter how his physical situation shifts and changes."[2] Pearce poetically considers the much greater effects of bonding as both a personal and universal process that permeates all of life when he writes:

> The bonded person can allow integration into wider circles of possibility . . . The bonded mother is in touch with the precursive, intuitive state and meets needs ahead of time. [Similarly,] the bonded person assumes the unfolding moment will meet all needs and is thus open and receptive . . . Bonding is displayed from the appearance of the first unit of matter, the smallest subatomic particle, on up through galaxies and universes and our own brain/minds.[3]

Most of us can easily understand that bonding is a natural, intuitive, even emotional experience, but it is also a very

171

concrete, psycho-physiological process. The most obvious example of bonding occurs when we see the mother tenderly holding or cuddling an infant, or breastfeeding. Any mother who has breast fed her child knows that babies naturally gaze for long periods of time into their mother's eyes while feeding, and this is a very important part of the bonding process. Every child has a legitimate narcissistic need for attention. In the first months of life an infant needs to be mirrored to, constantly, by his mother or primary caregiver. The mother gazes at the baby in her arms and the baby gazes back, finding him- or herself mirrored. These necessary elements of bonding don't stop at infancy, however. Bonding continues throughout childhood, and at each step of the child's development plays an important role in the psycho-physiological processes essential for the normal growth and development of the brain.

According to neuropsychologist and researcher Dr. James Prescott, the surest and quickest way to induce depression and alienation in an infant or child is to withhold touch and loving physical contact. Prescott has spent thirty years uncovering and correlating the relationship between bonding and the development of the functional, non-violent human being. For example, his experience with monkeys raised in cages and completely deprived of physical contact with mother or other monkeys led him to rename the "Maternal-Social Deprivation Syndrome" the "Somatosensory Affectional Deprivation" (SAD). He applies this term specifically to infants raised without adequate body-contact stimulation with their mothers. One significant result of this kind of deprivation, Prescott states, is abnormal development and function of the brain. In fact, during formative periods of brain growth, certain types of sensory deprivation—for example the absence of touch and rocking by the mother—causes the neuronal systems that control affection to be damaged or underdeveloped through a loss of the nerve-cell branches called dendrites.[4] Children who are not rocked and cuddled often have

172

incomplete development of the brain pathways that mediate pleasure. As adults, they cannot allow themselves to feel pleasure, or they simply cannot feel pleasure. They are more prone to frustration and exhibit a greater likelihood of drug or alcohol abuse and addiction.[5]

Studies conducted by Prescott and others have shown that mother-deprived adult monkeys tend to be pathologically violent and that this condition also is directly related to the undeveloped cerebellum and other brain structures that mediate pleasure.[6] Because the neuronal systems of the brain mediate pleasure, the unbonded individual has little physiological capacity to regulate the biochemical components related to depression and rage, which are, in the healthy individual, balanced through pleasure. "The failure to integrate pleasure into the higher brain centers associated with 'consciousness' (frontal lobes) is the principal neuropsychological condition for the expression of violence, particularly sexual violence."[7]

As Prescott explained,

> Those societies which give their infants the greatest amounts of physical affection were characterized by low theft, low infant physical pain . . . and negligible or absent killing, mutilating or torture of the enemy . . . The warmth of human touch and security of body contact, are without question, the most effective way to reduce violence in culture.[8]

The interplay of touch, bonding and violence is extremely relevant to our consideration of community. Touching is given little importance in our society, and in many families is even considered dangerous, immoral, deviant or threatening. For one who is identified with isolation and separation, a simple touch that communicates "I care for you," or "I'm here for you," or "I recognize and acknowledge you," or "I love you," may be a terrifying

173

confrontation. Touch may be like warm water on ice; but if we believe that we *are* the ice, then warm water becomes a threat to our very survival.

We are increasingly more isolated and cut off from each other because we have simply never learned what it means to be bonded to another human being in close and affectionate association and care. As children we learned that nobody was there for us, so now as adults, we stay closed off and alone, afraid and unwilling to reach out, certain that our fate will be the same now as it was then. As the extended family structure disintegrates and the psychological dysfunction of the nuclear family grows, the traditional, more instinctual arts of mothering are dissipated, even becoming obsolete or forgotten, hidden under layer upon layer of psychological angst and, in women, a kind of masculinized "femininity." More and more often, women with small children are forced by economic necessity into the work place, while children are raised in more institutional and sterile settings by, at best, childcare professionals, and at worst, by those who are there only because they need a job.

Bonding within community, then, becomes a necessary antidote to such alienation. Bonding is vital to the development of a sustainable culture of the heart. As we attempt to come into closer relations with our fellow human beings, a bonded community offers us the chance to heal and resolve, or at least manage, the anger, rage and pain that may erupt. How much easier it is to resolve conflict when it does arise, and to cooperate under the stressful demands of daily life, when we feel that we are together and united within a common agreement. We know that the pleasure bond between pairs is a basic element that sustains loving relationship and helps balance out the usual frustrations and conflicts that inevitably arise. In community, bonding with others who are not sexual partners also involves the sharing of mutual pleasure, albeit of a Platonic variety. The warmth of friendship, good will and mutual understanding—built through shared

174

purpose, laughter and enjoyment, as well as shared pathos—characterize the "pleasure bond" that exists among community members.

This felt bond among community members can pull us back to awareness at the level of the heart in the heat of disagreement or in the whirl of snared emotional reactions, so that we can say to ourselves, "I know Sally. I know where her heart really resides, and I know that there is alignment and caring between us in many areas." Remembering the closeness we share and have shared can be a tremendous impetus to relaxing the adversarial position in which we all too often find ourselves with others. The bond itself—which can grow deep enough to span all levels of one's being: physical, intellectual, emotional, spiritual—calls us back to the memory of our longing for closeness, for communion. Relationship itself becomes more important than "winning," competing or making the other wrong so that we can then be right.

Bonding grows as we live together, and living together includes rubbing up against each other's sharp edges—including our isolated determination to remain separate, to have our own way without consideration of others, to control and dominate, or to play the victim and manipulate through passive-aggressive dynamics (to name a few). Under stress, the other person can glibly be reduced to an object—nothing but "a pain in the ass." Yet, this very friction can eventually smooth out our character—much the way gemstones are polished by being placed together in a tumbler—so that we become brighter, softer, more cooperative and more available to reciprocal relationship and intimacy. Slowly, as our psychological facade is chipped away, our basic goodness, innocence and kindness shines forth as the ground from which we live in relationship with others.

For some, the bonding process may be primarily one of joy and pleasure, while for others it may be a more difficult road that demands one navigate through various degrees of childhood

175

trauma, abandonment and sorrow as we come up against the fears that closeness and intimacy can release. For most people, however, the bonding process in community will involve some measure of both. If we live a life of depth and passion, however, we can't *not* bond with people!

Certain events are ripe with the potential for bonding. Traveling together provides many such opportunities. After three months in India with my new community, I realized that I had shared intimately of all aspects of my life, and suddenly I was bonded, irrevocably. We bond through pleasure and through hardship. For instance, being sick and needing help allows friends to intervene, and builds the closeness among them. For me it's the day to day stuff; when I see someone in the kitchen and exchange a few words with them, I frequently realize how close we are, how they care about me, and the reality of this growing bond often catches me by surprise. When people know you and love you and care for you, they also then have the right to speak to you, directly and honestly, and to be involved in your growth and well-being. Such direct confrontation or feedback may involve "losing face," which becomes another precious chance for deeper bonding. If we stay present, instead of running away and hiding at such times, the degree of shared vulnerability strengthens our bonds.

It is important not to become disillusioned or disheartened by the difficulties that most people encounter in the process of building bonded relationships. Many of us experienced much less than optimal bonding as children, and so when we attempt to bond as adults, we encounter a great deal of resistance and upset in ourselves and in others. When we look at our culture at large, we see that even the bonded relationship of marriage is a great struggle for many people. The statistics of divorce have increased steadily over the last several decades, a mirror of our inability to bond as adults in a way that can persevere through the acid tests of postmodern stress. Too often the couple will split apart rather

176

than use the commitment of marriage to help remember their basic connection, and what vision sparked the marriage to begin with.

We may fiercely disagree, argue and "fight it out" in the midst of our bonding process, and all of that may be necessary and even very useful. However, we do recommend one rule that should be upheld at all times: no violence or abuse. There is never a good reason for violence, with the possible exception of clearly life-threatening situations that demand self-defense or defense of another. Physical violence and violent or abusive language or any other forms of psychological abuse are not part of the bonding process; they are pathological acts that are extremely difficult to heal or resolve once they have occurred between two people. The community can serve as a container for the tremendous heat, turmoil, intensity and alchemy of the bonding process, but at the same time it must be a strong enough container to defuse any explosive interactions that erupt in physical violence.

Safety and sanctuary for the nurturing of shared purpose cannot be maintained if violence is introduced or permitted. Violence and abuse destroy real bonds or the possibility of bondedness between people.

Bonding Through Our Woundedness

When they are expressed with vulnerability, rather than by attack or violence, bonded relationships are strong enough to witness and accept our deepest wounds, and to heal us. When I entered into a committed sexual relationship with my partner, I asked one of his friends who had known him for many years how I could best serve him. He responded by saying, "What a man needs is to be able to expose what he *thinks* is the weakest or ugliest part of himself, and for his lover to be willing to see it and not turn away." This is a truth that lies at the bottom of the bonded relationship—and certainly not just between intimate sexual partners.

177

Acceptance of the other's wounds means not trying to fix or change them through subtle or not-so-subtle emotional coercion. Our feedback must always be tempered with wisdom, as Chögyam Trungpa Rinpoche indicated when he said, "Being less helpful is more helpful than being helpful." This statement can be a koan for bonded relationship with others—knowing when to speak or intervene, and knowing when to remain silently supportive.

When we live and work together in community we are constantly challenged to examine our own woundedness to varying degrees, well beyond what we would encounter if we met once a week for a therapy group. In my experience, you don't really know someone until you've lived with them. In living together, sooner or later the acceptable masks come down, or begin to crack apart at the seams, and the pain underlying our anger, rage or drive to manipulate for the sake of power can no longer be contained. When the "honeymoon" of our first blush of love for community living is over, we then move into the stage of getting real with each other and ourselves.

Community holds up an immense mirror to us, and if we are willing to use it, we can see behind our masks and facades, sometimes with stark clarity. As Carl Jung stated: "The mirror does not flatter, it faithfully shows whatever looks into it; namely, the face we never show to the world because we cover it with the persona, the mask of the actor. But the mirror lies behind the mask and shows the true face." [9]

We must be willing to face the violence and rage that resides within the woundedness of our human condition. Namely, we must be willing to face the human shadow, which Carl Jung has said "is a moral problem that challenges the whole ego-personality, for no one can become conscious of the shadow without considerable moral effort." [10] If we are willing to accept that we are all interconnected, even at a global level, then we cannot hold ourselves separate in some idealized self-image, believing that we are personally free of violence or rage. If we do, we are in for a shock, sooner or later. Because of our interconnection we all carry around the seeds of all human emotions and feeling states. Therefore, what is in the unconscious of the whole—Jung called this the *collective unconscious*—is also in the unconscious of the individual. And, while most of us are painfully aware of the staggering amount of violence and war in the world today, we may not have encountered this violence in ourselves as yet. Given the right circumstances, however, rage and violence can be provoked in anyone. The bonding process that takes place within community can certainly be the catalyst for any number of emotions to arise—especially emotions that have been previously repressed or denied because they were socially unacceptable, or because our family system considered them taboo. When that emotional storm hits, the same bonding process or bondedness that provoked it can support us in dealing with the breakdown and pain that are its result.

Every person has "blind spots"—aspects of themselves that they simply can't see, and don't even know exist—which is another way of speaking of the human shadow. Because of our blind spots, we often act in ways that we are oblivious about. We project this unconscious shadow onto others—a constant function of the psyche that causes untold problems. According to Jung, withdrawing our projections and becoming conscious of the shadow is an immense undertaking that requires tremendous moral courage. One has to face what one has been told from childhood is sinful and wrong.

Bonded relationships can be of tremendous help to us in the self-clarity so necessary to personal growth. Our friends in community are able to see us as we are because they are not at the effect of *our* particular blind spots (although they certainly have their own). They can remind us of what they know to be true and what we often forget—namely, who and what we are, essentially. When I complained to a friend in community one day about how I had failed to meet a deadline because I had over-extended myself in other projects, she remarked lightly, "Oh, feeling rebellious again?" I was surprised that she had named my chronic tendency so perfectly. Such closely bonded friendships help us to realize how often we are kidding ourselves.

As we go further into this territory of allowing the bonded relationship to serve our efforts for self-honesty and self-clarity, we find that the less we try to hide our shortcomings—as most of us do, out of shame, guilt or pride—the more relaxation and freed up energy we have. There is no longer a reason to have a "secret life." Within the embracing net of community we can honestly, and with compassion and humor, share with others of like mind the foibles and challenges of our own individual struggle toward personal growth.

The Humor of It All

A sense of humor is tremendously important in the bonding process. Seeing the drama of the human condition enacted constantly around us and within us in community life, we learn not to take our habitual psychological patterns so seriously. Humor helps us bring perspective to our lives, to recognize that we are more than our ingrained habits and our neuroses, and to acknowledge that we are all really in the same boat. Those with whom we are bonded in relationships of mutual trust can help us to laugh at the illusory nature of some of our most annoying and even emotionally devastating habits. After all, when our habits are so transparent to those around us, how can we continue to identify with them so totally?

Humor can prevent us from locking ourselves into situations where we are at odds with our friends. If we can laugh at our exaggerated emotions and mechanical tendencies there is the chance to see how ridiculous the human condition can really be. Many of us can probably recall verbally fighting "tooth and nail" with someone, and then stopping suddenly, breaking into laughter. Perhaps in that moment we realized how untenable our "position" actually was; perhaps we were hit with the absurdity of being so angry and upset with someone we cared for and respected over something like how the lasagna should be cooked or the library painted! Nurturing a sense of humor can be the missing piece we need to stop alienating our friends and loved ones, and a huge relief to us as well! Humor is a magic potion that dispels any number of disturbances or conflicts, both inner and outer.

When traveling in Greece, at the Acropolis in Athens, I noticed a twelve-year-old boy sitting on the steps. He was pouting as he was having a disagreement with his father. The two were locked into an adversarial stance. Watching them I was reminded of what it was like to be twelve, and I could see clearly that it was just a game the boy was playing. At one point the boy looked up, caught my eye, and both of us broke into a spontaneous smile. For brief seconds we shared the mischievous spirit of the moment, and his mood with his father was broken. Remembering that he was supposed to be upset, however, he resumed his role of being serious and at odds with his dad. We all do this in our own way, no matter what our age!

Honoring the Bonds That Exist

While a mature community will open and stretch to embrace new members rather than making elite circles that are socially impenetrable, new members need to respect and honor the existing bonds, be willing to learn from them, and seek to enter them softly, with sensitivity, rather than blasting their way in. Marty had lived in community for only two years when she told the following story about her ongoing process of integrating into a well-established, intentional community.

Marty Speaks About Bonding

I was immediately attracted to the way the people in this community were together, and how committed they were to what they were doing. A few of them reached out to me, but I also noticed that it was a close-knit group, and I realized that it wouldn't be easy to approach. I have visited and lived for short periods of time in many communities around the world, and I have seen that it is always this way: people want to check you out and see if you're going to be an asset or a liability. They are protective of what they have together.

When I moved into the community residence two years ago, for several days few people even spoke to me except for a polite hello. This was hard, but what I tried to do—and what I've done everywhere I've gone—is that I just started working, seeing where I could help out in various ways. At the end of a long day's work when everybody is sweaty and tired, or in the thick of a project, there is less distance and defenses are typically down all around. When people are really into something together there's less space for judgement and trepidation.

On the flip side, people are also curious, and there were people who were genuinely interested, both in extending themselves so that I would have a good experience as a newcomer, and also because they were naturally oriented to befriend me. However, I realized quickly that really integrating and feeling comfortable was going to be a lengthy process.

It takes a tremendous amount of energy and time for a community to integrate a new person, and only time will tell whether or not a newcomer is going to give or take. People want to know that the new person is going to stick it out with them; at a really basic, personal level, people in community often feel that they don't want to invest a lot of energy into a friendship and then get burned when that person leaves or doesn't work out due to unresolvable conflicts. This isn't only true of intentional communities; people in cultural communities are the same way. For example, I lived in a community in southern India for a year, and at first people there were distant, even cold. After several months, friendships began to develop and people said to me, "Why were you so shy in the beginning?" This shocked me! I had thought it was them keeping me away, when in fact I was putting something out that kept them at a distance too.

Coming to my current community I have slowly begun to examine my own responsibility in how people receive me, and this is part of the process that is perhaps most difficult. As months and then a year and more went by, I got to see how other people integrated into the community. I had to look at the fact that other people had an easier time of it than I did. This gave me a lot to reflect on. Like most of us, I didn't want to have to scrutinize my own motives, fears and insecurities at the level that community demanded of me.

Jealousy plays a part in the bonding, or lack of bonding, in community. In any small group of people, it's a competition thing or a survival thing on both sides—the newcomers and the established members. Communities are a microcosm of our culture at large, so of course there are power struggles and often unacknowledged hierarchies. On one hand, you come in and see these well-established, deep bonds and friendships and systems, and wonder, "How am I going to make a life for myself here? They don't really need me, they have everything they need already." The others feel the new person's need, jealousy, fear and desire for power within the group, and they respond in varying ways. Everyone has to move over just a little, or a lot, to create room for you, so it requires a lot of giving and generosity on the part of the existing community. Some are more willing to do this than others. Some are very generous and others are openly jealous and hostile. The new person comes in with his or her added dynamics, with flaws and gifts, and all that has to be integrated into the chemistry of the group. That this process would be challenging is almost a given, but I think that we are rarely conscious of how intricate it is in a community. Naturally there is some fumbling and bumping up against one another. To make it through this process you have to want to live in a committed community, for better or worse.

I also found that the initial difficulty, which was substantial for me, changed over time. Many people in my community told me that there was no substitute or replacement for time. They would say, "Things will be different for you five years from now." I also have found that when people see that you are serious and committed, they want to like you and they want to welcome you. It took about a year for me to feel like I was really wanted in my community, but I was also battling my own childhood traumas in the process. It goes against my psychological conditioning to admit, "These people care about me."

Recently I was ill and both unable to tend to my usual work tasks and really wanting a break from them. So, for a few days I simply stayed in my room and rested. In the back of my mind I thought, "Nobody really notices that I'm gone, and if they do, they probably don't care very much." After only half a day, one friend came to visit and check in on me, and before she had even left, two more friends came by to see how I was doing. An hour later, someone else stopped by to see if I needed anything or if I was hungry, and I had to laugh at myself for believing that nobody cared if I was absent or sick. At the same time, those very people were willing to give me space to not show up at work or meals. Nobody complained or criticized, so I learned that there was that kind of space in community too. It was the first time I'd slowed down in two years of really working hard all the time, and I greatly appreciated that.

In community there is a combination of both being very integral and important, and also quite dispensable, because in community there are others who can do your job or fill in. When I left on community business for a week, I saw that the community functioned perfectly fine in my absence. The other side to that is the commitment that people have to caring for each other, whether you're the best friend or not, and in some cases whether they even like you or not. I've seen people who don't particularly like me or feel inclined to have any personal, intimate relationship with me, be very staunch advocates for me—willing to help me, to talk, to provide guidance. This example has struck me deeply, and I've been moved to do the same for others. It's like relationships are more objective, rather than being based on whether or not you are drawn to a person's chemistry. Because of that, compassion and help are offered just because you are another human being. I think this is one of the biggest lessons community has to teach new people, and it is a lesson that can totally change your life.

Realizing that bonding means we will be dealing with all aspects of each other, and that the more deeply bonded we are, the richer and more rewarding and ultimately successful in terms of a culture of the heart our community will be, we must ask ourselves this question: "Am I willing to take the risk involved in bonding, intimacy and vulnerability?"

Are we willing to expose ourselves beneath the masks we wear—the carefully crafted, culturally acceptable *personas* we have developed since childhood, which we keep so tightly in place on the surface of our lives? In every relationship someone must be first to take the risk, to admit their weaknesses, strengths, fears, pleasures, hopes and visions to themselves and others. It takes courage to be vulnerable, yet through this process one gains strength, certitude and self-respect, regardless of how one's vulnerability is met.

When we *are* met by others in a shared vulnerability there is a richness beyond words that takes place. This is the gift of relationship—an infinite possibility found everywhere in community.

CHAPTER EIGHT

On Men and Women

Driven by the force of love
the fragments of the world
seek each other that the world
may come into being.

—Teilhard de Chardin

Distinct sub-cultures for men and women are an important aspect of the bonded community found in all ancient and indigenous cultures. The value of such cultures has been virtually forgotten in the modern culture of the West. In our attempts to bring an egalitarian spirit to community we have often overlooked or denied the value of separate gender cultures. However, some communities today are beginning to experiment with rebuilding or revisioning these gender cultures, not as separative or sexist social devices, but as enhancements to the richness of relationships within community. Gender cultures are intended to honor and support the natural dispositions of each sex. Calling for support, intimacy and companionship from our male friends, if we are male, or our female friends if we are female, is a way of creating community within community.

The Gender Cultures

A wonderful children's book, *The Village of Round and Square Houses,* describes the creation of men's and women's culture in one African village. The story is told by a young girl who is explaining why in her village the men live in square houses and the women live in round houses, and why to her it seemed like the natural order of things.

According to this tribal myth, the nearby mountain called Old Naka, erupted and covered everyone and everything with ashes, so they could not tell who was who. When the chaos was over, only two houses were left standing: one round and one square. As the people stood around covered with ash, the village chief pointed to clusters of them, "You! Tall gray things! You go live in the square house! And you! Round gray things! Go live in the round house!" And so it was that the women lived in the round house with the children, where they "talked and laughed— preparing food for everyone," while the men stayed together in the square house and "told each other tall stories and planted yams and corn each day, in the new, rich soil."

The grandmother of the little girl explained why they had kept their village life this way in all the years since the volcano erupted. Simply, each group enjoyed the company of their own kind. "So you see, Osa," she said, "we live together peacefully here, because each one has a place to be apart, and a time to be together . . . And that is how our way came about and will continue—til Naka speaks again!" [1]

Throughout time, every culture to varying degrees has had some distinctions between male and female cultures. In modern-day U.S., college fraternities and sororities, women's clubs and men's clubs, the Freemasons or Ladies Auxiliary, sports teams, inner city gangs and exclusive cliques are an instinctual (though often shadowy and misguided) expression of same-sex bonding and nurturing. People today are seeking something that was inherent for tribal people, but without the gender cultures so basic to indigenous tribal life. In most ancient and indigenous cultures, the formal distinction between men and women was about acknowledging what was sacred and unique within each group, and regarding that as an archetypal expression of incarnated divinity. The rites of passage for adolescents that many

187

tribes still practice are examples of the flowering of distinct men's and women's cultures, as are birthing rituals, death rituals, hunting rituals, healing rituals and so on.

Within our own gender culture we can discover a sanctuary where we are not compelled to play the ordinary but deeply ingrained sexual games we have been taught to play in mixed company. These subtle, and not so subtle, games are indeed so commonplace that we accept them as " normal" when in fact they are quite neurotic. One of my mentors used to refer to himself and all of his students as the "normal neurotics," because neurosis is, in fact, the norm in our culture. The dynamics of competition, the power struggles and the convoluted projections of mother and father complexes, which so often characterize the casual, unconscious interactions between the sexes, do not bring dignity and honor to either sex. Nor do these projections and thinly veiled flirtations call forth what is truly Woman or Man in the highest sense.

Within our separate gender cultures we are much freer to let ourselves come through as we really are. Certainly many psychological complexities exist in relations with our own sex, but if we are willing to courageously navigate that labyrinth, we can find clarity and honesty in relationship with a member of our own sex that is biologically unavailable with a member of the opposite sex. We can get the feedback, the mirroring and the affirmation that only a woman can give to another woman, or a man can give to another man. It is not only a matter of friendships being easier and facades dropping; it sometimes is not even a matter of "liking" the other person. More objectively, a profound resonance that is archetypal at core can take place, beyond all other considerations, when women gather with other women and men gather with other men.

While living for a time in Germany I led two workshops on conscious childraising. Both entailed the same material and the same exercises, yet each produced distinctly different results.

One workshop was for mothers only, while the other had mothers and fathers. In the all-women group I noticed that a lot of the pretenses dropped, including my own. We weren't trying to prove something, and more easily spoke of our shared struggles as mothers and women. Tears and vulnerability came more easily to us. We much more quickly got down to business—to a gut level—and worked on what we all came to work on. The male-female group was also valuable, yet there was a marked difference in the mood, and I observed that we all kept our individual "masks" and distances more in place than when the group was gender specific.

African tribal spokesman Malidoma Somé has written and spoken at length about men's culture and women's culture in tribal Africa. Now that he lives in the West, Somé says that being together with men is the closest he can come to being with himself. In *Creating a Sense of Home—The Tribal Community of the Heart,* he writes:

> I like working with a group of men for the simple reason that it is the only circle in which I can get as close to myself as I can be in this hyper-developed country and culture. Why? Simply because every group I go to or I interact with reminds me of the very reason why there is a very powerful gender consciousness in the indigenous world I've left behind for this culture. You see, for an African who has gone through a certain amount of tradition education (which people like to call initiation) there is something that you become stamped with . . . the intolerable feeling that you experience each time you are trapped in isolation. There is a constant need for the other . . . of the same gender. [2]

According to Somé, tapping the natural urge that leads us to create "a certain sense of community, a certain sense of natural dependency upon each other for the grand purpose that Spirit determines for us" is the way to also "create a new sense of home in the middle of postmodernity." [3]

The Men's Movement / The Women's Movement

Where men are concerned, Somé affirms that initiation is not an option but an imperative—an absolutely necessary event of the human soul. The psyche and soul of man today has been crying out for initiatory experience. The contemporary men's movement, spearheaded by Robert Bly, James Hillman, Michael Mead and many others, has made a tremendous contribution toward revisioning and reclaiming authentic men's culture and initiation in a time when the emotional and spiritual alienation among men is at a tragic peak. For decades, men in Western culture have had no ritual form of initiation into manhood and almost no real friendship or intimacy among themselves. Instead, since the industrial revolution, men's relationships have been characterized by a ruthless drive to survive through competition, through analytical and separative thinking, and through the angst-ridden struggle over money and power.

Women, on the other hand, even in today's society, have maintained greater closeness with one another. By necessity, women come together to nourish and support life through their biologically and socially defined functions. For example, childbearing and homemaking more naturally nourish togetherness. This does not mean, however, that women today have an easier time developing a women's culture. The socially and biologically imposed closeness among women has often been based on patriarchal definitions of what it is to be a woman.

The women's movement that started in the 1960s has in some respects come full circle beyond the radical feminism of the 70s and the apathy of the 80s into a more soulful consideration of what it means to be a woman in contemporary times. This deeper reflection upon feminine psychology has brought many of us to a greater clarity about how masculinized we have become. At first we railed against being "male-defined," which meant typically that women were defined by men's needs and projections: "I want a woman who will serve my needs, who will be a sexual adornment to stand by my side and help my career, to have my babies and stay at home keeping the house together so I can be free to work and produce. Furthermore, you are my property and possession that I have total rights to control."

Next came equal opportunities—economically, educationally, in careers, in the business world, and so on. By the end of the 1980s, women began to realize that attempting to become liberated through assuming patriarchal values was cutting them off from a whole dimension of deeply feminine qualities: cooperation, creativity, sensitivity and empathy for others, nurturance, the ability to witness to birth and death, the ability to see the big picture and to care deeply and passionately for human life, the willingness to serve.

As men too have begun to feel a deep-rooted longing for these same qualities, collectively we have moved much closer to recognizing the need for a return to such values at a societal and planetary level.

Fear of Our Own Kind

When we first encounter the idea of men's and women's culture in actuality, we may feel a great deal of resistance. We may say, "No way am I going to get close to any of these people." But usually our fear and therefore our resistance is more cloaked and unconscious, and easily rationalized. We have lots of good reasons why we can't be trusting and vulnerable with members of our own sex. "Tony is too cynical. He's a hypocrite." "Rosemary scares me with her anger," or "She's so different than me—she talks incessantly and always has to have center stage."

191

We live with various degrees of deep-seated fear, hatred or ambivalence toward other women or men because our relationships with our mothers and fathers were unloving, rejecting, cold; we are too familiar with the themes of abandonment, abuse, betrayal or neglect experienced as children. To get closer to the heart of relationship, we have to be willing to look deeper than this—at ourselves and at others.

Mary, a psychotherapist who also conducts women's workshops and therapeutic groups, says it is not uncommon to hear women say, "I'm afraid of other women. I don't really like them. I get along better with men." Or, "My mother was a controlling bitch, and I find myself constantly battling with women over power." She also heard numerous stories of men whose relationships with their fathers were full of fear, rage and loathing. As adults, these men were unable to open up emotionally with other men, and often unconsciously arranged their lives so that they were constantly battling an oppressive male presence, especially in their professional lives.

With one client, David, his mother was his only reference point for love, acceptance or kindness. He was extremely dependent upon women, therefore, and this dependency often left him feeling powerless and angry in relationships with women. Although David became part of a community for a while, he eventually left because he was in conflict with several of the men there.

Most of us have to work through a lot to come fully into our own gender culture with some degree of trust and acceptance and vulnerability. In the following account, Lee, with the experience of twenty-five-plus years as the leader of a spiritual community, reflects on the psychological complexities of creating men's culture and community today.

Lee Speaks About Men's Culture

To varying degrees there is always some psychological "gamey-ness" between men and women—some exhibitionism that can be subtle and sophisticated or crude and obvious, or sometimes voyeuristic. So in men's culture within a community, a man gets to be who he is without having to subconsciously or unconsciously put on any kind of mating games—like when birds put their feathers up, or go through any hunting ritual. Literally, a different brain chemistry is activated when men are with men than the chemistry that is active when men are with women, so it creates a whole new possibility of understanding or consciousness to interact within one's gender culture.

Ostensibly, anyone involved in community would be involved for reasons beyond security, loneliness or some kind of social ideology; hopefully one would be involved because of a desire to really investigate the depths and heights of self-awareness. If this is what we are interested in, then men's culture or women's culture gives us a whole different possible insight into ourselves and our own gender which is literally not possible in that same way when one is relating with the opposite gender.

Unfortunately, however, one of the handicaps of men's culture—in my personal experience as a man—is that one can be a totally immature, sexist baby and get away with it in the presence of other men. Whereas, if one tries that in the presence of women, one gets criticized for being immature and politically incorrect. When my friends act immaturely about women, I feel like I'm in the wrong company, but sometimes I laugh anyway and pretend like this is acceptable behavior between grown men. I rarely confront them in those circumstances, because I think there is a time and place for confrontation, and every time someone demonstrates immature behavior is not necessarily the time. It is important to understand the other, and useful feedback is based upon an understanding of the psychology of the other. With some men, nothing their men friends can say will make them change anyway. Why talk until your are blue in the face if it doesn't make any difference?

In an informal culture of friends, therefore, I don't think one needs to get on a soapbox and preach, although I think there is a time for bringing other men into the awareness that their behavior is childish and inappropriate. To do that under informal circumstances with a bunch of friends all the time—you probably would not have many friends, and the ones you would have would be boring, controlled, uptight and superior. This is the unconscious of the Western white man's race we're dealing with—or the by-products of it. And, if you listen to rap music and they call the women "bitches" and "whores," the man will say, "But I don't mean anything derogatory." Then why not call them "sugar" and "molasses," if they don't mean "bitches" and "whores"? So this is a pervasive neurosis of our time. Men are immature; they don't grow up!

Women have their thing, their neuroses, too . . . but what do I know about that? (Although I think it has something to do with shopping.) As a matter of fact, feminist Cynthia Heimel agrees, at least in her column in Playboy, *which might just be humor— because she's very funny—or may be just to sell magazines. She said that when women get together they don't talk about men— that's a myth. They talk about food and shopping. When men get together they don't talk about women, their wives or girlfriends. The sexist jokes are just an unconscious habit based upon the crippling upbringing of twentieth-century society—of watching their mothers being manipulated and suppressed. It is totally an absorption from the culture they grew up in. Usually men talk about mechanical things, like cars, musical instruments, guns, computers.*

Because of the constant reminding factors having to do with the ideals of the intentional community, there are times when these ideals are considered in depth among the men, but those aren't the only times that lead to bonding. When men are building a stone fence and all they are talking about is building a fence—or even if they are building the stone fence and making sexist remarks all the while—there is still a very deep bonding that occurs because of the shared commonality of gender essence. So, just spending time together is actually very bonding.

No matter how immature a man is, he's not stupid. He may act like a little boy, but he still has an adult intelligence. So, men in general within community still have meaningful and responsible friendships based on deep bonding, just from spending time together, and from considering the difference between spending time with other men rather than spending time exclusively with their female partners.

To varying degrees some men take changes to heart. I've visited intentional communities in which non-sexism and non-prejudice is a high priority, and yet that kind of behavior is still common. Men are different around women because they have something to gain from the women that they don't have to gain from the men. Sexist attitudes are not going to handicap friendship with another man necessarily, but if a man is sexist in the company of woman, it will very well handicap the possibility of relationship. People's ability to manage their unconscious tendencies and attitudes under periods of stress is not necessarily in any way in alignment with their ideology, which in relatively stress-free periods may be acted out in a fairly consistent way. Look at what happened in the Vietnam War. Many moral, Christian farm boys from the cream of American culture were raping and killing when they got over there because that was what was expected, or was the general attitude in the war. Others of them were horrified and revolted and couldn't get with the program, which was total repression of the Vietcong through degradation.

That's the whole idea of the difference between community that really deals with self-knowledge as a necessary foundation for

195

political and social egalitarianism over and against a community where the primary aim is political and social egalitarianism, and self-knowledge is only talked about peripherally. In the latter case you get a lot of sophisticated intellectually-based behavior, but not real change in people's deep psychology. Yet it takes changes in one's deep psychology to have a relationship with the opposite sex that is non-manipulative and non-gamey, because it is in one's deep psychology where all the neurotic prejudices are operative, and stress tends to bring those hidden or underlying attitudes out of the closet, so to speak.

Scott Talks About Men In Community

The first thing men need to understand is that we have an instinctual need and drive for the company of other men. It's genetic. It's in the cells, It comes from being primates. If we are trying to build community or culture with other men then we will need to peel through all the layers of conditioning, which means a man has to examine himself inwardly because we are taught that men have to be strong loner types. It's a stereotype that we as men have to break through.

When men are able to be vulnerable with each other, we can offer each other ease, because there is a shared understanding of the difficulties of being a man. Men have fragile egos. We are really very sensitive creatures. For men to manifest their sensitivity they need the right kind of safe environment in which to do that. But relationships between men can very easily flip from kinship to aggression to hostility, so for men it's very important to have a space in which there's trust, and where hostility with other men is not an issue.

Trust has to be built, but once it is established it runs deeper than would make sense because it is nonlinear. There is a deeper trust than you would expect between men, a trust that is naturally there underneath all the culturally-defined role-playing. From the point of view of transformation, without the support of other men to make those breakthroughs, men will typically stay stuck in macho stereotypes. But men are looking for safety with other men. My hope is that community would have to be part of providing that safety.

The stress level of men's lives can either draw them closer together or make them rub each other the wrong way. Because of the close quarters we encounter in community—even just the emotional or psychic close quarters, if not physical close quarters—we can readily spark off each other and rub each other the wrong way. There is typically a lot of that happening in community before men are able to be together openly, easily.

Men tend to do macho posturing with each other ostensibly so that we don't look like we are afraid . . . afraid of each other, afraid of life. But I think fear is the greatest commonality that men have. I have found that when I stop trying not to look afraid, other men open up to me and admit that they are afraid too.

Men have a huge fear of failure. There are immense expectations laid upon us. How things look, how they are viewed, is very important for men. Ideally, community offers a place where you don't have to maintain the show. If you get to know each other well enough and "lose face" enough times and survive it, that creates the space of safety for men to bond through the shared experience of humiliation.

Fathers in our culture don't have any sense of the fragility of their sons, or they don't feel comfortable with it. What's underneath that discomfort is a compulsion to crush that fragility in other males, so they may even intentionally try to harden their sons and prepare them for the "cold cruel world." They can't stand the thought that if their son didn't grow up wounded, maybe they did not need to be wounded either. The wound feels so all encompassing that if someone shows you or tells you that it's not necessary, you can't bear that. But that is one of the greatest gifts a father today can give his son—an acceptance and maybe even a fostering,

197

if possible, of the son's fragility and sensitivity, so that he can grow up knowing that he is really okay in this regard.

As both Lee and Scott point out, we shouldn't let the intensity or difficulty of this healing process stop us from forging ahead into this territory of gender cultures within community, which is really ancient but wondrously new as well. Here is a similar perspective from a woman's experience. Maggie, a long-time community participant and activist in women's issues, particularly spirituality, shares her insights and experiences of women's culture.

Maggie on Women's Culture

In my community, gender culture isn't about a strict delegation of roles and responsibilities. Quite the contrary, in fact. We have some men who like to cook and provide childcare as well as maintain the cars or run the community business, and women who like to write books and manage our finances and sculpt as well as mother children or weave cloth or put up pickles. What characterizes our gender cultures is that women intentionally and specifically turn to other women for intimacy, help, advice, feedback, nurturance and affection, while the men go to other men for the same. I have seen tremendous leadership capacities and creative faculties nurtured and brought forth in both men and women through the incubation process of women's and men's cultures.

As a woman I cannot speak from first-hand experience of men's culture, although I have a great appreciation for what I can see of the men's culture in my community. I see that the men are steadily gaining solid ground together—ground that stands boldly new and distinct from conventional seeking for a competitive advantage; a ground that makes men stand taller and walk with the presence of essential life force, the way a true man walks on the earth—confident, noble, creative, willing to serve out of strength.

I think it is true that out of the true strength of manhood comes service to Life, and it is this quality that brings character to a man's being.

Being with women within my own gender culture has helped me face at a deeper level a lot of the issues that I've struggled with over a period of many years—issues with my mother, with other women and with the whole feminine aspect of my life in general. I've read many of the books on the feminine and the goddess within, and have been through years of feminine spirituality and feminism, including leading women's groups and therapy processes. Some of these books have been tremendously helpful, while some leave me wondering, "Where do these women live?" I hate to see the feminine get watered down and co-opted into some new-age cliché, and I see a lot of that going on, as if all we have to do to become the goddess is to wear some ancient emblem of Isis around our necks and dance to harps and flutes and drums; as if in touching the living reality of the divine feminine we wouldn't get our small, limited egos and illusory dreams of self-aggrandizement blown to smithereens in the blast of unmitigated raw truth.

It's been my observation that we women have a tremendously difficult time working through all the gargoyles at the various gates to find the real feminine within, much less to find real relationship between us as adult women. From my experience, this finding of the feminine takes a lifetime of very committed effort and damned hard inner work, along with a serious commitment to self-knowing.

There is no greater compassion or insight to be found for a woman on this path than from other women. Women are tremendously changeable, creative, volatile, passionate and complex creatures. Who can understand a woman better than another woman? That is sort of the bottom line in women's culture. Even the most sensitive men get weary of the unfolding panorama of creation and the awesome forces of nature that most women carry around as their basic impulses—the thunderstorms, the forest fires, hail, snow, sleet, tornadoes, hurricanes, sunrises, sunsets and high noons, as well as the long sunny afternoons when we languish in cool breezes. Like Venus, goddess of love and war, we women are both wildly ecstatic—from creation to destruction—and at the same time, dripping with the sweetest nectars that draw the bees and the bears near enough to us to beg for a taste. Another woman can both appreciate these moods and at the same time call us to task—to temperance, responsibility and the skillful means to channel these forces—when we are in the grip of the downside of these forces: the illusory, the raging or unproductive drama.

Living with many women in community as I do, I get to see all of my projections and the unresolved aspects of myself—the dark and the light of the feminine and the masculine—as they parade across the screen of my consciousness. This is true when I am looking at my women friends and am just overwhelmed by their radiant beauty, talent and sheer charm. This mirror can be quite wonderful, or it can be unpleasant to the extreme, but even on the wonderful side I get to see how unwilling I am to claim aspects of myself, including the beauty or giftedness that is there.

When I am at war with another women, it is like the bottom has dropped out from beneath my feet. My foundation is gone and I am at the mercy of the inner tempest unleashed. I may be raging with jealousy, revenge, envy and self-hatred. Whatever she has, I want—but I am sure that I don't have. I may be paralyzed with distrust and paranoia. Sometimes I am a hulking monster with lightning eyes, driving even the most stalwart friends away. Who can approach this kind of rage? This is a very miserable, abject state of affairs.

On the other hand, when I am thoroughly enchanted with one of my women friends, I sometimes want to follow her around like a child after her mother, seeking her approval and crying out for nourishment. I might be whining and reeling around in a whirl of self-pity and abandonment—the lost little girl. Or else I am the good girl who will do anything, say anything, to get mommy's love and approval. This little one sashays around with big wide eyes, begging for a crumb or a bone. This too can be hell in relationship, because it is a no-win situation: no one can ever change the fact of our lack of nourishment and love from our real bodily mothers. This kind of unconscious, desperate need cannot be met, and will usually only draw yet another scenario of rejection or abandonment from unwitting others. We have to accept the facts of our childhood, know it completely, stop projecting and re-running the same old scenarios over and over again, and go on as adults. We have to learn to approach our women friends for nurturance as adults in the here and now.

Another hell realm that I revisit again and again is when I am just controlling everything and everybody, and my women friends and I are locked into a very masculinized psychology in which we are going to fight to the death over some shred of territory. That territory may be who will use the shower first on a busy morning, or who is going to facilitate (or dominate) the meeting today, or who is going to get a certain person's attention, especially when that attention involves sexual energy at any level.

Some idealists may say, "Oh you are really exaggerating; we've gone beyond all that stuff!" I say, look deeper and get off of that cloud, my friend. We need to get our feet firmly planted back in the earth of reality, not some fantasy of how we wish it would be. If we are honest with ourselves, we see that our motivations are not always as altruistic as we would like them to be, and that we are in fact fighting it out with each other, often at the most base levels. These repressed or denied aspects of ourselves come out most often under stress, when we are emotionally charged by primal passions. If we have any hope of really discovering ourselves as women, individually and together, we must have the vision, fortitude and guts to look in the mirror and see the very real dark side of Hecate, Lilith, Hera or Artemis. Jealous, scheming, raging, insatiable, petty, gossiping and revengeful! Only when we have

201

faced all of this can we know the sublime and transformative side of the feminine.

I have also learned from my women friends that there is a place where women can meet in an enjoyment of life that is extraordinarily free, exquisite, fruitful, and that springs from radical understanding. This does not mean that we agree about everything. It means that we have the skills, insight and courage to live what we know to be true within the framework of our most serious commitments in life. We live together what the soul calls us to be, to embody, to witness, create or speak. We encourage each other to flourish, and we uphold each other when times are hard. We are traveling companions walking down a road whose surface changes don't really matter, because it is for the joy of the company and the journey itself that we are singing and walking in strength and wisdom and sobriety and sometimes uproarious gaiety.

One of the things that women excel at naturally is "witnessing and blessing" the other in relationship. This is an authentic expression of loving-kindness. The real loving-kindness for which the feminine is so famous is not sickly sweet, insidiously nice and good, but like a liquid which has been clarified in the high heat of ruthless self-honesty. This loving-kindness captures the brilliance of light and flows in smooth streams that are startlingly refreshing, so much so that it can take our breath away or even cause a shock. Because of this translucence, a truly mature, self-realized woman is a very rare occurrence, a wonder of nature in fact, the long draught of which is nothing less than liberating to one who is willing to drink fully.

Maggie's words inspire me, but they also terrify me. At the beginning of establishing links within a men's or women's culture many of us find our feelings confusing and even terrifying as we hit pockets of psychological disturbance rooted in our relationships with mother or father. But, as we clear away the debris, we will come to understand the value of these new flavors of intimacy in friendship.

I first experienced the power of the bond that can exist between women who are not related by blood ties when I lived and worked within a small healing community in the Northeast. Initially, I was scared, a little put off—I didn't know what to make of these strange feelings. Distrust and confusion often clouded this growing intimacy. Soon, however, the reality of living in community revealed that the essential new feeling was a natural and organic expression of connectedness among women, and since those early days I have found my relationships with close women friends to be a bottomless well of nurturance, strength and love. The possibility of this kind of communion is our birthright.

Beyond the Solitary Couple

Culturally, we have been "taught" to seek nurturing almost exclusively from our sexual partners. While our partners—whether in a heterosexual or homosexual relationship— certainly can offer a particular intimacy that reaches to our innermost core, too much turning exclusively to the other can eat away at the relationship. Expecting our sexual partner to be our sole source of nurturing, support and objective feedback limits us and them.

By the same token, we are sometimes too emotionally tied in to our partner to objectively hear and accept what they are offering. Too often we find ourselves in a feedback loop based on enmeshed mutual neuroses. Men's and women's cultures can significantly help with breaking this cycle of unhealthy dependence within a couple, bring new insight and fresh energy to seed new growth, and generally break up the mutual covert agreement of codependency.

When human beings come together in intimate relationship already feeling complete, already saturated in the knowledge that they are loved, having received that from the like company of men and women, then they have room for delight and ecstasy with each other. This realization builds a passion that ultimately serves the whole community. As a married woman and a mother, Jean talks about women's culture for her, noting the support it lends her relationship with her husband.

Jean Reflects on Couples and Gender Cultures

My husband Dennis and I went over to a friend's house one night for dinner and there were a number of couples there and a few children. We sat around the living room talking together for a while, and then we decided to play bridge. There was a great sense of enjoyment and closeness and very naturally the women gravitated to play bridge with the women and the men with the men. There was no dissonance between the two groups, but the mood of the men's game was different than that of the women's game, and they seemed to complement each other. Delightedly, the children ran back and forth between the two games. The way we all were together as one, but also as part of our separate cultures felt so rich and so right. It wasn't contrived ahead of time, but was simply part of our flow together. A great evening!

Being in a mated relationship, I've found that having gender cultures is invaluable. Observing Dennis working with the other men, I get a renewed appreciation for who he is; I get to see some little aspect or something about him that deepens my respect and fondness and regard for this man who is my husband. It adds an element of richness or depth to my relationship with him to see these other facets of him.

My relationship with him is served as I get clearer about who I am, and where Love comes from. As a teenager and young adult, my relationship with my mother was always rocky and adversarial. As I've gotten older, had a child of my own and become more mature, I've become aware of how absent my mother was as a guiding force and true presence in my life. There was a real lack of deep bonding with her, and I have no memories of being held, rocked, hugged or really nurtured by her. I never had a feeling of safety associated with her as my mother. However, being in women's culture now has provided what I didn't get then. It's like going back and slipping in the foundation that was never given to me. The feelings of trust and nurturing and the world as a safe place—all that basic ego-building stuff that should have happened when I was a growing child—is happening now with my women friends, sometimes in very subtle ways. The result of all that nurturance and trust allows me to be present to my husband with clarity, certainly with less dependency.

In my own case, living in community for the past fifteen-plus years, I have been involved in a coupled relationship, but most of my time has been spent as a "single" woman. Consequently, I readily learned that I could turn to the women around me for their friendship, support and nurturing. After beginning a relationship with my male partner, however, I tended to access the women's culture less. My necessity for women's culture was clouded for a time by the newness of love and sexual intimacy. The further we got into this new relationship without spending time with our respective gender cultures, the emptier we began to feel, until we realized what was happening. Within the matrix of community life, then, we were able to turn this situation around. We learned by experience that even in a strong, positive relationship we still needed the individual support that comes from women's and men's cultures.

Continually turning to my partner for all of my emotional needs didn't satisfy me. I was actually looking to him for the unconditional love I didn't get from my parents when I was young. I desperately wanted to know that love was not scarce, but rather all pervading and unceasing. I was trying to use my partner to heal that primary wound of separation (even from God); and to heal the wounds of childhood.

What I have found is that there is no relationship—with a partner, a friend, or anybody—that can do that for me now as an adult. Ultimately, I must discover this unconditional love within myself. I sometimes still search for this love within my gender culture as well as with my partner. But my search among my women friends is often less caught up with my own psychological history, so that their nurturing can have a more direct effect on me.

Men and women simply handle things differently. A wise woman once said to me, "Men seek space and women seek relationship, and so thank God for community!" In my coupled relationship, between the two of us, I like to talk things out while he often likes to work things out internally. If I didn't have others to turn to I'd be seeking something from him that he simply would not be able to offer me.

This is all very easy to say, but having been raised in the heart and bowels of American culture, the conflict between our conditioning and our vision sometimes feels like torture. When a dear friend of mine suggested that I "surrender" to my mate and not ask him for anything, only be responsive to him, and that I go to other women for nurturing, I thought she was out to get me! I was paranoid and then disbelieving, yet I knew her to be a wise person whom I also trusted. I found myself running to her every fifteen minutes saying, "Surely I must have misunderstood you!" Fortunately and unfortunately I hadn't misunderstood her. I only had to go against most of my conditioning to find the truth beneath it all.

I thank God for the wisdom of my women friends. When we are attempting to live so differently than the mainstream cultural neurosis demands that we live, we need a support structure in which to do so. Men's and women's culture together make a strong foundation for that challenge to be met, to discover a more sane and enlivening way to live.

Eros: Sex and Celibacy

Anyone who has participated in any form of community knows that sexuality and sexual energy are big concerns of the group. This is true whether the community is heterosexual, gay or lesbian. Sexual tensions, jealousy, indiscriminate and unconscious eroticism, negative patterns of sexual addiction and love affairs gone astray can wreak havoc in the cohesion and stability of community, especially within small communities. Indeed, sex and all its related issues can severely undermine the fabric of context, communion and sanctuary within any community.

Gay and lesbian as well as heterosexual communities are faced with the challenge of how to consciously manage sexual energy in a way that is not repressive and allows the creative flow of relationship and energy, while at the same time maintaining appropriate boundaries—so that the culture of community is not damaged by the shadow side of sexuality. But, developing gender cultures is not the panacea for dealing with the complexities of sexual energy and how it is expressed within community. It certainly is not the answer for gay or lesbian communities because these communities are already gender specific.

To explain what I mean by the shadow side of sex, I will turn to psychiatrist Wilhelm Reich, a protégé of Sigmund Freud, who developed a profound view of sexual energy, which he called *orgone energy* or primal life force—what the ancient Greeks deified as Eros. According to Reich, sexual energy is that force which lies at the core of all creativity, healing and health. When repressed, denied and shamed (as happens in the authoritarian family system, for instance, well described in Alice Miller's work) this same energy is expressed through violence, rage, rape, war, disease and aggression—the shadow side of Eros.

Sex, eroticism and sexual energy—the entire domain of Eros—is interwoven with all other aspects of life. Without Eros we would have no art, song, dance or ideas, no science, no philosophy, no great architecture, no culture, and of course, no future humanity. No community effort of any kind is separate from this primal energy; if we attempt to build and sustain community without a conscious consideration of sexual energy and sexual ethics (rather than morality) we are naively and dangerously denying the basics of human life. Sex will rear its many-faceted, beautiful, ugly, sacred and profane head whether we like it or not!

A radical shift of context is fundamentally necessary to create sanctuary within community with regard to sexual energy and sexual interplay. This context includes a commitment to self-awareness, responsibility and to defining what is appropriate, healthful and sane. Such a perspective goes beyond morality, judgement and deep-seated religious concepts of sin and guilt toward a truly human ethic (and even spirituality) of sexual energy.

In most religious or spiritual communities there are specific rules with regard to sexual conduct within committed relationships, or to celibacy, and participation in the community assumes that these agreements have been made. For the secular community, coming to terms with how the individual will deal with sexuality is a different matter since these issues are regarded as highly personal and cannot be legislated by the group. Nonetheless, the secular community can still make certain agreements to support its members and provide sanctuary in relationship. For example, members can agree that sexual abuse, harassment or even casual physical contact without clear verbal agreement between two parties is not acceptable to the ethic of the community at large. An example of this would be to discourage so-called "casual" affection, i.e., "casual" bodily contact and embraces. This does not preclude affection and appreciation between individuals, but it would mean that a woman who does not want to be hugged or touched by a man (or another woman) without her permission, would not be hugged or touched, and

208

vice versa. Every woman I know has at least one story of having been physically approached by a man who assumed that he had access to her affections when his actions were neither appreciated nor condoned by her; this includes being grabbed and hugged when a handshake would have been adequate. My partner and his male friends confirm that this is true for men as well: there are times when a man would prefer not to be hugged or touched by a woman in a situation in which he was left little choice, given basic courtesy, but to yield to someone's advances which were cloaked under the guise of casual friendship.

"Oh, it's so nice to have met you!" Many people in New Age and other sub-cultural networks feel that they have been given *carte blanche* to reach out, grab and hug someone after an afternoon workshop or lecture, without waiting for cues from the other person as to whether or not she or he is willing to physically embrace. Mixed social gatherings are often infected with the unconscious sexuality of individuals who are carrying a kind of vagrant eroticism or voyeurism tangled up with the current ideals of free expression, "sharing," and casual but intrusive affection between comparative strangers. This is one of the biggest social traps in which real intimacy and trust gets co-opted into something that is inauthentic. This kind of inauthentic affection is a cheap substitute for the deeper trust and respect that comes with time and experience together, which gives real meaning and warmth to shared affection. Once we realize that this kind of behavior is often a neurotic use of sexual energy, we naturally begin to want to draw more firm personal boundaries, and to say a simple "No" to sharing our bodies unconsciously, even in a seemingly innocuous hug.

Honoring and respecting Eros in our lives does not mean that we become dry and prudish; on the contrary, we can become juicier and more real. When we decide to make certain distinctions and draw personal boundaries around sexual energy and how we use it, we are freed up to laugh heartily at a bawdy joke.

We are no longer coy about sex; we are clear because we have enquired deeply about sex, and that self-knowledge and self-honesty sets us free in many ways. We stand by what we know to be true for ourselves and we keep healthy, integral personal boundaries as a result of that clarity.

When we start to redefine sex, energy and relationship within community, we find that we are no longer willing to fritter away this creative energy. Rather, we want to contain it so that when it *is* expressed—in our enthusiasm for life, in our art, in the creative pathways of our lives, in friendship and affection, or in sexual union with a partner—it is not watered down, but potentized, made more profound and even wildly exciting. When we begin to change our way of looking at sex and erotic energy, we naturally begin to chose different ways to manage sexual energy within community. If we are not consumed with hidden and covert eroticism, tied up in neurosis and unconscious interactions with others, then a true, natural eroticism is free to shine out—both from us and to us from the natural world. The vegetable garden, the fruit trees in full blossom, a particularly vibrant and textured sunset, a misty day or a thunderstorm, a swiftly flowing river or the ocean at high tide can all be experienced as profoundly erotic. One could spend prolonged ecstatic moments, or hours, just contemplating a tidal pool or the tender inner throat of a fragrant, lush flower. Music, dance, meditation and art all become enlivened and imbued with the power of Eros in a way that is both pure and tremendously pleasurable.

All of this should be very familiar terrain to anyone who has chosen celibacy as a conscious way of life. Celibacy must be based on self-knowledge, honesty and clarity—not on repression, denial, fear, shame or guilt, or any other ambiguous negative feelings about sex in general. Celibacy should be entered into with a sense of purpose and clarity, the details of which is a highly individual matter. I have personally known some celibates who were unconsciously radiating sexual "hooks"—that is, they were flirting and interacting in energetic and subtle ways that indicated they had not done their psychological and spiritual "homework" to make celibacy a conscious, meaningful choice in their lives.

To have a conscious practice of celibacy means, in part, that the sublimation (making sublime) of sexual energy is done in a way that is regenerative. With such a practice, sexual energy is contained within the individual's emotional/nervous system, and actually imbues the individual with a juicy aliveness at the feeling level of the body.

"The fruit of celibacy is hospitality," said a Benedictine nun. Many religious and spiritual communities are celibate, and find that in celibacy, their members are indeed free to develop parts of themselves that would be unavailable otherwise. Kathleen Norris speaks of celibacy in her book, *The Cloister Walk*, in which she questions the cultural prejudice that celibates are perverse or stunted in some way. In her friendships with monks and nuns who practice celibacy in which sexual energy is sublimated toward another purpose than procreation and sexual intercourse, she finds an unusual degree of sanctuary in relationship:

> I've seen . . . many wise old monks and nuns whose lengthy formation in the celibacy practice has allowed them to incarnate hospitality in the deepest sense. In them, the constraints of celibacy have somehow been transformed into an openness that attracts people of all ages, all social classes. They exude a sense of freedom. They also genderbend, at least in my dreams. Sister Jeremy will appear as a warrior on horseback, Father Robert as a wise old woman tending a fire.[4]

Norris goes on to say that her younger celibate friends are "more edgy" and still dealing with their biochemical urges. In addition to that struggle, these younger celibates have to contend

211

with the cultural bias against celibacy, so that their loneliness is exacerbated and they sometimes feel like their work and efforts are meaningless.

Norris argues that celibacy is necessary to the vision of some communities when she writes: "Monastic people are celibate for a very practical reason: the kind of community life to which they aspire can't be sustained if people are pairing off." For freedom-loving Americans of the post-sexual revolution era, this is an idea worth considering deeply, and actually is tied into our previous considerations of creating gender cultures.

I am not advocating celibacy or strictly enforced monogamy —these are very important individual decisions and commitments. Yet, the great majority of us who are sexually active can stand to gain much insight about our own quality of life and the creation of culture from celibate communities. One of the things that interests me the most is the quality of friendship or hospitality that becomes available when sexual energy is managed among celibates. Such relationships are freed of hidden motivations and the desire for personal emotional gain. Norris tells the story of a young woman who after being raped healed her relationship with men by spending time in the company of celibate monks as a guest at their monastery.

All of these principles for management of sexual energy apply within monogamy or marriage as well. One would hope that the discipline, commitment and inspiration of the committed, monogamous relationship would also result in an environment of healing, a greater capacity for friendship, and the cultivation of unmotivated, unselfish attention that actually amounts to true hospitality in human interaction.

In September 1994, my friend Regina and I had the wonderful opportunity to interview Mother Tessa Bielecki—a Carmelite nun who is the co-founder (with Father William McNamara) of the Spiritual Life Institute, and the abbess of several monastic hermitage foundations. As a living representative of the "earthy mysticism" which is so integral to her community's life and practice, Mother Tessa has been a tremendous inspiration to many people in spiritual communities across the U.S. Her depth of perspective, along with a marvelous sense of humor on the subject of celibacy and sublimation of sexual energy, is refreshing and hearty. I quote here from that interview, as it is reported in Regina's book, *The Woman Awake: Feminine Wisdom for Spiritual Life.*[7]

Mother Tessa Speaks About Celibacy

I think celibacy is one of the greatest gifts, one of the greatest joys in life, but it's one of the hardest things initially. When Father William suggested to me that I had a call to celibacy I literally screamed and ran away, I was so horrified. Finally I calmed down and came back and I said: "All right, I'll do it." And in his wisdom, Father William said, "Well, why don't you just make a temporary vow for three months and then you can renew it for another three months, and then renew it for another six months."

I think that celibacy is one of the most marvelous, humanly congenial ways of being that exist—and talk about being underrated! I'd like to talk about the asceticism of celibacy first, because it begins as a type of asceticism and becomes mysticism. It begins as an agony and then becomes a tremendous ecstasy, which I would not trade for the world.

At first, the most obvious sacrifice is the sacrifice of genital activity, which I think is harder for men, initially. I think it's easier for women, or it used to be easier for women before so-called "sexual liberation." Now I think there's a new breed of women who find the genital sacrifice more difficult. But I just turned fifty, and for women of my era, where chastity and purity were more acceptable socially, and politically correct, this was not such a hard sacrifice. The harder sacrifice for women, I think, is the giving up of one special other who was all for you, and you are all for him.

213

Closer to mid-life, this "special other" becomes a harder sacrifice for men. But I don't think they feel that at first . . . and it varies from person to person.

The sacrifice of physical motherhood and fatherhood for me was not a sacrifice. Somehow I never felt strongly called to physical motherhood and was so fulfilled in terms of being a spiritual mother. For the true celibate, there is a fecundity—a great fruitfulness; a tremendous regeneration that comes both personally and then spills over to other people . . . .

I think there needs to be a very radical, graphic preparation for celibacy so that we know exactly what's involved. You need to know what's going to happen psychologically, what's going to happen emotionally.

Whether you're celibate or not you're sexual . . . .

The witness of a person who has done it, who is fulfilled having done it, who has no regrets having done it, who is not cold, not dried up, not bitter, not repressed; that is the strongest statement for the positive value of celibacy.

So you need happy, joyous celibates to serve as guides. And you need a great sense of humor. It needs to be out in the open. We live in a mixed community [both women and men], so if you're not open and light-hearted and honest about this, it could be pretty tricky. We are rather hilarious about our celibacy . . . .

People in our community are trained to see celibacy's connection with prayer and the spousal love of God. You see, traditionally there's been too much emphasis on, the expression is "apostolic efficacy." In other words, the idea that you can serve better as a celibate because you are not distracted by spouse and family. Well, that is true, but it's not going to get you through a bad night when you're all alone and you don't want to be alone . . . . You have to understand celibacy in terms of the mystical graces, the mystical blessings of this, and then you have to pray out of that understanding. . . .

Now also, another thing I love about it is the freedom—that it is absolutely clear who I am and what my lifestyle is . . . for me, friendship can immediately go very deep into the soul things that matter, because all that other stuff [the distraction of promiscuity] is just not part of the picture. When there is that kind of real commitment to chastity and purity, then the "sparks" also are tremendous. It's great fun, because you're very clear about what you do and what you don't do, what you say and what you don't say. There's a lot of energy there that's just great fun. I enjoy it. I enjoy being a highly erotic, passionate woman. The spark is there, but it's all in the context of chastity and purity and celibacy which I think makes life much more interesting, because then you can be much more creative with it . . . I mean celibacy leads to many more interesting ways of expressing love and passion than ending up in bed.

Celibacy, Eros and sex are good topics for open discussion among the members of a bonded community. Taking responsibility for our own sexual energy and how it is expressed must always be guided by the principles, the context and the vision of what our community is about, so that the vast resources of Eros can be harnessed toward our mutual aims and purpose.

CHAPTER NINE

The Continuity of Life

Serving children is a great practice for learning to serve God.

—Lee Lozowick

A true culture is one that embraces, nurtures and sustains all of its constituents—regardless of age, sex, ability, or wealth. Children are a necessary dimension of natural human life, and in tribal cultures children and elders are considered blessings to the spiritual life of the whole group. There might be particular spaces, rituals or tasks that are the domain of adults alone, but this is not a matter of exclusion or rejection of children. Rather, it is a means of designing what best serves and maintains the entire culture. Contemporary communities that do not enjoy or welcome children in their midst as a matter of policy—with the possible exception of some ashrams, monasteries or spiritual retreats—represent digressions from what I envision as a culture of all-embracing wholeness. I see such groups as missing out on a profound opportunity, a responsibility, and a vast field of transformational potential.

A Culture of Orphans

There is a great necessity today for childraising beyond the form of the nuclear family and within the sanctuary of community. In community we have the support to create a loving culture and an environment in which children can grow and flourish in the focused attention and wise guidance of many caring adults. So many single parents today, as well as parents in families where both must work, suffer the heartache and remorse of having to leave their children day after day with relative strangers in an impersonal daycare situation. Robert Bly reports in *The Sibling Society* that the majority of babies born in the U.S. are placed by working parents in full-time day care within a year of birth, commonly within the first two or three months. As they outgrow the need for daycare, many children come home from school to an empty house and the solace of the TV. Only too often their parents return from work frazzled, exhausted, and angry. How can they experience any quality time with their waiting and eager children in this state? Consequently, many children are virtually orphaned in mainstream culture, experiencing profound degrees of emotional abandonment.

Anne told me an incident from her life at four years old. She made a necklace for her mother one afternoon when her mother was at work, carefully stringing together the red and pink four o'clocks she had picked in the yard. All day Anne had been missing her mother, and could hardly wait until she came home. This flower necklace was her childlike way of expressing her love and longing for an absent parent. When her mother finally arrived, Anne excitedly presented her with this labor of love, but her exhausted mother was too tired to pay any attention. She barely said hello to Anne, nodded absent-mindedly at the necklace and didn't even reach out to take it from the child.

In relating this story to me, Anne confided that her disappointment and sense of rejection was overwhelming—probably greater than anything an adult can imagine. After that incident, Anne adapted to her mother's needs by never again making a flower necklace for her mom. Of course if her mother had realized this, she probably would have been grief-stricken. But she never knew how her four-year-old daughter felt, because she was too consumed by the need to survive and provide for her two kids.

When the quality of relationship between parents and children suffers in this way, children are literally cast adrift without real guidance, affection or attention. This creates a vicious cycle—children begin to seek the attention they need and deserve by acting out negative behaviors, to which the adults may respond with more criticism, cold reproach and inappropriate discipline. Our priorities are misplaced when the best of who we are as adults is poured into the devouring, inhuman machine of business or industry. For most, however, this prioritization of energy and time is not a choice—it is a matter of raw survival. Ultimately the price of this lack of vision as a culture will be paid in future generations and in the eroding heart and soul of the world.

Lacking the continuity of life that community can provide, a large percentage of children today are growing up in a state of loss created by the absence of family, and absence of spiritual and cultural meaning and enrichment. This feeling of loss is reflected in the current trend of deep cynicism and nihilism within the youth—the "Generation X" of popular American culture. Young people who are entering early adulthood now are faced with a void. Where there should be excitement and enthusiasm for entering into the stream of a productive and satisfying life, they are often filled with existential angst and despair at the state of the world. What do they have to look forward to as they enter into adulthood? Based on what they see in their parents and in the society at large, they face only deeper alienation and feelings of isolation. In addition, they are burdened with the ecological tragedy that the generations before them have left behind.

A legitimate kind of pessimism about the future is warranted. The natural world is dying, and much of the ecological damage that has been done is now irreversible. Such a terrible legacy is only complicated by the fact that young adults are expected to prove themselves by breaking away from their families into a world that is, for many, hostile and threatening both socially and economically. Such a break-away is the opposite of what tribal and indigenous peoples have been doing for thousands of years. As one anthropologist puts it, "In the West we speak of young people growing up, leaving their parents, and 'starting a family.' To most of the world, including parts of Europe, this notion seems strange. Individuals do not start families, they are born into them and stay in them until death or even beyond. In those societies you cannot leave your family without becoming a social misfit, a person of no account." [1]

In traditional cultures, the young members of the culture are embraced; there is a meaningful place waiting for them when they arrive at adulthood, when they are accepted as valuable members in the continuity of life, a vital link in the living chain from ancestors to progeny.

Transition and Initiation

Youth of today have no way to become initiated into adulthood. As we mentioned in the previous chapter, in traditional tribal societies a child's transition into adulthood would be complete when his or her essential nature, gifts and unique contribution were witnessed by and ritually acknowledged by the group, clan or tribe. Then the emerging young adult would be ready to take his or her place in the fabric of daily life, to unfold his unique potential and contribute to the ongoing well being of all.

As David Maybury-Lewis points out, most of these tribal initiations involve shocking experiences that force the individual to leap to the next phase of maturity; they can be life or death situations, long period of solitude and physical hardship, followed by a celebration of the individual's triumph over these circumstances.

The tribal transition to maturity is made cleanly and is marked with great ceremony. In Western societies families dither over their often resentful young, suggesting that they may be old enough but not mature enough, mature enough but not yet secure enough, equivocating and putting adolescents through an obstacle course that keeps being prolonged . . . . Initiation rituals are intended to provoke anxiety. They act out the death and rebirth of the initiate. His old self dies, and while he is in limbo he learns the mysteries of his society—instruction that is enhanced by fear and deprivation and by the atmosphere of awe that his teachers seek to create. [2]

Sometimes the ceremonies involved with initiation are not centered around pain or terror, but are celebratory acknowledgements of a threshold that has been passed through. For example, the Navajo rite of passage for a young girl who has become a woman—by virtue of the fact that she has started menstruating—is a week-long celebration, including ritual washing and combing of the hair, singing, dancing and feasting. The men of the tribe sing to the young woman of her entry into the stream of the tribe as a bearer of life. This is one of the more gentle forms of initiation rites. Maybury-Lewis states that some initiation rites for girls can be as terrifying and intense as those for boys, which often involve circumcision and other ordeals.

In the Bemba tribe of Zambia, the girls' ritual lasts for a month and transmits certain long-held beliefs and attitudes to its participants—respect for age and elders, for the spiritual bonds between husband and wife, the mystical properties of forces such as fire, sex and blood. The young Bemba female is initiated into the secret names for things that only women—the bearers of sacred knowledge—of the tribe know. Since the Bemba tribe traces descent through the female line, the mothers of daughters who are undergoing initiation must give up their daughters to the community during this time as well.[3] What is built into this and all initiation rites is a sense of individual dignity, strength and

220

self-worth, as well as a more conscious connection with all of life. The individual comes through the initiation process changed, much like the butterfly emerging from the chrysalis.

When we are part of a bonded culture that provides this transformational experience of initiation, we know who we are, we know our place in the great scheme of things, and we have a relationship to right timing, or the unfolding of life in a way that is in perfect harmony with the needs of the moment.

A good example of what happens when traditions are disturbed was relayed by Helena Hodge, a British woman who lived for many years in Ladakh, a tiny country in the Himalayas. Prior to the time when Westernized education came to Ladakh, the children grew up nurtured by the social and spiritual values that were indigenous to their village life, with a great emphasis on ideals like compassion, nonviolence and harmony in relationship with all things. As a result, virtually every adolescent boy and girl knew how to raise food, mend clothes, care for animals, build houses, construct complete irrigation systems, and generally were capable and ready to contribute to both the moral and social fabric of the community.[4]

Since the onslaught of Westernized technology, ideas and "progress" into Ladakh, thousands of children are removed from their villages, crammed into classrooms to memorize facts and recite their times tables. They no longer learn in a natural way from their grandparents, parents, aunts, uncles; they no longer share the responsibility for the well-being of the village in producing food, shelter and child care, even though by Western terms, they now have a more privileged childhood based on educational standards imported from the industrialized world. But, as Ms. Hodge reports, when these children are "educated" and then returned to their villages, they are essentially unable to fit into the scheme of life in a productive way; they are useless to the life of the village, in a typical clash of cultures which has been seen time and time again as the Western world has intruded into

221

Third World cultures. These children are cut off from the treasure of their own culture—the wealth of values, skills and traditions that have made the Ladakhis a happy, productive and peaceful people for hundreds of years. Many of these young adults who are now strung out between two conflicting cultures migrate into large cities in India or Nepal, and there find no other way to support themselves than prostitution or selling and using drugs. At best they may find a place for themselves as laborers, working for a pittance which supports a subsistence lifestyle of unimaginably poor quality.[5] There has been no help in bridging the gap from a rapidly evolving modern culture that can somehow also be founded in the roots of tradition as well. This cycle of despair, hopelessness and meaningless that is perpetuated as their children are then caught in the struggle to survive outside of their ancestral traditions only contributes further to the decay and decline of real human values on the planet as a whole.

It is the natural evolution of a human spirit to seek initiation as it moves through levels of maturity. When initiation is not offered to us through accepted cultural forms, we will unconsciously seek our own process of self-initiation—often the most painful kind, such as addictions, obsessions, psychological dysfunction and other kinds of self-destructive behaviors. The individual is trying to feel, to be pierced or shaken into an awakened relationship to life. Unfortunately, his or her route into the archetypal realm is through the danger and intensity of the addictive process.

On the other hand, addictions also give one either momentary relief from the tremendous inner conflict and tension that results from feeling meaningless and empty, or they give a very short-lived false sense of wholeness and well-being. In this case one finds oneself caught in a vicious circle, never coming to the completion of the initiation process in which he or she can connect with a sense of radically true wholeness, aided by the rewarding experience of deep recognition and honoring by the tribe or community. Without initiation we continue searching for our lost and separated selves; we need to find out who we are, to experience another who truly knows and recognizes that wholeness in us. We are looking for a place to rest, to stop searching; what we are needing is to rest in the hands and heart of community. We are longing for a kind of *relatedness,* a communication or communion with other human beings that witnesses and honors and acknowledges our deepest nature.

Conscious Childraising Within Community

Child raising is one of the most fundamental human experiences that connects us all. It is one of the great equalizers in life, and another area in which we may rediscover and benefit from our interconnectedness. Community can make it possible for children to become an integral part of the life of the adults, rather than a forgotten, lonely by-product by providing childcare options and the warmth and care of extended family. But there is another aspect that community can provide for children and parents alike: the opportunity for conscious childraising. This means allowing our children to receive all the nurturing support we possibly give them; allowing them to grow into their innate potential without being shamed, or forced to accept our own conditioning upon them.

Some communities do not include children, but for those that do, the work of conscious childraising provides an immediate, living feedback mechanism of our ability to manifest our vision. The care and education of children is an area where what we do makes an absolute and immediate difference: for example, our attention and commitment to conscious childraising can be the difference between sustained or shattered innocence in a small child. We must have ruthless self-honesty and a willingness to face the wounds of our own past if we don't want to pass on to our children what has been unconsciously given to us. In the

223

same way, it takes a great deal of conscious awareness, self-observation and desire to change in order to treat our children differently than we were treated as children. Our own cultural and familial assumptions, hidden beliefs, attitudes and expectations—if they continue unobserved—communicate to our children in our glance, in our tone of voice, and in what is *not* said. Children respond to the unspoken as much, and maybe more, than to the spoken. We broadcast our underlying assumptions about life at a subtle but very real level, and children pick up on this. When we have brought clarity to our own destructive, obsolete belief systems, we are no longer unconsciously compelled to pass on the same pain to our children.

In community we have the opportunity to see that we can not give a child all that he or she needs by ourselves, and that we need the help and support of others to fulfill our vision of what it means to be responsible to our children. Many parents are horrified by some of their reactions to children. Small children can be especially challenging, particularly if we are attempting to allow them to freely explore anger, selfishness and the totally natural self-centeredness of their developmental stage. When rage and the impulse to spank our children or otherwise physically (or emotionally) coerce them into compliance and obedience surfaces, many adults are filled with shame and doubt about their ability to parent. It is important at this point to have some compassion for ourselves. These are the same emotional states that we as children absorbed from our own parents who did not stop at *wanting* to spank or shame us, but did so rather routinely as a basic part of the parenting package of the times and culture in which we were raised.

At the time when we have lost patience with a demanding three-year-old, we can call on others in community to bring the kindness and compassion to the situation that we feel we have run out of—both for ourselves and for the child or children involved, as the next story demonstrates.

Elizabeth Reflects on Childraising

When my daughter Amy was little, she had regular, hysterical tantrums up until age five. She would lay on the floor and scream and kick her feet while her whole body writhed with rage. She would pound her fists on the concrete or on the floor, and really attempt to harm herself. It took tremendous discipline not to be authoritarian with her at these times, nor to shame her into quieting down. She would scream for me, and go rigid in my arms, and I was the only person who could manage her and keep her from hurting herself. It had become a kind of convoluted "prison" for us both.

For years I dealt with her tantrums by appeasing her, holding her and trying to reason with her, but I had reached a point of frustration and anger that was making it hellish for me. None of the things I had tried over the years were working, and the situation was getting worse.

Then I moved into a community and the situation was taken out of our insular nuclear family when some wise-elder mothers suggested that this was a manipulative dynamic between mother and daughter that had to be broken for both of our sakes, but especially for Amy's. We were far too hooked into each other in unhealthy ways for me to be able to guide Amy out of this self-destructive dynamic. They recommended that whenever Amy had a tantrum I should leave her in the capable, loving hands of other women in the community, who would then hold, nurture and speak softly with Amy until she was able to relax out of the tantrum. Amy was able to hear these women when they explained to her that this was not the most effective or healthy way for her to get her needs met.

The first time I had to walk away from the scene when Amy was having a tantrum I felt as if I would die. I felt that I was abandoning my daughter. It was tremendously difficult! But the women took over and really made a difference in Amy's life. I could have never have broken my side of this negative pattern with my child without the tremendous trust, support, love, and sacrifice, of the women in my community. Amy grew out of that behavior, and I have moved on to many years of a wonderful, nurturing relationship with my daughter.

Since I work with community children as a schoolteacher, I too appreciate the help I've gotten from my friends that has allowed me to drop my stubborn stance with a child. In this way community members offer each other a mirror to more conscious self-reflection. In the company of others we are more attentive to our mechanical behavior, and the ways in which we may unconsciously be passing on unnecessary or painful dynamics to the children we love.

In its immature stages, this element of mirroring and self-reflection that community adults do for one another can sometimes amount to "policing" each other, an activity that brings no strength to community or conscious childraising. If, on the other hand, we remember to bring compassion and vulnerability to another's need, help can be offered and received in a mood of mutual acknowledgement, rather than with criticism and defense. We can stand together in the awareness of our shortcomings and of our need of one another, instead of hiding behind the mask of isolated self-reliance.

It is truly a gift to be living with other parents (and if we are really lucky, supportive and wise grandparents) who can help us to realize and understand the phases that children and parents go through. After you have seen several two years olds go through the natural developmental stage of asserting their independence and discovering the word "NO!" you don't take it as personally anymore when a child does that with you. When our older children need to express their anger or tell us what they don't like, or if they are just having a hard day, in community we can get a "reality check" from other adults. This helps parents from getting emotionally burned out from taking it all so seriously and too personally when our kids just need to rebel at authority.

This kind of help makes a greater impact than reading a book on childraising. It reconnects us to the natural patterns of life, the continuity of tribe and clan, where a child may be nurtured by and learn from many different people. This wider circle of connections and intimacy gives a child a place to go if mother or father is having a bad day, or a friend to turn to when mom and dad just can't quite understand. It also gives a child many resources and avenues for being mentored and guided. Children model after adults, and having a wide range of adult behavior to witness and connect with gives a child a much broader range of options.

Another pitfall of the isolated nuclear family is that when we have nowhere to turn for nurturing and support as adults we may be inclined to turn to our children to get our emotional needs met. To draw on our children to meet our emotional needs forces them to "take care" of us in a way that is not the responsibility of a child. This kind of emotional dependency between adult and child is sometimes called creating a "surrogate spouse." The child is emotionally forced to take on an adult role in relationship to his or her primary caregiver, a psychological entanglement that does profound harm to the growing child. Adapting to meet the adult's emotional needs becomes a matter of survival for the child who has received the subtle message from his or her parent, "If you aren't good for me (or make good grades or play the right sports or listen to my problems or pay attention to my needs or do the chores the right way or act sweet and compliant so I don't get more stressed out than I already am), then I will not be there for you." Thus the parent effectively "goes away"—disappears behind a cold, angry mask; becomes rejecting and critical, or raging and physically abusive. This is manipulation and coercion at its worst.

Many adults fall into variations of this psychological drama with their children only because they have no support to live differently. They may not be aware of or educated as to alternatives and healthier ways to parent, or they may be so caught up in survival in the rat race that they feel they have no other options.

Community can give struggling parents emotional support, encouragement and education when and as it is needed. I cannot overemphasize the value and importance of community in this role to parents who wish for and hope to provide a healthier, more humane and creative environment for their children than they themselves were given. Full participation in community may effect a healing process, but where our parenting skills are concerned it takes an immense commitment and a great deal of vision and courage to stay in the fire that such healing generates.

If we live in an environment from which we can seek our nurturing and support from other adults (including but not limited to our partners), then we have the opportunity to relate with our children from the wholeness of our lives. Rather than seeking or needing anything from them, we relate to them from a position of abundance and plenitude.

Community children have access to a wide range of individuals who can serve as enlightened witnesses of their process of growth and development. "Enlightened witness" is a term coined by psychotherapist and author Alice Miller. It refers to that person in a child's life who affirms the child's basic selfhood and therefore protects the child's innocence and wholeness when many forces are at play to fragment or deny that innate wholeness. These enlightened witnesses can acknowledge what a child may be going through that a parent may miss simply because he or she can't see the forest for the trees. I have found that, within community where children are an integral part of daily life, the kids know who to go to for more rough and tumble play, who they like to snuggle with and who will read with them when Mom is out of time or patience. It can be a happy and playful flow for children to go from one adult to another when they don't have to rely solely on their parents for all of their needs for attention, and it can be a gift for other adults to reach out and serve them in this way. And as all parents know, children need—and rightfully so— a lot of quality attention. Malidoma Somé speaks about the love and attention his people give to children within tribal culture:

> Grandfather's respect and love for children was universal in the tribe. To the Dagara, children are the most impor- tant members of the society, the community's most pre- cious treasures. We have a saying that it takes the whole tribe to raise a child. Homes have doorless entrances to allow children to go in and out wherever they want, and it is common for a mother to not see her child for days and nights because he or she is enjoying the care and love of other people. When the mother really needs to be with her child, she will go from home to home searching for it. [6]

It is a great gift for children to have many different role models so that they are exposed to a richness of people, manifes- tations and shortcomings—a healthy spectrum of human life! When we have a particular area of personal weakness we can offer our children the model of someone else who has strength in the same area. I am deeply grateful when I can honestly tell the children in my life that I don't know the answer to their question, but can direct them to someone who is able to provide it. It is also very heartening to have a teenager's trust and confidence when he or she is needing to break away from parental authority, but still needs adult guidance.

Writing about the Makom kibbutz in the wonderful book about community, *In the Company of Others,* communal cost accountant Amia Lieblich talks about the economic life and extraordinary stability and success of the kibbutz, and finally says,

> I don't think that our economic intuition is our secret charm; it's our social spirit which preserved us. I believe our most profitable undertaking is rearing children. The core of people who first settled this location were an outstanding intellectual elite . . . . Every single one of them could easily have become an administrator or a branch coordinator, yet this kibbutz decided to allocate its best people to education and child care.[7]

He goes on to say that their childbirth rate went from .80 per member to 1.25 children per member. This meant that a lot of adults had to work in childcare. "We suffered a lot," Amia went on. "We ate only half a egg, but we raised a lot of good children and provided them with the best possible education. This is our kibbutz talisman, our secret." [8] As a result, he says, sixty to seventy percent of the adult members of the Makom kibbutz today are the sons and daughters who were born or educated there, and their "imported" spouses. The fact that these children chose as adults to continue living in the community is an amazing testimony to the quality of life, attention and care which these children experienced growing up on the kibbutz.

Children who are raised by conscious adults adopt a very different view of the world at an early age. A child learns to walk by watching and imitating others; a child learns to talk by imitating those who are talking; in community a child learns compassion for others, enthusiasm for life, cooperation and service by watching the adults in his or her environment live and interact with others. In the process of living with other children they learn many skills of relationship and interaction, including compassion, cooperation and nurturing. In a community that has a highly developed culture, children get to be part of that culture from infancy; they may get to experience an active men's and women's culture, to see children being born, to see adults supporting each other, the cultivation of food that is eaten, perhaps people dying and buried, to experience that the adult world may go through breakdown, but also breakthrough as natural cycles in life—all these elements of life that they might not have the chance to experience without community.

Children's Culture and Education

Part of this continuum and people-oriented environment can include an active children's culture. When raised in community together, modern children naturally develop a children's culture, a place for them to grow and develop with each other's help, so that children are interacting, playing and learning with other children of all ages. The older kids help and guide the younger kids, which provides value for both ages.

In one community I know, the children are schooled "at home"—in a formal program run by community members which also meets state educational standards. The children range in age from three to thirteen, at which time they often opt to enter into public school to engage more social opportunities. In home schooling, besides being exposed to traditional curriculum, children participate and interact with adult activities within community in a way that is highly educational, so that learning is a very experiential process. Individual adults can serve in mentorship programs, giving the children hands-on, one-on-one guidance in a vast range of academic subjects as well as occupational skills.

Communities that are self-supporting through cottage industries or small businesses also give the option of incorporating children into the daily life and work of community so that the family is not fragmented in day care or childcare situations. Children learn immensely from this kind of contact with and observation of the adult work world, and many values are instilled through this process as well.

I know a five-year-old who has been going through a phase of wanting to take things apart and see how they work. This means he loves what others would consider junk and has piles of old machines, spare parts and odds and ends from the woodworking shop in his room. The other day he discovered a doorknob he wanted to take apart. None of us, including his father and the resident handyman, could figure out how this particular doorknob came apart, but we have a man in our community who was a master woodworker and used to make custom doors in a former woodcrafting business. He had the tools and the knowledge to help take the doorknob apart. Similarly, it is very gratifying to see the children cook with a woman who used to manage a restaurant, or weave with the resident weaver, or participate in similar opportunities in which they can learn things by doing them in a context that is applicable to life.

As author and child-advocate Jean Liedloff writes,

> Children ought to be able to accompany adults wherever they go. In cultures like ours, where this is largely impossible, schools and teachers might learn to take fuller advantage of the tendencies of children to imitate and practice skills on their own initiative rather than have them "taught." [9]

She calls the kind of culture that incorporates children completely in daily life a "continuum society" in which generations live under the same roof to take advantage of and incorporate into the culture the special gifts offered by all ages and stages of life.

> Grandparents would help as much as they could and people at the height of their working powers would not

begrudge support to their elders any more than to their children. But again, the truly enriching cohabitation of the generations depends upon their having fulfilled personalities and not pulling, as most of us would, at one another's emotions to satisfy leftover infantile needs for attention and care.[10]

This kind of integration between the generations requires a maturity of both individual and tribal or community context that is rare in the Western world today.

Boundaries and Choices

Throughout their development, children need positive education and role modeling about why the adults in their lives are making the choices they make. As adults, we have to provide guidance to young children who are not in a position to discriminate for themselves, but our decisions should be backed up with information rather than authoritatively justified with the arbitrary but familiar, "Because I say so." For example, when it comes to playing with toy guns (or a BB gun) or with Barbie dolls, I know many parents who have had to explain time and again the reasons they have chosen to limit or omit those activities that simulate violence or that foster an unrealistic and unhealthy body image. In my community we replace television by focusing on relationship with our children are playing games, talking, hiking, learning crafts together. Despite their earlier dissatisfaction with this and other elements of our lifestyle, some of the college-age teenagers and young adults who grew up in my community have candidly reported that they are now glad that their parents stood firm in these principles during their formative years. It is helpful to know that this can be the case if your ten-year-old is complaining about not getting to watch MTV every afternoon after school.

As children grow older they sometimes want to make lifestyles choices that are different from those of their parents. Some examples might be: wanting to eat different food than the community serves; wanting to watch television if the community doesn't have or support television; preferring to interact with outside friends in a non-communal environment. When their objections are raised, parents or other primary caregivers need to listen, both with a willingness to exercise flexibility and with clarity about their own commitment. I have found that it is necessary and wise to allow young people more leeway to make these decisions for themselves. For example, we may give them the option at a certain age to decide whether they would like to continue in the community school or enroll in public school.

I know parents who made the difficult choice to leave the residence of the intentional community because their children wanted to live a more conventional lifestyle during their high-school years. After that, the parents moved back into the community residence. This was a tough decision for these adults to make, but they deemed it the best decision for the children. Their three children are now well-adjusted, loving and sensitive young adults who have a great deal of respect and admiration for their parents and for the community in which their parents live. Sometimes community is not the best place for children during certain years of development. This can be true if the community only has one or two children and is in a rural setting, in which case the child may need more social input and experience in order to grow and develop. Arrangements may need to be made to make sure the children get their needs met in the greater community of the world-at-large.

As our children grow, parents and extended family caregivers must be willing to let go and to trust the ethical and moral foundation that has been provided for the child in the early years of his or her development. If children have a healthy, secure, loving relationship of mutual respect with their parents, then most

234

children will make healthy, appropriate decisions as they grow and experiment. A secure foundation of love and respect creates a similar inner culture within the child, from which they may grow into self-respecting, wise and happy adults.

In return for the commitment and energy we put into making sure that our children in community get their needs fully met—even when it involves significant sacrifice on the part of adults—we receive a tremendous amount back. Children can be our best teachers in many instances. Children are endless sources of enthusiasm and creativity; they teach us to be more resourceful and spontaneous, and they call us back to a state of innocence. They are the constant mirror of our humanity, where we have been and where we are going, and they are one of the surest barometers of where we are now.

The Wisdom of Elders

In the way that children can teach us through their innocence and spontaneity, elders have much to teach us from the wisdom of their experience and a kind of innocence regained. A person who has lived through many years and passed through many trials, learnings and initiations is like a living artifact, and in many cultures is treated as such, with great veneration as the source of wisdom and the living link to the ancestral line. This has not been the case in Western culture, where elders have been hidden away in old age homes because they are too much of a blatant reminder of our own mortality, the cycles of birth, renewal, death and decay in a strangely youth-oriented culture. Elders have lived long enough to have a perspective which we, who are in earlier stages of life, do not have. Elders are on the other side of striving, seeking and attaining; they have seen many things come and go, and have learned a lot about change, the transient nature of life, and simple acceptance. Many elders in their wisdom—and through trial and error—have learned to

235

understand and listen to their instincts, or that "still, small voice within."

In making a place for elders we bring balance to community. Malidoma Somé in his audio tape entitled, "Habits of the Heart—Building Tribal Community," talks about how youth represent fire and elders represent water. According to his perspective, if community is made up of only youth, and there is not an honoring of elders (as in our modern society today), then we have a community whose nature is exclusively fiery, and will burn itself up. He sites our present nuclear stockpiles as an example of this fiery nature over-running all common sense, sensitivity or wisdom.

There is a Polynesian myth that says the tribe or community is like a dragon. The youth—adolescents and young adults—represent the head and nose of the dragon, always sniffing out new possibilities. The legs and body, with their strength and momentum, represent the adults and prime of life power of the tribe. The tail, which guides the direction of the dragon, represents the wisdom and vision of the elders of the tribe. This completes the dragon, keeps it moving on a steady course that is at the same time always open to new potentials. This is the most wonderful metaphor I have encountered for understanding the necessary place of the wise elder within the matrix of community.

So many of our elders have lived conventional lives and now find themselves at the effect of mainstream attitudes in such a way that prohibits or limits their availability to community and alternative living. Because of this, many of us working and/or living in community feel the loss of having wise elders within our communities, many of which are made up of people whose ages span from young adulthood, the early twenties, to middle age or the fifties at most. My friend Mary has on many occasions commented to friends in her community, where the oldest residential member is fifty-five years old and the median age is about thirty-five, "I often feel the loss of having elders in the community, and then I also realize that we will not have elders until we become the elders of our community in the next twenty years!" In this way many who have been involved in the resurgence in community since the late sixties once again find themselves pioneering a new path in community life, as we re-establish a conscious relationship to old age through the growing body of elders who will evolve out of the baby-boom generation during the next few decades.

The wisdom of the initiated lies not in telling us how to complete the path. They can't tell us how to walk our path, but they can teach us how to listen and respond to the universe, how to relate with the world in a way that brings clarity and heartful understanding. Elders cannot keep us from making our own mistakes, but they can help guide us through difficult and obscure pathways of life by sharing their experiences. There are no tricks, there is no skipping of the process of maturation, but we can listen to what is offered by those who have already walked the path that we are presently on. This is one way we are served by the presence of elders in community.

The following story was taken in an interview with Leah, who at age thirty-five began working and traveling with elders. This turned out to be a remarkably enriching experience for her, and one that I immensely enjoyed hearing about.

Leah Speaks About Learning from Elders

When I first met Amos he was eighty-seven, a visiting trustee at the university law school where I was working. My boss assigned me to be Amos's secretary while he was teaching for two months. Before I met him they said, "We've heard that he is one of the worst people in the world to work for—he's really hard on secretaries."

"Oh great," I said, "I can't wait!" But I soon found out the reason why he had such a reputation: no one had been able or willing to really communicate with him. No one was really relating with him, or responsive enough to know him. He had been treated

237

like a god for many years because of who he was in his field—a renowned scholar and an incredibly successful lawyer. He was like a worldly genius in a way, and on top of that, he was an elderly man who appeared to be senile or irrational and who was certainly very demanding.

Somehow I just clicked with him. I had a natural affinity for and a native understanding of him. I was willing to surrender to his demands in a way because I could see that I had a lot to learn from this extraordinary person. I appreciated the depth and variety and opportunity of his sophisticated but old-fashioned lifestyle. In spite of his tremendous wealth and power, he lived in a way that was balanced and moderate, never excessive—and he was elegant. Amos had used his mind to study how life is around the world and how things are set up in various cultures. He had traveled all over and had a vast knowledge of how governments are run, as well as about different cultures and their laws. He was like a walking encyclopedia. While other people may have more of a "folk mind" about what's happened around them, Amos thought very big—about whole systems, rather than just about pieces—and I was deeply interested in "sitting at the feet" of this elder. That was where I put myself.

I learned how to interact with him on an equal footing, as a person, and because of the efforts that I made to understand him and to move based on his rhythms and needs, he was not senile or irrational. He was able to be different. When you take care of old people you are paid to slow down; you have to have the patience to go as slowly as they are. You have to be able to be with yourself while they are doing their thing; it takes them a long time to get things done that you can do in one second. It's such a creative and beautiful thing—it stops time when you can really be with an old person.

Amos was incapacitated by the brittleness of his bones. He couldn't lift himself up out of his chair, and he had to have a cane with him all the time. His whole orientation was toward his cane

238

because it was a necessary appendage for walking, so the cane took on tremendous importance as a symbol of what little independence he could still have. A lot of his irascibility, I came to understand, was because he had already lost so much control of his own life, and was facing nothing but the prospect of losing more as death stalked him on a daily basis.

After working for him for two years I accompanied him (by then eighty-nine years old) and his eighty-six-year-old wife Mary Helen on a three week trip to Turkey, which included a cruise in the Mediterranean. I was their traveling companion and helper. While we were there in Turkey, people reacted to us in a very interesting way. In the most conservative city of Konya—which is where the Sufi saint Jalalludin Rumi is buried and where devout religiosity is practiced almost fanatically, so much so that tourism is discouraged in this city in spite of economic need—people frequently stopped to help me with Mary Helen and Amos. They helped us in and out of the car . . . into the restaurants . . . . At one point, as we were getting out of an elevator, I noticed a man watching me very closely. "Allah is smiling on you," he said, "because you are taking care of her. She's an angel," he said, looking at Mary Helen. And at Rumi's tomb, three peasant women who were praying there came over to Mary Helen, stroked her and touched her head tenderly. They obviously honored her old and crippled state to a great degree. "Allah is happy for you, Allah is pleased with you," they said to me, clearly because I was taking care of this old one. Their veneration was deeply moving, and I was so grateful to be with them.

Amos lost his balance and fell at the Hagia Sophia—one of the seven ancient wonders of the world. We immediately went back to the hotel. This was the one time I lost patience and resented him. I wanted to get to see the Hagia Sophia, of course, and he had disrupted my trip! At the hotel I had some difficulty in helping him into his chair, so I handled him somewhat brusquely, sort of pushing a little on him to get him into the position he needed to be in to sit down and back. I was instantly shocked into realizing how easily one could lose control and lose the context of service to someone who was very vulnerable. "You don't have to be so rough," Amos said, and I was immediately overcome with my own shame and sorrow at having let my intention to be nothing but kind and understanding slip through my fingers for a moment. It was the only time something like that happened.

Every morning I was their human alarm clock. One morning Amos was sleeping so soundly that I got Mary Helen up and did her bathroom rituals while he slept. When she was ready for the day, she said, "I want to go wake up my husband." She couldn't do it by herself, but I was there to assist. I helped her walk over to the bed and stand over him as he slept. She leaned over him, shook him gently and spoke an endearment in German to wake him; he opened his eyes and saw her there. What an amazing moment between two people who had been together for sixty-six years! For that instant there was real happiness between them, and I was grateful to be there to witness it.

Amos and Mary Helen had such tremendous dignity; it was almost like people who passed by them were receiving their blessings. Perhaps once you get old all you have to offer to others is your ability to bless and witness. It's like the elixir of all the years inside your being distills itself into a quality of presence, a blessing force. I've come to understand more through Amos and Mary Helen that there is a transcendent power that exists in spite of any hard edges—like Amos's tyranny and impatience and his demanding, irrational behaviors.

It seems like we don't allow ourselves to receive this blessing force from elders because we are afraid. Elders can be very confronting to our fear about survival, because they don't care about conventional forms anymore. As a much younger person, the people I typically want to be in contact with are the people whose reflection I want to be, and who represent the things I want to see in myself. I want to be with the beautiful people, those who have fun, those who are exciting, dynamic; I don't want to be faced with my greatest fears of disintegration and death when I am talking to someone. With very elderly people you have to face yourself in a way because they are not surviving—they are obviously on the way out, and into decay and decline. If they aren't surviving, then you have to be the one who offers them life, even though your own disintegration and future decay is right there in your face, and that is a big demand and emotional responsibility.

Throughout our trip together, even when I had opportunities to do other things, or eat dinner with other people, I just wanted to stay with Amos and Mary Helen. I realized that they had quickly become family to me; they fulfilled my need for community too. I felt safe and deeply bonded with them, based on a relationship of trust I had developed with Amos over time, and developed later with Mary Helen because she was so kind to me, and because she was helpless and dependent on me. Amos and Mary Helen were old and in need, but they were providing something precious and invaluable for me; an education in the classics of life. But for me the real reward for making this kind of commitment to serving two elders came in this discovery: once you have served in that human capacity with someone, it starts to spread out in your behavior toward everyone else. And even greater is the satisfaction of seeing that other people are affected by the generosity you show in service toward these old people. Seeing you, they want to do the same.

Up until the later half of the twentieth century, the continuity between younger generations and elders was still intact, even in the highly-industrialized and socially-fragmented U.S. Unlike many of us, my friend Mary grew up in the 1950s in close relationship with the elders of her family. In the interview that follows she shares a part of her heritage that we would all do well to honor and acknowledge.

Mary Speaks About Continuity With Elders

As a child growing up in the fifties in a Southern town of about 30,000, I lived in the warm, exciting, sometimes loud and strident but always affectionate atmosphere of an old-fashioned extended family. My mother, sister and I lived in the same house with my grandmother and grandfather—the very same house where my mother, her sisters and her brother were born and grew up. My grandparents' grown children—my mother's three siblings—also lived in the same town with their husbands or wives and kids.

My parents were divorced when I was three and my sister ten; so I was extremely lucky to have the unconditional love and support of my grandparents and extended family to help us through our growing up years. I know that my extended family situation was rare, but even more rare was the chance to have had elders as a strong physical and spiritual presence and foundation throughout my childhood. My mother had to work full-time to support us, and so she was gone a lot; consequently, it was my grandmother who was there for me during the days. She made my breakfast and braided my hair in the morning and dressed me up in layers of warm clothes for school. She was there after school as well, and when I had scarlet fever or flu or got my tonsils removed. It was my grandmother who cooked all of our delicious family meals day after day, sometimes with my mother's help, and it was my grandmother who provided the ample spiritual foundation that would serve me throughout my own search in later years.

My grandmother was the Irish matriarch of our family. People acknowledged my grandmother as a wise woman; she had already birthed and raised four children, and had weathered many storms in her own life, living through two World Wars, the great depression, the murder of her beloved younger sister at age twenty-five, the deaths of her parents and many others. Her loving arms were always available, and most every night she rocked me to sleep in a rocking chair until I was a very big girl, to the consternation of my

242

cousins! She was the magnetic center of our household, and of the extended family. Everyone basked in her presence and wanted her attention, but she was no sentimental or gushing granny-type; she could be tough whenever she chose to be, and had no problem with discipline or drawing boundaries for us kids. She demanded a fierce honesty from us all, and was perfectly able to recount our faults as well as our virtues. There was nothing mawkish or maudlin about her love for us; it was always well tempered with a profound, earthy sanity and common sense, and it was this combination of unconditional love and impeccable toughness that earned our undying loyalty.

My grandfather was half-French, half-German, and had been born in New York City only hours after his parents arrived by ship as immigrants from Europe late in the nineteenth century. Sixty years later, his grandchildren gave him the name "Big Daddy." His parents were professional classical musicians, and so he had grown up traveling around the South, mostly New Orleans and Mobile, Alabama, hopping from theatre to theatre where they performed in vaudeville acts. He had performed "Madame Butterfly" and other operas as a young man growing up, and loved music of all kinds. Because he had such an unusual and unsettled childhood, he was fiercely protective of his own children and home, and wanted nothing more than to settle down and provide a solid foundation for his kids. This he did, both in his own philosophy of life and in practical ways. I can remember Big Daddy saying to me— the fatherless granddaughter—on very specific occasions, "You always have a home here with your grandmother and me, as long as I'm alive."

Our neighborhood had once been my grandmother's parent's farm. They were Irish immigrants who traveled across the South in a covered wagon with their five kids in tow. These were memories I loved to hear my grandmother recount: how they'd traveled through Tennessee and almost settled there, but then went on through Texas to circle around and head back to the old South again. Later, after the First World War, the farm had been sold to various second and third cousins and a few newcomers to town over the years. When my grandmother talked about "a house down the street on the corner," that house was lived in by either one of our relatives—like my grandmother's brother and his wife, or their grown children and their families—or someone she had known for fifty years. My great uncle had a small corner grocery market just around the block, one of the last of its kind in a growing urban environment. These great aunts and uncles and second and third cousins made for an even larger circle of family within the close-knit immediate family that centered around my grandparents.

My grandparents were deeply rooted in the earthy values of their generation and the generations that came before them: hard work, responsibility, fidelity, church, family ties and service to the greater community. Together they had each known a great deal of happiness, but also sorrow and hard times, and all of this had forged their characters and deepened their spiritual lives over the decades. Both of my grandparents put in many hours of service within their community, particularly at church. Until her death eighty-three, my grandmother was revered within the church as an old-time member of the community and as a valued elder. When she died, the whole community came out to honor the passing of this woman who had given so freely to them. At her funeral, the large church sanctuary—full of lilies, roses and gladiolus—was crowded with people who had come to pay their respects. Back at her oldest daughter's home, the food was abundant, and people laughed and cried together, remembering her. I was twenty-three at the time and my son was only two. I was so grateful that he had the opportunity to meet her and be rocked in her arms during those two years before she died, even though he probably wouldn't remember it as an adult. Held in the arms of his great-grandmother, his young life was blessed by the continuity of his living ancestors.

Six months after she died my son and I moved to my first residential intentional community—a communal farm in the deep woods where about twenty-five people lived. It was 1973, and indeed the times had changed. My grandmother's house on First Street was sold, and all of the second or third cousins had moved away. My mother had remarried years before, and now lived in Texas with her husband. The older first cousins were all out of college and pursuing their careers and raising children; none of them lived in our hometown or even in the state. Big Daddy had died in 1966, and now with the death of my grandmother, the family was scattered to the wind. It was as if she held the last key to an older, infinitely more communal and earthy life, rooted in family, community and clan.

My mother used to say that my grandmother was much more lenient, understanding and flexible with her grandchildren than she was with her own children. This flexibility and unconditional acceptance was always apparent in my grandmother's relationship with me, and consistently so. When I was eighteen my allegiance to my family and its traditions was deeply shaken as I became radicalized by the Vietnam War and current events like Kent State. As a whole, my family couldn't or wouldn't understand the changes I was going through or that my generation was going through. I became deeply alienated from them at age twenty, as my changing spiritual and political beliefs and my radical lifestyle became more pronounced. My grandmother was the only member of my family who didn't chastise or reject me in any way for my different beliefs or for my tearing away from the family tradition. She was never threatened by my changes, but continued to be the nurturing, accepting and unconditionally-loving person I had always known her to be, even when she knew I was experimenting with psychedelic drugs. I was never alienated from her at any time, even though I went through years of serious alienation from the rest of my family, until I grew older, more compassionate and more accepting of the differences between people.

245

An intimate friend who knows me very well said to me some years ago, "Your grandmother was your 'enlightened witness' as a child." He was using the term coined by Alice Miller that refers to that person in a child's life who can see and acknowledge and affirm the essence of the child, and because of this witnessing of the real being, helps to preserve the child's essential nature and innocence in the face of familial or societal repression. To me, this is part of the wisdom and blessings that elders bestow upon us all; life has tempered and softened the hard ore of their personalities so that the gold can shine through. Because they have stormed and rejoiced through triumph and disaster, they have a perspective— born out of raw experience—which is unique to old age.

We could say that growing old is a spiritual path in and of itself. If one lives with honesty, heartfulness and some degree of concern for others, then insight and wisdom is bound to dawn upon us simply because life itself is a great spiritual teacher. But certainly I felt a strong connection with my grandmother because of her state of consciousness as an elder, which in some ways was not dissimilar to my state as a child. She had a receptivity and softness, combined with a stability and soulful substance born of time that made me feel safe.

The year before my grandmother died, she was full of peace and even ecstasy at times. A light seemed to shine out from her; this radiance is a kind of inner beauty that one sees in elders who have lived fully and are ready to embark on their next great adventure. About a year before she died, I asked her if she felt ready for death, or if she was afraid. She was eighty-two at the time, with pure white hair and shining, very bright blue eyes still sharp and steady. "Why yes, I'm ready," she'd say. "What do I have to be afraid of? I'm ready to go whenever the Lord calls me. I'm just here now because He hasn't called me yet!" These words were spoken with the simple, direct truth that was the foundation of her life. Her faith and constancy was a palpable presence around her. Holding her incredibly thin hands, both soft and bony, like ivory but veined and spotted with age, I said plaintively—at age twenty-two, still not wanting to grow up yet and in defiance of the inevitable, "Mama, I don't want you to die!" She'd laughed. "Everybody's got to die! I've lived a long, wonderful life, and you shouldn't be sad when I die, you should be happy! You should know that I'm at peace."

Sitting at her feet as I had many times over the years, I asked her one of the last questions I would ever have the opportunity to ask—"How is it that you are so peaceful and serene?" She replied, "Because I have accepted everything. The only way you can have peace in your life is through acceptance." I've never forgotten that piece of wisdom, and as I grow into my own middle years, the memory of her wisdom gleams like a jewel in the landscape of my life experience. I count myself among the very fortunate to have had the influence of my grandmother and grandfather and extended family in my life, to have had the opportunity to know what it is like to grow up in the company of wise elders.

Elders and Children Together

There is much to learn from tribal peoples about the necessary wisdom and place of elders and a wide circle of extended family within human culture and community. The subject of the important place that elders occupy in the web of life is inexhaustible. One thing we modern Westerners so pervasively fail to see is the natural connection between children and elders. There is something a child can receive from an elder than he or she cannot get from any person in another stage of life. Malidoma Somé speaks about elders, and about the connection between elders and children in his book, *Of Water and the Spirit: Ritual, Magic, and Initiation into the Life of an African Shaman,* with the authority of authentic knowledge, the kind that one earns through life experience:

247

When I was twenty-two, my elders came to me and asked me to return to the white man's world, to share with him what I had learned about my own spiritual tradition through my initiation. For me, initiation had eliminated my confusion, helplessness, and pain and opened the door to a powerful understanding of the link between my own life purpose and the will of my ancestors. I had come to understand the sacred relationship between children and old people, between fathers and their adolescent sons, between mothers and daughters. I knew especially why my people have such a deep respect for old age, and why a strong, functioning community is essential for the maintenance of an individual's sense of identity, meaning and purpose.

Wealth among the Dagara is determined not by how many things you have, but by how many people you have around you. A person's happiness is directly linked to the amount of attention and love coming to him or her from other people. In this, the elder is the most blessed because he is in the most visible position to receive a lot of attention. The child is too, because it "belongs" to the whole community. [12]

In most intentional communities today this continuity between the extended blood family and community is greatly fragmented by philosophical, political and spiritual differences between generations of the family of origin. The Sunrise Community in Colorado has over one hundred members, of which approximately twenty-five are elders, some in their seventies and eighties. This is much closer to the natural stream of life as it has been in the world for generations upon generations going back in time. Many other communities are only just now coming into a substantial population of elders, as communitarians age within their chosen life situation in community. Even in Native

248

American communities, where the span of ages has been kept intact in the tribal way of life, this continuity of life is threatened as the last stronghold in the Western world of a truly organic culture of many generations living in harmony, cooperation and respect. When Joanne visited a reservation in Arizona, she came back with many impressions about continuity.

Joanne Speaks About Continuity Among the Hopis

Walking into the Hopi village was like walking back in time. As we walked along the dirt road, the structures were progressively older and as we neared the plaza we found ourselves speaking softly and trying to be as invisible as possible. The dances were already underway in the central plaza that was formed by a rectangle of row houses with a small opening at the narrow end. The plaza was lined with rows of chairs, benches, and milk crates surrounding the central area where the dances were taking place. The spectators ranged in age from newborn infants to elderly Hopi men and women, whose faces bore the lines of their years in the Arizona sun. The flat roofs were covered with more families watching the dancers and sharing food and conversation. Children of all ages ran around, and it was clear that any adult in the community was available to soothe a hurt or provide some discipline if necessary. Everyone knew everyone. It felt like one big extended family, and in many ways that is probably true. The homes have been lived in by generation after generation of the same family, and the neighbors are also generation after generation of the same families. Quarrels may erupt, but there is no way to avoid each other.

The dances themselves were a living demonstration of the meaning of community. There were dances done by small children, in which the elders played drums and chanted as the children performed the movements with quiet pride and dignity. In the middle of a dance done by a group of teenagers, several elderly women got up and joined the dancers. Rather than creating a disturbance or

249

annoyance, the teenagers simply made room for the elders and continued to perform the movements of their dance as the old women shuffled along next to them. As the teenagers exited the plaza an old man pressed something into the leader's palm and blessed him. It was clear that the youth was both honored and moved to receive his blessing.

The overall feeling was of a community of people who had lived and worked and suffered and celebrated together for generation after generation. They have lived so closely together that they know each other's virtues and their faults as well, and have transcended both in their relationships with one another. It was a rich food being provided to the children of the community, but at the same time, one diluted by exposure to the temptations of the outside world. Many of the oldest adobe homes sprouted TV antennas and one had a satellite dish. On many reservations, income from gambling and sale of natural resources is resulting in huge amounts of income for the native peoples. I am glad to see these people who were taken from their traditional homelands and placed in some of the most barren and infertile land, have the last laugh. But I am saddened at the thought of how that money may erode the very values and qualities that have created such rich and vibrant communities. The Hopis and their ancestors have lived there for thousands of years, and many of the buildings on the tops of the mesas are hundreds of years old. Knowing how their lives and their lands have been contaminated by extensive exposure to the fragmentation of dominant white culture, I wondered how long this example of tribal community would continue to live in the world.

Conclusion

Elders have something to teach us—that we do not know now—about the transformation and spiritual growth that is inherently possible through the organic experience of growing old. Life is a mysterious and awesome process, from birth to death, and there are challenges and ever-new wonders to be discovered at every stage of the way. For many people, the action and speed of one's middle years obscures this wonder and awe at the grandeur of life . . . and perhaps that too is as it should be. Each stage of life is equally worthy of respect and reverence. Perhaps in our elder years, as we sink back into the bare essentials of life, as what is superfluous falls away, as we let go of what was, to be fully present to what is, we will again comprehend the beauty of life. And this wisdom, this vision that is both old and new, will be our contribution toward the transformation of others. As Bo Lozoff has written, everyone at every stage of life needs to make a contribution toward the common good, and children and elderly people are no exceptions to this need:

By sheltering children and putting the elderly out to pasture, we have unwittingly created an angry, aimless younger generation and a lonely, unappreciated older generation. Many Americans assume this is simply what it means to be young or to be old. But anyone who has traveled in other cultures knows this is not true. Children can be happy, respectful, capable. The elderly can be radiantly peaceful, lucid, venerated. We need younger, middle-aged and older people around us, not just others our own age. We are ever and always part of each other. We either walk into Heaven arm in arm or we don't get in at all. [13]

CHAPTER TEN

The Healing Power of Community

> *The Cure comes from the medicine*
> *and the art of medicine*
> *originates in charity.*
> *Hence,*
> *to be cured is not a work of Faith*
> *but one of sympathy.*
> *The true ground of medicine is love.*
> —Paracelsus

Community life generates a tremendous potential or force for healing. By "healing force" I don't necessarily mean the cure of aches, pains and illnesses, although that can be part of the healing power of community. By healing force I mean the combined power of human hearts joined together in a way that is transformative. There is a force transmitted between human beings that cannot be measured and controlled by outside forces and we can let ourselves be vehicles for it. It can not be replaced with the most advanced allopathic or naturopathic medicines. The healing power of community is a result of the living web of relationship, commitment, shared purpose and the tender and sometimes terrifying aspects of bonded relationships. A bonded group creates a magic, an alchemy, based on the synergy of many different energies interwoven and working together. This alchemy works on us both from the outside and the inside. It generates a healing power that can make a very real difference in individual lives.

252

Healing is not always good, nice, sweet and attractive to us. If it is real, it is also raw, potent and sometimes shocking or frightening. All true healing leads us to a greater or deeper realization of our innate wholeness, and sometimes that is found in death and dying, or in illness and recovery. We find breakdown, illness, death and decay frightening only if we are denying our own mortality and the natural cycles of life. Embracing these aspects of life does not mean that we won't still feel fear or be afraid to die, but that we are big enough to accept life as it is— fear, uncertainty and all. In community we have the opportunity and the support to embrace these facts of life in a greater way, and to heal each other and ourselves simultaneously because we are bonded, and because we live a little closer to—with a little more awareness of—our basic connectedness as human beings. What one person experiences becomes available to all in a way, so that the voice or vision or knowledge of the individual is reflected back into the collective, and vice versa.

An example of the healing power of community is described in Dennis Jaffe's book, *Healing From Within.* In the early 1960s, medical researchers were astounded by the uncharacteristic health of the residents of Roseto, Pennsylvania. A comprehensive study of this highly bonded Italian-American community showed that Roseto residents had an amazingly low incidence of all of the most common diseases of civilization. For instance, compared to the national average of 3.5 per 1000, only 1 per 1000 men in Roseto died of heart attacks, and the rate for the women was even less, compared to the national average.

Doctors found that the people of Roseto had all the same risk factors for heart disease: they were comparatively overweight, and consumed the same amounts of animal fats as people in neighboring towns. They had serum cholesterol, hypertension and diabetes levels comparable to other nearby communities, and their smoking and exercise patterns were about the same. Still, their overall physical health was much better. Why?

After ruling out genetic and ethnic factors, researches came to the conclusion that it was the supportive culture—the community structure of their lives—that created an environment in which greater health was achieved. Stewart Wolf, vice-president for medical affairs at St. Luke's Hospital in Bethlehem, Pennsylvania said that Roseto's culture "reflected tenaciously held old-world values and customs. We found that family relationships were extremely close and mutually supportive. This cohesive quality extended to neighbors and to the community as a whole." [1] Researchers also noted that the elderly were loved, respected and cared for in the homes of their families when they were sick, and that whenever a family or an individual had financial problems, relatives and even the community-at-large pitched in to offer assistance.

By 1965, however, Roseto had changed. Many younger residents were becoming dissatisfied with the tradition and social isolation of their community. They began to seek more middle-class American goals and values: success, status, career, money, material possessions. This took quite a toll on the community. Wolf noted that the younger adults "joined country clubs in the nearby Poconos; they bought Cadillacs; they replaced old, tradition-rich wooden houses with sprawling suburban ranch-style structures; they began attending outside churches, or no church at all . . . It seemed like a capsulized, accelerated fulfillment of the American dream." [2] While this was going on, another notable change occurred for the Roseto residents. The heart-attack death rate rose significantly, especially among men below fifty-five. Researchers drew the conclusion that the breakdown of family life and sense of community purpose and closeness was the reason for the increase.[3]

Other studies have also revealed a connection between an individual's health and their relationship within community. For example, one study states that "voluntary exclusion or forced expulsion from a community or group coincided, with astonishing frequency, with the onset or the relapse of a peptic ulcer." [4] Another study revealed that tuberculosis occurred more frequently in " 'marginal' people who had been deprived of meaningful social contact. Men and women who lived alone, who were single or divorced, who were members of minority groups, or who moved frequently and consequently felt displaced were more likely to get TB. This same finding applied to schizophrenia." [5]

Research has also shown that despondency and depression and lack of will to live is often the precursor to the onset of cancer or death by some other cause. This kind of depression, hopelessness or despair is commonly found in the bereaved, and in those who have been through a trauma like war, a major accident that involved serious loss, and even through the more common losses experienced in divorce or loss of a job. The growing field of psychoneuroimmunology—which traces the connecting pathways between emotions, feelings and the immune and nervous systems—scientifically demonstrates the undeniable relationship between being dislocated, disaffected and disillusioned and one's state of health. When one feels shattered by events and disconnected from life, the body's natural defenses are weakened by concomitant emotional plunges. That is when illness often sets in.

The process of healing is one in which the balance of wholeness, harmony, inner unity and integration is restored. Often this occurs when one reconnects with a sense of purpose, and often a spiritually-oriented purpose. One study of people suffering from heart attacks found that in five out of ten individuals, recovery was clearly linked with a "transcendental redirection" or an experience of spiritual rebirth and transformation, which they felt had made a great impact upon their healing process. [6]

When psychologist Carl Rogers sought those qualities that made psychotherapists most effective in the healing process with clients, he found that unconditional positive regard, warmth and deep empathy were the prime ingredients of healing. At bottom, the ideal healing relationship between client and therapist, regardless of what technique or therapy was used, was founded upon intimacy, caring concern and a sense of partnership. These are the qualities and attitudes that can be found in abundance in a group of individuals who make a conscious effort to create community. Community generates meaning and connectedness in our lives, and these are part of the basic building-blocks of psychological and physical wholeness and well-being.

Pain, Illness and Death as Part of the Healing Process

Community is a great place to practice kindness, generosity and compassion and at the same time not to be attached to the outcome of this practice. Because I was trained as a child to deny pain, discomfort or anything that threatened my security, I often feel uncomfortable with the pain of another, and that discomfort compels me to try to take away the pain. Making it all better as fast as possible by jumping to the rescue, or trying to gloss over the facts of someone's pain with joviality or glib statements can be very misguided and deeply unconscious gestures. Attempting to take away pain may interrupt a process that is necessary to the overall well being of the individual. What is needed is to *be with* another in his or her pain, to go through it together in compassion (to "suffer with") and to come out on the other side. This is usually the hardest thing to do, and requires a great deal of surrender and trust. I have to let my heart be touched by another's pain. While this can stir up and bring me in touch with my own pain, we both come out stronger in the end.

It is a sign of the maturity of the community when we are not fixing, rescuing and altering one another's process, but instead supporting each other through it. A real safety and trust is created when we give each other space to do whatever is needed, and when we hold a context of wholeness for one another regardless of the details of the healing crisis we may be experiencing.

Jenny Speaks About Death in a Healing Circle

When Rosemary first came to our community she was about thirty. Diagnosed with breast cancer five years earlier, she had already been through a radical mastectomy, chemotherapy and radiation treatment. She was rail thin. Her hair was finally growing out a little, so it was about one-inch long and stuck out in nut-brown spikes all over her head. Rosemary had a toothy smile in her bony, thin-lipped face, but her eyes were kind and understanding, and we were quickly warmed by her eager friendliness and her vulnerability.

Rosemary had been told that her cancer was in remission, but six weeks after she arrived the pain returned and when she went back to the doctor she learned that the cancer had metastasized. More chemotherapy was recommended. Rosemary absolutely believed she could heal herself and live, but she needed a lot of help to do that. She wanted to enter into a very intense program of natural healing combined with positive thinking and visualization. In response to her need for care, a team of five or six of us women came together to form what we called a "healing circle." At her request, we agreed to hold a positive outcome for her. For the next six months, this was almost all we did.

Rosemary couldn't care for herself, because she had weakened a great deal, so we assisted with all of her treatments, herbs, teas, massages, special diet and so on, all of which took a tremendous amount of energy and time. For instance, she drank wheat grass juice, and the grass had to be grown, harvested and juiced by us. We had to buy special, organically-grown grape juice by the gallon for her, which she took with chlorophyll that we got from a place one hundred miles away. And she had to have someone with her twenty-four hours a day.

At first, it seemed like we might be able to stave off the growth of the cancer in Rosemary's body. Besides religiously managing her herbal and dietary program, we meditated together, chanted

257

and sang songs, hung crystals in her window to fill the room with rainbows, and brought our guitars, flutes and drums in for music. We told stories, read to her and hung out together. At one point when she left the land to spend two weeks at a special healing institute, we took turns staying with her there. Nonetheless, after about five months of these efforts, we couldn't deny what our eyes and senses were telling us: Rosemary was getting much worse. She could barely turn herself over in bed, and although she still insisted on dragging herself (with two people helping) into the bathroom, she was a skeleton with a skin covering. Her lips were dried out from dehydration—no matter how many liquids we offered to her—because her ability to drink had diminished significantly. When I massaged her back, with a sinking heart I felt the literally hundreds of small tumors that were growing just underneath the skin. Clearly her body was riddled with cancer, but Rosemary was still completely unwilling to admit that she was dying.

Her denial was fierce and very unsettling to those of us in her healing circle because we felt we had to live a lie with her. We hoped that she would be able to embrace the fact somehow, come to peace with it and begin to consciously let go. One afternoon, as several of us sat quietly with her, singing and talking, it was as if a window opened out onto a vast, infinite field of peaceful emptiness. Rosemary felt it too, and she called me to come close to her until my face was right next to hers. "Come with me," she whispered in a hoarse voice. "Let's take the journey together." I held her hand gently as a tear ran down my face. "I can't go with you, Rosemary. I don't know how to go with you," was all I could manage to say.

Often she was very angry with us all—perhaps because our lives went on about her while she was dying. After all, we were healthy, young, independent, flighty at times, and coming and going in a flurry of activities while she was confined to bed, in pain. On the other hand, because she was so ill, she had a direct connection to the profound value and the fragility of life itself.

258

Rosemary was quick to criticize our selfish and self-destructive behaviors. She chastised us frequently for being so careless of our own health or irresponsible about aspects of our lives or relationships.

One day, shortly before she died, she became more and more irascible and angry. "You are all killing me! You don't believe that I can be healed, so I am dying!" She raged on hysterically. This was extremely painful to us all, because we loved her dearly. We cried in each other's arms, we tried to reason with her, but we never confronted her denial about her impending death directly. Out of respect for her process, we didn't come out and say, "Rosemary, your body is going." Wanting her to die with equanimity and peace was, in retrospect, one of the most selfish attitudes of all.

Finally, the kind, young medical doctor who was helping us with her care talked to her, at our request. When he was done, Rosemary asked us to call her mother who lived in Florida. She wanted to see her one last time, maybe to make peace with her since they had been estranged for many years because Rosemary was a lesbian.

Her mother came immediately, and since she was the only blood relative present, she had the legal authority to take Rosemary out of our care. At this point Rosemary was in no condition to be able to speak for herself; she was barely conscious, and although we knew that she preferred to die at home in her own bed, there was nothing we could do to persuade her mother, a nurse, to let her stay with us.

Once at the hospital Rosemary immediately lapsed into a deep coma and did not speak again. Twelve hours after she was admitted I was alone with her, standing at the foot of her bed and gazing at her still, shrunken form. It felt like time for her to die. "I came to say goodbye my friend. It's time to let go, Rosemary. We all love you and wish you well in your journey. You can go in peace now." I said this several times until I felt a subtle response from her still form—barely perceptible, and yet just the briefest whisper of a

*touch in my heart. I walked out into the hallway and looked out
at the gorgeous orange sunset and blue evening sky. Not five minutes after I had whispered my goodbye to Rosemary, one of our
friends walked up and said, "Rosemary just died." Instantly I felt
a soaring happiness. She was flying in the colors of that sunset and
across the vast sky. She was all around me, free and ecstatic.
Somehow I could hear her saying, "This is the healing I sought. I
am finally liberated."*

*After Rosemary's death her mother had a change of heart.
When she first arrived she was suspicious of us and deeply disturbed by her daughter's imminent death. But we had won her over
with our obvious love of Rosemary, and as she came to realize what
we had gone through with her daughter, she decided to give us permission to bury her daughter in the fashion that Rosemary would
have preferred.*

*By state law a body had to be embalmed, but we took
Rosemary's body as quickly as possible and placed it in a beautiful, handmade pine casket that a woman in our community had
made for her. On the way to her burial, with her casket in our Ford
Bronco, we spontaneously sang holy songs, with high spirits and
joy rebounding among us. Once on community land where she
would be buried, we removed her body from the casket, anointed
her with sweet oils and then wrapped her in a white cotton sheet
with flowers tucked in here and there. The grave was dug deep,
and we lowered her stiff, cold body into the grave. Each woman
had the opportunity to toss in a symbolic object—flowers, a cowrie
shell representing the Divine Mother as the gateway to birth and
death, a piece of amethyst.*

*Rosemary's spirit was everywhere around us, flying in the
wind, dancing across the spacious vastness of the sky, in last fall's
tall gold grasses that bent and swayed in the wind. It was so clear
that she was there with us, and that she was free, healed, whole.
All of our dark moments when she was angry with us and paranoid
because we couldn't heal her of cancer, her moments of terror and*

denial, her sorrow at having to leave so early in her young life with so much untasted and unfinished were gone—completely. Now the rest was up to us: to live in a way that would do justice to and honor the gifts of the spirit she had given us. It was our responsibility to recognize the tremendous healing and even transformation we had all gone through together, and to make that a part of our lives in service to others who might cross our paths in the years to come.

Many communities provide this kind of hospice care for the dying, and hospice organizations themselves often serve as community for those who participate at various levels. There is community formed among volunteers, healthcare providers, patient and family members during the period of illness and the subsequent bereavement. "Let death be your advisor," advised Don Juan, a Yaqui shaman and man of knowledge, to his apprentice Carlos Castaneda, and indeed any situation in which we are caring for the seriously ill, the dying or the newly bereaved has a tremendous amount to teach us about living. It is commonly held by many who work with the dying that "we die the same way that we have lived." A sobering thought to meditate. As a caregiver witnessing the process of illness and dying a tremendous opening of the heart may occur in our own lives. We may come into a more conscious relationship to our own mortality, realizing the precious gift that life is, and this may inspire us to make changes for ourselves. Relationships can become more important to us, as we admit that we don't want to squander precious time in chronic defensiveness or needing to be right at the sacrifice of communion within others. We may start to clean up our interactions with others, to use our energy more wisely, to stop rushing around at breakneck speed, blindly denying the delicate beauty of life itself. We may cry more easily, and find that our hearts are touched by strange and bittersweet things, and at odd times. And all of this can make us more available, more vulnerable to what life has to offer.

One mystery that community reveals is that when we serve others in a healing capacity we also heal ourselves. Most of us have a reference point for finding joy, regeneration, personal renewal in this kind of giving. One friend of mine used to say that whenever she got depressed or upset or felt despairing about her own situation or problems in life, she would shift her focus onto doing something for someone else. This always dispelled her own problem- and self-centered clouds, and brought light and joy into what was dark and gloomy before. When I give of myself fully, the "I" that I think myself to be is forgotten and there is just the service at hand. What a relief and a joy when we are relieved of our own suffering by serving someone else!

I had an experience similar to Jenny's when a member of my community died in 1994. For the last six months of her life she required twenty-four-hour-a-day care, and so a group of community members took shifts caring for her. We changed her diapers when she became incontinent, sponge-bathed her daily, read to her, prepared her special foods, medicines and liquids, and carried her around on a litter that a friend made for her when she wanted to attend community activities and could no longer walk. We were with her through all the emotional processes of death, in which she mimicked us, yelled at us enraged, blessed us, transported us during her raptures and ecstasies, laughed with us and questioned the meaning of life, death and the Divine with us in achingly sober moments or in moments that were sweet with a heavenly kind of longing. We went hand in hand with her throughout, and in the end we bathed and cared for her dead body, wrapped it in muslin cloth and buried her on our community land amidst quiet singing and wafts of incense.

A strange thing happened the day our friend died. We had a snowstorm that was so severe that the power was out for the entire day, and the water pump was not functioning. We had to melt snow on the gas stove to make water for washing her body. While some of us prepared her body for burial, others meditated together and a crew dug the grave out of frozen, rocky ground amidst the pine and cedar groves on our property. Fifty people were present that day, and each one clearly felt that it was a gift to them to have had the opportunity to serve her. As we left the gravesite strewn with flowers and petals, we crossed the sandy arroyo to walk back through the snow toward our houses when someone threw a snowball. Soon several people were joyously zinging snowballs back and forth in high spirits while the sun went down in a blaze of orange and red in the western sky. She would have jumped into this kind of fun too, a fitting display of the joy of life at the time of her transition. In some intangible way, this snowball fight was an important and poignant part of our goodbye. We were all healed in some unfathomable way by her life, death and transition into the unknown.

Healing Through Personal Change

A great deal of the healing that becomes possible in community takes place in the emotional, psychological or spiritual realms. Often this healing process is almost invisible because it happens slowly, over time, as we change, grow and outgrow old negative patterns. One day we look back over five, ten or fifteen years and realize that we *have* changed, in spite of our hardheaded resistance! Community is a fire that transforms us, but it is also like water on a rock—over the long haul it wears away new contours in the landscape of our psyches. In this way, community is like an alchemical vessel for transformation within the individual. I know many people who have dropped one or more addictions because of the healing power of community. Twelve Step groups are an obvious example of the healing power of community in the area of addictions, but I am specifically referring here to residential communities, both secular and spiritual or religious, that have made it possible for individuals to really let go completely of addictive substances, relationships or patterns.

Mary Grace, for example, has lived and worked in communities, both residential and non-residential, for twenty-five years. Ten years ago when she found her home in a spiritual community, her struggle with alcohol simply fell away and has not recurred, replaced by a life of spiritual practice—daily meditation, prayer, dietary discipline, exercise and study. Many people find that community life feeds their spiritual being so that the impulses underlying their addictions—driven by emptiness and meaninglessness—are satisfied by a kind of transformational or healing "substance" that is present within the bonded community. Addiction is one of the most physically, psychologically and spiritually ravaging illnesses of our times, and so this is not a small accomplishment in any group.

Not long ago I participated in a support group for Roberta, a woman in my community who has had tremendous difficulty for many years in controlling her anger. Roberta has acted this anger out in many circumstances with other members and with her own children. On this particular day, the group had reached its limit of patience, resources and hope for being able to break through the hard shell of angry and hostile defensiveness that Roberta was demonstrating, to everyone's great sadness. We were ready to throw our hands up in the air when Delores said quietly, "I stopped hitting my son, and if I can do that, Roberta, then you can control your anger." We could hear a pin drop in this moment, as everyone's attention along with our hearts went to Delores. "I just made a decision one day," Delores continued, "and I stopped doing it, that was all. I guess it was a combination of getting so much help from so many people." We were dumbfounded, not because Delores had struck her son—we knew that she had struggled with these anger issues too—but because of the power that her simple statement about her personal transformation within community contained for each of us.

264

I also know many cases of families who have stayed together when they would have fallen apart without community. I have seen rebellious, discontented teenagers circumvent some very rocky roads because of the support and understanding they received within community. In one instance, a mother of two children needed to leave the community residence to move to a city where she could work with a particular psychotherapist. The psychological wounds that prevented her from being whole with her husband and children and within the community-at-large were such that she needed professional help. In order to make this possible, the community rallied and created a situation in which the father was able to stay on the community property and raise the children while the mother took care of her own healing process. This involved two years in which the community provided support, co-parenting, and nurturing childcare, as well as emotional support to both adults in the family. Without the help of community, this family could have gone through a serious breakdown that might have inflicted a great deal of psychological damage on the children.

To Love is To Bless, To Bless is To Heal

How we feel about one another and the thoughts and energy that we project onto each other can either heal or harm. The difference that we feel between spending time with friends whom we greatly enjoy and spending time in situations of conflict is tangible. Most of us have had the experience of being with a person who has complained, viciously gossiped and made negative comments for two hours, after which we have come away feeling drained and exhausted.

Scientific research confirms that happy emotions or pleasure trigger an immune response that is powerful for good health. Someone who is sick or ailing can come among loving friends and family and be "loved well." We literally have the power to "love a person alive," as Lila, a long-time healer in my community, words it. When we are happy to see each other, we are profoundly affected, and this stimulates a certain brain chemistry that enhances health. We all have the usually unacknowledged capacity to bless each other with love, attention, energy, time, feelings of mutual regard, respect, trust and concern. These intangible blessings that are flowing between us as invisible energies are the daily messengers of the community's power to heal and promote health among its members.

In the same way, feelings of anxiety, lack of self-worth, confrontations and angry interactions have a degenerative effect on one's health. I've had times of running far beyond my personal reserves, on the edge of falling ill, and after spending time with a close, loving friend felt myself "loved alive." But if someone is abusive to me or withdraws their care and regard, I can feel very depressed. The more attached and intimate I am with the person, the stronger the effects of our interactions for good or ill.

When it comes to the synergetic dynamics of community, this principle of people affecting one another multiples exponentially. Therefore, it is wise to examine together what the group's attitudes, both conscious and unconscious, are toward health and healing, and to acknowledge consciously the effect we have on each other in this way. Acknowledging this makes each one responsible in relationship to the others. As we become more sensitive and receptive, this kind of individual responsibility for the well being of the group becomes urgently real. Our capacity to bless and heal is another aspect of hospitality in relationship—that we consciously extend good will to our fellows because we realize that we in fact are not separate from them. This is another doorway into the transformative effects of living in community in a way that embraces our oneness and unity as beings.

Self-Healing, Self-Responsibility

Health and healing are subjects that are terrifying for some of us. In community they have to be approached with sensitivity to each other's various levels of willingness to take responsibility. Modern allopathic medicine has not fostered the idea that each individual is responsible for their own healing and health, and we as a culture have given our power away to the medical establishment.

Natural healing methods seek to approach health and healing from a holistic perspective that includes mind, emotions, body and soul. Unfortunately, one can be equally passive and dependent upon these healing modalities as they are on more conventional doctors and therapeutic approaches. The important point is to take responsibility for one's own healing process and inner power to heal, regenerate and transform.

Community can support us as individuals in taking this responsibility, but there is a delicate balance to consider here: community can educate, nurture and bless, but community should not legislate "right and wrong" with regard to health and healing. Health and healing is, and needs to remain, very personal and intimate. Yet at the same time, each individual needs to realize that we are all part of a greater body. What we do, think and feel has a profound impact on that greater body. When we do not take responsibility for our own health and healing, others in our "larger body" will suffer for and with us.

John, for example, had a chronic, degenerative illness that could be significantly arrested and managed by a maintenance program of exercise and dietary changes. He also had a lifetime habit of depression and lack of self-worth, and would go to his room to brood alone when cycles of despair and uncertainty hit him. Despite these emotional problems, his sensitivity and kindness made him the person in the community that others often went to when they needed someone to listen in a nurturing way.

267

It was extremely painful to his friends and loved ones that John refused to make the simple lifestyle changes that would alleviate his physical suffering, even though they knew this behavior was another symptom of his shaky emotional health. The community had two choices: to confront him lovingly but directly about his self-destructive choices and behaviors, or to ignore the situation. Finally, a group of his close men friends within the community asked to meet with him and honestly laid out their concerns. At first John was defensive. He felt threatened believing that people were trying to control him by prying into his personal business.

After some weeks of discussion and input, however, John finally heard what people were saying—that everyone was suffering along with him. The impact of this recognition was the catalyst for his personal change—a process that took time and effort on his part. With the nurturing support of the community, John started down the long road of healing.

Often we can do things for others whom we love and respect that we cannot do for ourselves. Carla smoked cigarettes when she was in her twenties and early thirties. One day her son, then ten years old, came home from school and told her about the film he had seen about what nicotine does to the lungs. "I'm worried about you. I really want you to stop smoking," he said. Carla never smoked another cigarette. In this same way community can become the catalyst for the individual to turn toward greater self-regard and self-respect. By changing negative attitudes and making concrete gestures toward self-responsibility in health and healing, we actually serve others.

Any intentional community might consider setting aside a day or two once a year to explore this vital area of health together, as an ongoing opportunity for education, bonding and self-responsibility. This kind of "health retreat" could be structured around lectures and discussions, plus ample doses of music and dance—some of the best preventive medicine available! Informal discussion, in which people are sincerely invited to explore their underlying fears and anxieties about issues like health, illness and death, can be tremendously important in revealing those attitudes that undermine our efforts to live in a way that is conscious and transformative. The community might come to new and creative agreements about preventive health also. Exercise programs, meditation, diet, and positive, life-serving attitudes are all significant factors in determining health and vitality. Having group support in these areas can make a big difference. For example, the community might decide that money be allocated for an exercise room to support the health of individuals.

The community may find that it is strong in one area of health maintenance, but needs work in others. For instance, if exercise is part of the daily flow of life but meditation is not, we can explore and question together how can the group can support its members to move toward incorporating this important and natural aspect of a healthy life.

There is a peace that comes with being naturally and organically connected within the human family, and this itself is a powerful agent of healing. This peace, combined with the acknowledgement of one's uniqueness, which is part and parcel of community life, is one of the great keys to quality of life and the transformational possibility.

CHAPTER ELEVEN

Celebration and Ritual

*The wisdom of a true community often seems miraculous
. . . This is one of the reasons why the feeling of joy is such
a frequent concomitant of the spirit of community. The
members feel that they have been temporarily—at least
partially—transported out of the mundane world of ordinary pre-occupations. For the moment it is as if heaven
and earth had somehow met.*

—M. Scott Peck

The harder we work together the harder we play
and pray together. Celebration and ritual season the rich hearty
stew of community life. They feed the spirit and soul, reminding
us of the joy naturally present in existence and of our initial joy
in coming together in a shared purpose and commitment to what
matters deeply to us. Often celebration and ritual are intertwined,
while at other times they are quite distinct moods or events. For
our purposes here we will separate them in order to consider their
unique aspects.

Celebration

Celebration can have many moods, from silly and
mundane to sublime and extraordinary. It may involve playing
with the children, watching movies, doing humorous skits, having
cookies and tea and sitting around, or making a bonfire and roast-
ing marshmallows. A picnic, a softball game, a cookout, a wed-
ding, the birth of a child—these human events and moments

within the matrix of relationship lend themselves to the celebratory mood, as does playing music and dancing until the wee hours of the morning. Celebrations can be any form of activity (or contemplation) that brings us together. It may not really matter what our celebrations are—only that we have them, and have them completely!

Certainly we may find celebration within our daily work, but typically we tend to think of celebration as that time when we set aside work and focus on what is playful, restorative to the soul, and that which renews our energy for another day. One monastic community designates their weekly Friday night spaghetti dinner as a form of celebration. These festive meals are one of the ways that these celibate monks and nuns, who spend several days a week in solitude and ritual silence, celebrate their lives and their commitment together. In another spiritual community, in the midst of the austerities of building a new ashram, when many of the comforts of everyday life were suspended, the simple act of gathering to chant some traditional Indian *bhajans* became a mini-celebration. The adults and children also created celebrations together twice a week in front of a roaring fireplace in the chilly evenings over ample bowls of hot popcorn. For other groups, celebrations may revolve around weekly potluck dinners, or traditional secular or spiritual holidays like Christmas, Easter, Hanukah, Summer Solstice or Thanksgiving.

Often celebration happens spontaneously. We simply find ourselves together in a mood infused with communion and joy. Often humor is present as well, and in fact is one of the most important aspects of celebration and renewal. We all feel uplifted in these moments, and our cares and struggles are washed away, temporarily suspended or even transformed by the healing power of fun, laughter, song and camaraderie. In celebration we offer our gratitude for the chance to live and work and play together in community.

Music has always been integral to celebration. My community has two bands: a rock & roll band and a traditional blues group, and one or both groups often play at our celebratory events. On one memorable occasion, the women and children were dancing to the music while most of the men watched from the sidelines. While there was lots of fun and enjoyment in this, something was still missing. Then the men got up, crowding the dance floor and increasing the heat of sweaty bodies, already lost to the rhythmic enchantment. As the men joined in the music and dance a happy pandemonium broke out, and an undeniable energy spontaneously burst forth from everyone. Suddenly the whole of community was present and together, and the happy mood was magnified. Swept up in the fun, I thought to myself, "This is the mood of celebration in community at its best!"

Celebratory events may require a lot of focused time, energy and resources. Cooking for one hundred people and orchestrating the details of a sacred or secular space, whether around a meal or a day of meditation or a community meeting, calls us to work together in ways that can be transformational. Some of the most profound moments I've shared with others have occurred over piles of dishes, or in the heat of the kitchen when the meal is about to be served and a dozen decisions come rushing at the cooks all at once. From experience I know that when the kitchen and staff goes into breakdown—too much water in the rice, the chickens seem like they aren't going to be done on time, the bread isn't rising as it should—that if I persevere in good faith, things somehow turn out right in the end. I have experienced some miraculous recoveries in the communal kitchen: someone who knows how to make the *dosas* (Indian pancakes) shows up at the last minute when all of our attempts have failed; somehow the soup extends itself to serve the extra ten people who have arrived at the last minute!

Part of the joy of celebration comes through service to others, because someone has to scour the pots, wash and dress the chickens, laboriously peel garlic and chop onions with tears streaming down the face, or take out the compost and mop the floor while others go on to the next scheduled event. Those of us born and bred in the West often have a hard time realizing the transformational effects of such selfless service. For me, it is all worth it when I peek into the dining room and look out upon a sea of shining faces, where enjoyment and communion is so obviously present in my friends and loved ones, at least in part due to my efforts.

At times, a more informal celebratory event opens us to a deeper appreciation of our lives—our commitments and sacrifices. Such celebration may then overflow into or mingle with ritual in a most natural way. Kathleen Norris describes the mood of celebration she experienced among the Benedictine nuns at St. John's Abbey when a celebratory meal was being prepared and enjoyed. After a busy day she changed into more festive attire and hurried to join the group. "God, the laughter," she wrote, noticing this first when she entered the communal kitchen where women were preparing vegetables, cooking, washing dishes. She had brought homemade bread and champagne as an offering, which was joyfully accepted. Over the meal, the conversation moved into the subject of the deeper meaning of their life.

> . . . discussion turns toward something I've noticed that Benedictines seldom talk about, that is, the angelic nature of their calling. Their Liturgy of the Hours is, at root, a symbolic act, an emulation of and a joining with the choirs in heaven who sing the praise of God unceasingly. To most people even to think of such things seem foolish, and Benedictines are well aware that their motives are easily misinterpreted, labeled as romanticist or escapist. "Anyone who knows us knows we're down to earth," one sister says. "We have to be, to live in community as we do."

But one of the Australian sisters insists that Benedictines "be willing to admit to the angelic charism. The best thing we can do," she says, "is to praise." I tell the story of a monk I know who dreamed one night that armed men in uniform had entered the abbey church, and when he tried to stop them from approaching the altar, they shot him. As he lay by the altar, he saw Christ standing before him. "Am I dead?" the monk asked, and Christ nodded and answered, gravely, "Yes." "Well, what do I do now?" the monk inquired, and Christ shrugged and said, "I guess you should go back to choir."

The laughter comes as blessing; women, youthful and aged, with nubile limbs and thick, unsteady ankles, graceful, busy hands and gnarled fingers slowed by arthritis, making a joyful noise. Our talk is light-hearted, easy as we clear the table.[1]

The Need for Ritual

Rituals have been enacted since time began. There is a time for private rituals, done in solitude, and there is a time for communing and coming together in ritual acts. Ritual tends to be a formal and focused act, in which our attention is exclusively placed on a specific purpose—particularly *to invoke* the presence of the Divine. Community provides the bonded matrix for empowering a group ritual far beyond what can happen when ritual is done in a group of strangers. As Jesus once said, "If two or more are gathered *in my name*, there will I be also." This is the basic principle of "invocation through ritual" in community. Through such a ritual, the Divine becomes a palpable presence that imbues each person with blessings, grace and the renewal of purpose, inspiration and commitment to the shared vision and hope of the community. When brought into life through action, thought, word and deed, this sanctified vision benefits the greater design of Life at the heart of the world.

The rituals of religious communities are usually grounded in hundreds or even thousands of years of traditions. Christianity, Judaism, Hinduism, Buddhism, Islam, Sufism and indigenous tribal cultures—African, Native American, Aboriginal, for example—all contain profound rituals, and communities that are centered around any of these great traditions have tremendous wealth to draw from. Secular communities that create their rituals (as Mary will describe below) often borrow from other traditions, synthesizing, innovating and coming up with an often eclectic blend. These rituals may have an interior focus, expressed as in simple prayers or meditation, or more active and external focus accompanied by singing or dancing.

Like the celebrations that often accompany them, community rituals may revolve around specific events like the birth of a child, or the death of a community member; they may be connected to the flow of the seasons and solar system, such as on the summer or winter solstices or fall or vernal equinoxes. Rituals may also mark a rite of passage within the maturation process in community, such as a teenager's rite of passage out of childhood, a marriage ceremony or a pregnancy. We can create and enact ritual in our daily lives when we are moved.

Rituals are necessary to our spiritual health. Such ceremonies feed the spiritual dimension or soul in very direct, immediate ways, and is always connected to some kind of living mythology, in which symbols act as a bridge from the seen to the unseen, from the concreteness of ordinary life to the multidimensional, subtle life of the soul. The symbols that characterize our rituals must have a living meaning and resonance to us personally, whether these are the Christian or the Celtic cross, totem spirits or animals, or the elements of earth, air, fire and water. Yet these symbols are completely impersonal as well in that ritual transcends the personal to become the supra-personal—they link

275

the individual with the collective, or with the ultimate unity of life. In this way we go from diversity to unity in the One.

Mary Speaks about Community Rituals

When I first came to Medicine Pipe Ranch I fell in love with the wide open, spacious urge toward a native or innate spirituality that I instinctively felt to be present there. We all had permission to personally create this spirituality for ourselves; no one was laying a trip on anyone else about some rigid form of religion or worship, though each one had personal interests and inclinations. We had a ritual at the beginning of every evening meal: after the bell was rung on the porch steps, everyone came in and gathered around the table, joined hands and sat in silence for an indefinite period of time, until someone felt called to gently squeeze the hand next to his or hers in the signal that the communion had come to a natural close. Our lives were also filled with informal rituals.

One especially loved formal ritual that we created was that of the sweat lodge. We built the fire and selected the rocks (no river stones) very intentionally and with great care and attention. We covered the bent and lashed willow branch skeleton of the round sweat lodge with canvas tucked in tight around the bottom and held down with large stones, and we dug a hole in the earth in the center of the lodge. Then we hung fresh sage from the garden and wild cedar inside the lodge from the ceiling of arched willow poles, and placed two large buckets of cold spring water on the ground inside. The fire burned all day long, usually for eight hours, or until the rocks were white hot. That night, under the cold stars in winter or warm moonlight in summer, we would strip down naked to bend and stoop and crawl into the lodge, which held about thirteen people snugly. There we sat in silence for sometimes as long as thirty or forty-five minutes, while one or two people sprinkled water on the hot rocks and almost unbearably hot steam swooshed up over our bodies and faces. Then sweat began to drip. Sitting on

276

the ground, with the dark earth pressing small pebbles into our flesh, sweat began to roll in long streaks down our backs and chests and arms and legs. The steam was so hot we began to suffer, and this is the best part of the sweat; the inner purification that one undergoes if a sweat lodge is properly done, because the intense heat on flesh, the hot moisture of the in-breath into the lungs, caused us to touch our inner pain; there is something to be said for having the discipline to stay in the lodge even when it is so hot it hurts, and the urge is to run out, get out, claw your way out. Instead, we sit, we stay. Through this kind of relatively insignificant but potently symbolic physical suffering induced in the sweat lodge, one then connects to the deeper suffering of the soul. The suffering of the pain of separation—our uncertainties, our grief, our fear and rage and sorrow.

Sooner or later, as we swooned and dripped with sweat, and when the silence could no longer bear the intensity of the space, someone would start a low hum, almost a groan, and as one voice after another joined in, the hum grew and floated from one inchoate melody to another until a coherent "song" appeared in the midst of the rising voices that intertwined. This was like a river; once the dam was opened, a torrent came rushing through. This song was a prayer, a prayer of purification and gratitude and supplication also.

For us the primal symbolism of this ritual was a powerful fact. Each sweat lodge was like a death and resurrection, a purification through darkness, fire and water. After the sweat, warm and dry back inside the house and gathered around the blazing wood stove with cups of hot tea, we were made shiny and new, reborn. Love and harmony flowed like wine among us at these times after the sweat, and we were happy and sane and connected. The sweat lodge was a ritual ordeal that brought spiritual renewal to us all, and around which we were able to drop any of our disagreements or separateness or isolated problems to unite in something that took

*us out of our small individuality and into the greater world of the
purely collective, human event of the soul.*

Malidoma Somé writes and speaks about ritual a great deal,
having come from a culture in which ritual is incorporated as a
fundamental aspect of daily tribal life. Linking ritual, art and
healing, he makes the important point that no one can practice
the "magical arts" of ritual without a stable and supportive community that "reflects the laws of nature and dances with them.
Within this framework, art, because it celebrates the powers of
the underworld, where the true nature of the natural order is
administered by the gods, becomes the greatest healing tool that
a community can have." [2] Somé tells of how his mother always
made two servings of food, one for the women and one for the
men. His mother would then preside over the women's meal and
his father over the men's meal. This activity ritualized the gender
culture practice in a way that was highly empowering for each.

Dinner always began with a hand-washing ceremony, then
the first bite of food was offered to the spirit of the Earth shrine.
This he called the "clearance bite," a ritual always performed by
his father, who then took a second bite for himself, held it in his
mouth for a few seconds, and then swallowed it, signifying that
the meal was safe to eat. Then everyone dove into the communal
dishes. There is no private dish of food for each person in the
Dagara meal ritual because, according to Somé, in the context of
a real community separate dishes cultivate separateness.

He comments that his brothers had a tremendous elegance
and agility in eating with their hands, carrying even liquid food
to their mouths in a way that seemed almost religious, and was
certainly artful, "as if the food were a living entity performing a
lifework on behalf of someone who needed it." [3] All these
aspects—the gender-specific nature of the meal, the ceremonial
form, the communal sharing of the bowl—all added meaning,
depth and richness to the ritual of eating.

Rituals require our time and energy if we want them to be effective. A meditation hall or prayer chapel, for example, needs to be kept immaculately clean—a service that requires daily maintenance. Flowers, if they are used, should be fresh and well-placed; incense or other ritual substances have to be kept stocked and available; ritual implements need to be cared for appropriately. Careful consideration must be given to what makes a sacred space work or not work. For example, if we find that a space requires silence in order to build a mood that most enhances a ritual, then we need to agree upon and keep that silence. If the person who cares for the meditation hall oversleeps and the room is dark and freezing when everyone arrives for the early morning meditation, then the possibilities normally inherent in that space may be hampered. If the purchaser did not order sufficient candles, or anything else needed for the ritual, then we have another breakdown of systems. If we want to create a sense of elegance in a space, we might agree to wear a specific type of clothing for ritual activities, rather than our worn out and much-patched blue jeans and favorite flannel shirt. All of this requires group cooperation and agreement at basic levels, but contributes toward the possible transformational atmosphere or event that can be created through ritual in community.

Bernadette Comments on Ritual

As a nun, I joined with the other members of the community five or six different times a day for ritualized prayer, which was the core of our lives. We started the day with the chanting of the Divine Office, then followed that with silent group meditation, and then the Mass—the epitome of communal prayer in the Catholic Church. The Mass has all the elements of prayer in it: invocation, emptying of self, confession of our unworthiness and inability to receive the mystery that is about to be bestowed; in the Mass you ask forgiveness of all whom you have harmed in order to come to the table of bread and wine, and you sing Gloria In Excelsis Deo, *so that your prayer is not only praise of the Divine, but also an invocation of divine intercession for the good of the whole Church. When we spoke of the whole Church, the entire body of Creation was implicitly understood—the recognition was that we were connecting ourselves with humanity. Throughout the Mass there is an offering of gifts—the fruits of your labors are laid at the altar, symbolically—but nonetheless if you do it with consciousness you are laying your life there, and you have the opportunity for* kenosis, *which is the Greek word for emptying, so that you can then receive the Holy Spirit.*

The Mass is actually a prayer that is a communal feast, the remembrance of the passion, death and resurrection of Christ, and the Last Supper in which Christ offered his body and blood is integral to that. The Mass is such an elegant prayer, and such a communal prayer. I think that a lot of people used to misuse the Mass in a way, as a form of personal devotion—not that that's bad, but I think the structure of the Mass is really a calling together of the community to jointly witness this celebration of God, and then together to participate in this communal symbolic meal. It is a meal that signifies spiritual incarnation. Your own possibility for spiritual incarnation, for the Divine to be incarnated in your case, is nourished. You are actually partaking of the body of God, and therefore you can no longer claim to be separate. When we do that as a communal body how can we turn and be spiteful to the person next to us? Or ignore the needs of others? When we sit together and consume this sacred meal, how can we hold ourselves apart from others or from God?

I was steeped in this tradition of prayer from the time I was a child, so ritual invocation and prayer was always very attractive for me. These years steeped in the ritual prayer of the Catholic Church were the beginnings of my hunger for a relationship to fully incarnated prayer.

Rituals have been enacted since time began. There is a time for private rituals, done in solitude, and there is a time for communing and coming together in ritual acts. Community provides the bonded matrix for empowering a group ritual far beyond what can happen when ritual is done in a group of strangers.

Ritual is the form that facilitates our journey into integration and wholeness. It is a healing process in spiritual terms. Each time we enter into the field or form of ritual, we bring back this renewed sense of wholeness into the "thousand things of life" once again.

CHAPTER TWELVE

Of Spirit and Soul

Two birds,
inseparable companions,
perch on the same tree.
One eats the fruit,
the other looks on.

The first bird is our individual self,
feeding on the pleasures and pains of this world.
The other is the universal Self,
silently witnessing all.
> —Mundaka Upanishad, 5th Century B.C.E.

Meaning is connected to purpose when purpose is very
deeply understood in relationship to a person's soul.
> —Malidoma Somé

Community is inherently spiritual. If we enter deeply enough into community life—living this path of heart with passion, fidelity and faith—we may discover that we have been "called" to a "spiritual path," a way that is much more profound than we may have imagined at the beginning. We may find that we have entered into a process of transformation; a process that connects us with an essential longing for the world of the soul. As we glimpse this domain, we are imbued with a sense of hidden meaning that reveals itself slowly over time, and becomes the beacon that calls us forward even while we carry on in our daily commitment.

282

To embrace this sense of being "called" we must expand our definitions of what this may mean. Kathleen Norris quotes Walter Brueggeman from his book *Hopeful Imagination* as saying, "A sense of call in our time is profoundly countercultural . . . the ideology of our time is that we can live 'an uncalled live,' one not referred to any purpose beyond one's self." Anyone who has felt a yearning for greater connectedness within the human family; anyone who has grieved the shattered self, or been struck by meaninglessness and lack of higher purpose, or who feels deeply the suffering in the world and what Malidoma Somé calls the "tyranny of modernity;" anyone who has come into some form of community life because of these sometimes inarticulate longings has felt a "calling." It is the call to unity and a depth of perception and vision of human possibility as not separate, isolated or strange but completely, innately integral within the life of the other, the world at large, the universe and even the cosmos.

This calling is not necessarily a formal religious process *per se,* but it is a deeply spiritual process that leads us into relationship with the realm of the sacred. Hearing the "call," we begin to live in such a way that the other is no longer the stranger—separate and alien from ourselves. Rather, we know that the other is linked to the same pulse that beats within our own hearts. Community becomes the vessel that contains and invokes the ingredients to catalyze this kind of change.

Community life is inherently about unity, bonded relationship and self-discovery—ideas that run counter to a culture focused on consumerism, avoidance of intimacy and the cult of the almighty individual set against the world. In these disparate and degenerate times, community is a choice that goes against mainstream culture; embracing community makes us radical in a way, because the vast momentum of the majority in the West is toward alienation and separation rather than unity and solidarity.

I often think of those who are committed within community as artists regardless of whether they produce formal or concrete art forms like poems, stories, painting, pottery or songs. They are artists because of the vision that calls them to a radical choice in which they struggle against the tide of countless of millions of their peers who are going in the opposite direction. This radical choice places us squarely in the realm of the "necessary other"— what Kathleen Norris calls the poets and prophets, contemplatives and renunciates, visionaries and artists of our times. The intangible realms of the soul that are nourished in these vocations and avocations are beyond our reckoning in value to human life. Who can say what is useful about the spiritually contemplative or artistic life? Often the real fruits of this kind of calling are invisible.

To experience a calling is to follow one's deepest, most heartfelt impulse. For many this is not necessarily an easy choice. It often involves tremendous sacrifice—of an old life or habits, of youthful dreams, of basic wishes and desires—made for the good of a higher vision. A calling is "revolutionary" in essence because it leads us against the flow of the status quo and re-establishes us in new territory. Anyone who has followed such a calling has felt the backlash from friends, relatives and the societal world, because such choices or lifestyles are a threat to living the unexamined life that is the norm. Of course, this has always been the case throughout history, as the stories of the world's visionaries, poets and saints testify. A true calling—in the way I am using this word, as arising from the depths of one's spiritual essence—overturns the old structures and begins a process that has the potential to radically transform all aspects of being. This process can be gentle, or it can involve an inner war, in which the individual must slowly or quickly come to terms with the new internal "order" which has been established by the revolutionary forces of change.

A true calling is what commits one to the unitive and self-revelatory principles of community. Because we have been called to community through our prophetic and poetic vision (which may seem more political or psychological at the beginning) we are thrust into the grand design of the world, where community becomes the vessel through which we too may enact the creation of the world anew. Community connects us to the heart of the world, and sooner or later in our sojourn into community, through perseverance, persistence and commitment, we are led into the realm of radical self-knowledge, and to the archetypal and mythological worlds of the spirit and the soul.

No matter how unclear it may be, or how much mystery we find in our own unfolding, generally a calling just won't leave us alone. It is not always clear that certain simple acts may have profound long-term effects, or that a call has been sounded in the depths of the soul. Now, however, many of us can look back at pivotal moments in our lives, knowing that something essential was catalyzed in us years ago. Perhaps that pivotal moment happened when we got together with a group of friends or neighbors and planned our first communal garden, or because we bonded into the community of our church, or because we were drawn to live radically in community and make fundamental lifestyle changes. Perhaps it occurred when we experienced an opening of the heart simply because someone in our group touched us deeply in a moment of rare vulnerability, and a whole new trust and faith in the goodness and wonder of life sprang from that touch. Norris comments further on the idea of being called:

> I suspect that this idol of the autonomous, uncalled life has a shadow side that demands that we resist the notion that another might be different, might indeed experience a call. Our idol of the autonomous individual is a sham; the truth is we expect everyone to be the same, and dismiss as elitist those who are working through a call to any genuine vocation ... By what authority does the poet, or prophet, speak? How dare the poet say, "I" and not mean the self? How dare the prophet say 'Thus says the Lord'?

It is the authority of experience, but by this I do not mean experience used as an idol, as if an individual's experience of the world were its truest measure. I mean experience tested in isolation, as by the desert fathers and mothers, and also tried in the crucible of community. I mean a "call" taken to heart, and over years of apprenticeship to an artistic discipline, developed into something that speaks to others.[1]

Indeed, community is an apprenticeship to life itself, to humanity, and to the crucible of relationship, self-knowledge and revelatory insight. Through our commitment, we become changed, and through this process, we come to understand that we are called to a greater life—a life of spirit, if you will; a life that intersects with the sacred on a daily basis. In this way community can be a circle: it initiates us into the call to spirit, it mentors and teaches us about the call of spirit, and it provides a haven and sanctuary for a life rich in the possibility of relationship to spirit, in a way that is evolutionary to the individual soul itself. And coming full circle, we find that there are no strangers here. The flourishing soul feeds community, and community feeds the heart and soul of the world and even the Divine. As Jung wrote, "But God himself cannot flourish if man's soul is starved." [2]

We may tend to think of the soul, and the spirit that nourishes soul, as something very private—an affair between God and individual. This is true of course, but community also provides the alembic for the heat of the inner life as well. The life of the soul is so necessary and integral to community that we could say that spirit is the breath of community. Without the food of the spirit and the life of the soul, there would be no evolving consciousness through which community may grow or be inspired and guided. If we go further using the metaphor of the breath, we can see that spiritual food is not only what keeps the organism alive, but what keeps the organism an open system, exchanging necessary life force with the greater environment of the world and the universe.

> *And what is the life breath?*
> *It is pure consciousness.*
> *And what is pure consciousness?*
> *It is the life breath.*
> —Kaushitaki Upanishad

Religious and spiritual communities are designed for this purpose—to generate the necessary elements, the breath and heat and heartbeat, for spiritual transformation. But all communities tap into and are naturally connected with the elements that create a transformative possibility. Some secular communities are more inclined in this way than others, but whether or not secular community becomes a transformative vessel depends on the intention of the individual. Any individual can make use of the naturally spiritual elements of a community situation, or can foster a context of community within themselves in such a way that will spark the creative process of the spiritual journey simply because there is an inherent sacredness in our coming together.

The soul is perhaps the least tangible and obvious dimension of community—certainly less tangible than the body or mind. Or maybe we tend to give it less attention. Yet the soul is the invisible fiber of community, interwoven with all other aspects. It is the soul that gives substance to form, that ignites our vision and longing for a greater life, and that gives community a lasting strength and ongoing possibility for creation. In the same way that we must have food for body, mind and heart, so does soul need the food of the spirit.

Some of the foods of the spirit within community are contemplation and meditation, solitude, service, a willingness to surrender to one another, prayer, true imagination and art,

287

compassion and wisdom. Wisdom begins with knowing that we truly are not separate from one another. Realizing the inherent unity that underlies the phenomenal world creates a foundation for the spiritual heights and depths of meditation, contemplation and service. We will not always be able to live from this realization as fully as we want to. But our intention to live toward this realization of unity feeds the soul of community. We have each been born into separate bodies, we have separate identities, personalities, habits, beliefs, patterns of life that we believe to be the definitive parameters of our selfhood. Yet all spiritual traditions tell us that there is much more to the human being—a vast, even infinite divine possibility in fact—but what it takes to open that door is much more demanding and arduous than most people are willing to consider. Those of us who participate in community discover, sooner or later, that inherent in the call to community is the call to greater self-realization. It is up to us individually how we will respond to that call.

As Nietzsche pointed out, our greatest sin is our belief that we are separate. If we are separate from one another we are not responsible to one another. This belief that we are separate numbs the conscience and barricades the heart, and lies at the root of countless merciless wars and acts of horror, violence, vengeance and insanity. The belief that we are separate from each other and from God is found at the core of the perennial philosophy and all great spiritual teachings as the fundamental illusion of the separative ego, which blinds us to the fact of the unity of all existence in the ground of being.

One definition of gossip is "to speak of someone as if he or she is separate from you." If we are separate from the universe, we forget its natural and organic workings and our place in them. All of the suffering in modern society is related to this fundamental inner split, this exile from the true Self, essence, or *Atman* as it is called in traditional Advaita Vedanta Hinduism. But as the ancient *Vedas* tell us, the individuated Self cannot be discovered

288

unless we accept on faith that truly we are all connected because of the fact that all beings are sparks of the same unitive Divine ground, or Brahman. It is this union that Jesus of Nazareth expressed when he said, "I and my father are one."

> *First accept that the Self exists,*
> *and accept that it can be known.*
> *Then Its real nature is open to experience.*
> —Katha Upanishad VI. 13

With an unyielding commitment to creating community in the persistent company of others, we come up against every illusory belief we falsely hold to be true, and particularly the belief that we are separate from each other. Thus, false beliefs may wear away and our sense of the truth grow stronger, but this process must be actively sought and encouraged in community, in spite of the sometimes glaring differences that become painfully obvious, or the often raging disputes that arise between ourselves and others. We cannot allow ourselves to become discouraged and cynical, but must continually find the courage to surrender to the transforming grace of community life, hard edges and all. The questions then become: How will our lives be different if we realize that we are not separate from others, from the universe, from the Divine—if we allow ourselves to know, on a gut level, how completely intertwined we are with one another? And how would the human evolutionary course be effected?

Lee Speaks About Individual and Collective Evolution in Community

That one can realize the truth of the nature of reality is implicit in the experience of community, but community is not necessary for such a realization. The value of community is that the probability of integrating and living out of that realization is protected and

289

nurtured, whereas in society-at-large such a realization is too often considered dangerous, as if it were a virus that needs to be destroyed. Someone who is trying to live that vision genuinely and organically in society is putting themselves in a position of being scorned and distrusted; and thus their possibility of being able to live from such a realization is infinitesimally small. In community, such a vision or spiritual realization is strengthened. In community, the individual is supported to build a foundation and a tenacity for that realization that can sustain tremendous amounts of inevitable stress.

At the place our society is at now, the traditional values of what it is to be a conscious human being and what it is to live in a nurturing human society are being obliterated. The Industrial Revolution was the beginning of the end. On the information highway that we are on now, contemporary technologic breakthroughs are totally destroying everything that is humane in us. The information age is literally using the extraordinary intellectual capacity of the brain to so dominate the other aspects of brain capacity—of what it is to be an organic, self-conscious being— that we're essentially looking at the possible destruction of the entire human race. (In cosmic terms, so what! Big deal! That doesn't mean much. Perhaps in another 50,000 years we would just become like the dinosaurs!) But if we are interested in capitalizing upon the possibility that is the human race, it is crucial that we demonstrate an ongoing evolutionary maturity at all levels of human existence: not just intellect, but the emotional body, the feeling body, the moving body, instinct and so on.

In that sense, community is vital. By its very nature it not only idealizes but demonstrates a lot of the qualities of conscious humanness that have become at best trite and at worst non-existent in human society in this time and place. Such things as compassionate and affectionate care of one another, a recognition of the organic integrity of each human being, recognition of the other as self are non-existent at the level of intellect or mind alone. The obvious demonstration of service, of love, of common nurturing, of non-abusive, non-violent relationships—all that is the evolution of what it is to be human.

Being fully human demands that we incorporate the growth of the intellect into a conscious relationship with those other aspects—feeling, service, love and so on. In ancient tribal society, when the intellect was at a level of potential but not yet highly developed, one could look at the universe and imagine the stars to be holes in the roof of the earth. Now that we understand the physics of astronomy and galaxies and all that, our universal view is not as naive or as primal. But our scientific knowledge has got to be incorporated into the primal aspects of care for the family, the integrity of the tribe, the nature of healing, health, wisdom, and the desires of the heart and the body. Outside of community, the likelihood of that complete vision dawning within people is not small, but the practicality of applying the vision is very unlikely. The probability of it being applied is very small because society's demand to conform in our contemporary age is too seductive and manipulative to resist without the support of community.

One of the criticisms of community is that it is insular, and in one sense it is, but that insularity serves as a protection against the "poisons" of our culture and as a protection for all that is human and heartful. In Chögyam Trungpa Rinpoche's poem offered to his son upon his son's initiation into leadership, one of the lines was "discipline is endless." One of the reasons discipline is endless is because seductions and distractions in our culture and society are endless. In community, qualities such as discipline, discernment, strength of integrity, responsibility and reliability, trustworthiness, integrity of creative vision, compassion, non-abusive relationship, also non-intrusive and non-abusive healing practices—all of those things are supported and encouraged. In community we are educated in those things. These are the kinds of things that are often held in and by community as having great value and sanctity.

291

Whereas in our society-at-large, those things may be given some kind of lip service, but when it comes right down to it they aren't valued at all, because the only things valued are productivity and profit and submission to the politics of the state—regardless of how inhuman and inconsiderate and violent those politics are. Of course in one sense, the state is a community of a large and extended nature. But I am referring to community that is based on the essence of what it means to be a human being, not community based on the flux of social and political waves and what we have created in our ignorance. I am referring to community based on the values of what it means to be fully human.

I absolutely don't think there is any hope for Western society if we don't return to the values of bonded human community. Look at the prophesies for example: in terms of the Hopi prophesy we have already gone beyond the final stage in which the Hopi elder visionaries state that if "this" doesn't happen, it's all over. We're past the point of no return in terms of the prophesies of many sacred cultures, in fact; so if we listen to the prophesies of the greatest oracular traditions in history, society is already finished.

Small bonded communities are like survival capsules, because when society as we know it breaks down, those who have been living in community will not be helpless in the face of doubt, confusion, despair or chaos, and will have tremendous opportunities to serve and assist others with those very qualities of humanness that have been cultivated in community.

The Heart of Compassion

When we live in community with an openness of heart and being, the dawning realization that we are not separate calls forth compassion and the desire to serve in a way we have never experienced before. We begin to deeply experience the inner demand to demonstrate this realization in the details of our everyday lives. The more clearly we see the nature of human

292

beings—through radical self-knowledge—the more profoundly compassion will deepen and mature in us. We do not just know compassion with the intellect or mind, but feel completely, whole bodily, the pain and unconsciousness that we as human beings are living through, and the sorrow and grief we perpetrate upon each other. In feeling this completely, we may glimpse with clarity the freedom that lies beyond that pain and unconsciousness. To walk this tightrope between deep feeling and clarity is compassion.

In compassion we are moved beyond our individual considerations to serve others in whatever way is needed. This doesn't mean we won't have days when we are just completely irritated and impatient with others, when we feel resentful and unwilling to serve. Our understanding sometimes runs out and we forget our vision. Then we must begin again to rebuild our connection with others by going within and reconnecting with our own original vision and sense of higher context and purpose. We cannot overemphasize that this dance between opposites is an ongoing part of the process of community, of life, of individual evolution and of the universe. Just as the universe expands, it also contracts, and so there are cycles of death and birth at all levels of life; in the human sphere, at the same time we recognize our oneness, we are still living and functioning in the world of opposites or polarities. We cannot expect ourselves to never feel anger or hate because these are the other side of a coin called peace and love. The poet Rilke reminded us that if we cast out our demons we cast out our angels also. If we keep our purpose consciously before us, the impulse of the heart will soften our hard edges again and bring us back into alignment with the context of our lives in community. Pseudo-Macarius, a fourth-century Christian monk said it this way: "The heart itself is a small vessel, yet dragons are there, and there are also lions; there are poisonous beasts and all the treasures of evil. But there too is God, the angels, the life and the kingdom, the light and the apostles, the heavenly cities and the treasuries of grace—all things are there." [3]

In Mahayana Buddhism many spiritual practitioners take a vow of compassion called the Bodhisattva Vow. This is a commitment to continue in the cycles of incarnation, through birth and death and rebirth, until all sentient beings have awakened to the liberated condition. This principle can be applied at all levels in our here and now relationships within community, within family, within friendships as we are called daily to put our own needs and wishes aside for the sake of another's more pressing need. Compassion and the recognition of our interrelatedness builds community consciousness, and community consciousness feeds back into the maturation of compassion and sense of oneness with all life within the individual. These spiritual principles— oneness, compassion, unity with all life—are called forth daily within community life, but bringing our glimpses of a greater reality into the field of action and relationship is the key to real fulfillment in life.

Not Outside the Ordinary

Many people today are so desperately seeking a sense of unity, or of spiritual meaning and depth, in lives that are essentially devoid of meaning—cut off from the sacred—that they often search in all the wrong places. Spirituality has become a big business in the U.S., where spiritual artifacts and objects have become commonplace consumer goods; consumerism and marketing strategies mislead us to believe that owning objects or having possessions will imbue our lives with real spiritual meaning. We also seek spiritual substance in the workshop circuit. We think that if we experience a brief high or a passing insight or bliss in a workshop that we have encountered the sacred in a way that will bring some lasting satisfaction to us. Unfortunately, when we return to our daily lives we discover that we are really no different, and that nothing has changed. Malidoma Somé commented on this in one of his lectures:

> . . . some people spend thousands and thousands of dollars every year in spiritual pursuit and they feel like they are just turning in circles. They're not going anywhere. Their spiritual pursuit has become like they're shopping in a mall. They go here to try this out, they try that out, they try this out . . . in the end they don't even know what they have. And so this is the sad part, this initiation over a weekend is really the biggest rip-off one can ever think of, because it damages a soul that is actually sincerely seeking deep transformation. [4]

That longing for deep transformation will only come through an embrace of those gifts of the spirit that, when tended and guarded within the crucible of daily life, will bear the fruits of a soulful life. The great secret of a life made sacred is that the extraordinary is found within the ordinary. This is the opportunity and the gift that is offered to us again and again in community. Where else would the presence of the Divine be, but in the nitty-gritty of day-to-day life? Where else could spiritual transformation be found but in the countless opportunities that present themselves daily to be of service to our families, friends, communities, the greater ecosystem and being of the Earth, and even to the universal or the Divine. There are endless daily chances in community to remember that the Divine is not separate from us but is a part of everything. In the intimate company of others this remembrance of the immanent Divine seems to rise to the surface much more quickly. Each human being is a reflection of the Divine in ordinary life, both roughly and softly reminding us within the texture of the day to listen, to be still, to be receptive to the gifts of the inner life.

Brahman, Thou art One.
Though formless,
through Thine own power,
and for Thine own unfathomable purpose,
Thou givest rise to the many forms.
Though createst the whole Universe from Thyself,
and, at the end of time,
drawest it back within Thyself.
O Brahman, Give us clear understanding.

Thou art woman,
Thou art man.
Thou art the youth,
Thou art the maiden.
Thou art the old man tottering along with his stick.
Having taken form, Thou facest in every direction.

Thou art the deep blue butterfly.
Thou art the parrot, green with red eyes.
Thou art the father of lightning.
Thou art the seasons and the seas.
Unborn,
Thou art everywhere,
And all that is, is born from Thee.
— Shvetashvatara Upanishad IV.1, 3 & 4

Solitude and Contemplation

I call the high and light aspects of my being spirit and the dark and heavy aspect soul. Soul is at home in the deep, shaded valleys. Heavy torpid flowers saturated with black grow there. The rivers flow like warm syrup. They empty into huge oceans of soul. Spirit is a land of high, white peaks and glittering jewel-like lakes and flowers. Life is

sparse and sounds travel great distances. There is soul
music, soul food, soul dancing and soul love . . . When
the soul triumphed, the herdsmen came to the lamaseries,
for soul is communal and loves humming in unison. But
the creative soul craves spirit. Out of the jungles of the
lamasery, the most beautiful monks one day bid farewell
to their comrades and go to make their solitary journey
toward the peaks, there to mate with the cosmos . . .
People need to climb the mountain not simply because it
is there but because the soulful divinity needs to be
mated with the spirit . . .[5]

—The Fourteenth Dalai Lama

Self-knowledge begins by going within—into
silence, into solitude and contemplation, into those moments that
feed the soul but may not be easy to access or to endure. When
we first embark upon the journey within, we have no idea how
difficult it will be to settle down, to shake off the worn mantle of
the frantic world, the obsessive doing, doing, doing, the drive to
win, to get results, to maintain and enhance our "successful" and
"worthy" personhood as society has defined it.

Most of us assume that what we desire or want is "outside"
of our limited selves, and that we must go somewhere else, and
do yet more to get what we need. We are ceaselessly seeking,
looking and hoping for more, when the real life of the spirit is
already present, full and overflowing. It is "something very near
to you, already in your mouths and in your hearts; you only have
to carry it out." (Deut. 13:14) And as Jesus said, "The kingdom
of God is within you." (Luke 17:21) If we stop running around
desperately looking for something outside of ourselves to fix us,
stop trying to design a problem-free life and to relieve our fears,
we can relax, go within and inquire there of the inner life. Such
inquiry leads to self-knowledge through pathways both
profoundly full of wonder and joy and profoundly fierce with

297

heartbreak, uncertainty and darkness. Doing this requires that we be willing to embrace the fact that what we are actually running from—fear, emptiness, uncertainty and even anger and hate—in our endless search for the illusive goal, is an unavoidable part of life. The key to this is what we human beings do with fear, emptiness, anger or hate when it arises in us. Problems arise with these so-called "negative" feelings when we deny them out of self-loathing and then project them on to others. The simple alternative is to "own" these feeling, claim them as our own and then take responsibility for working with them and through them in a way that can feed the fires of our inner life. These very feelings that we run from become grist for the mill of self-awareness and transformation. But in order to enter into this kind of alchemical relationship with all our feelings and emotions we must be willing to experience solitude.

Solitude is sacred. I am not speaking only of being physically alone, but also of being alone internally while in the midst of others. Most of us have a reference point for this kind of experience when at a gathering or party, on the busy street corner or at work we have suddenly glimpsed our aloneness. Neither am I speaking here of loneliness, a very different state of being that typically connotes separation and angst. While being alone may be poignant and bittersweet, perhaps tinged with sorrow at the suffering of humanity, to realize that we are alone even in the midst of the crowded "marketplace" is inherently joyful because in true aloneness we are complete, whole and therefore paradoxically connected to the greater whole.

By nature, community is contemplative. In the company of others we find, if given space, that there is a natural self-reflective mechanism that arises within us—we begin to reflect more deeply on the nature of life, on relationship, and on our own identity within the web of community. The members of all communities, religious or secular, would do well to consciously advocate space and place for their members to contemplate: "space" meaning psychic space and conscious, intentional support for the mood of contemplation; and "place" meaning meditation hall or yoga room, chapel, prayer room, retreat cabins or healing center, or just a room of one's own. To contemplate means to reflect with attention, to gaze intently upon something, or to meditate. When we contemplate we not only bring awareness and clarity to ourselves, we bring the fruits of contemplation back to the whole group.

As human beings we always have the choice of where to place our attention—in other words, what we will contemplate. Whatever we place our attention on strengthens and grows through the nourishing energy brought to bear upon it. In community, where a huge demand exists for one's time and attention—there is always work to be done, someone to care for, some way in which we are called to serve—the workaholics and the social butterflies among us, particularly, must make a serious commitment to making time for meditation or contemplation and to fostering the mood of self-reflection. I actually find that constant activity can be a great impetus toward the contemplation that brings balance and harmony to the whole day. Once we have tasted this kind of harmony and the sweetness that contemplation can bring, then we naturally begin to hunger for more. If I do not carve out the time for inner work, to nourish the soul, I can easily become lost in the concrete forms of a busy life, forms which seem to multiply themselves continuously as I finish one thing and three more stand in its place.

I have talked to many mothers of young children who would love to go off into the desert or forest for a week or two and cannot. I am sure we have all had the desire to spend time in seclusion when our circumstance does not permit it. In this case, our lives demand that we cultivate a state of awareness that offers interior solitude and the contemplative spirit that can underlie activity. In this state of being, where we are not separate from others, physically or otherwise, we stand whole unto ourselves, complete. For many people contemplation means "being in the world but not of the world," so that we are experiencing solitude and inner silence even when our children are playing rambunctiously all around us, the phones are ringing off their hooks, a major project has to be finished by a deadline and three people are talking to us at once. Some spiritual communities recommend solitary retreat for members only after one is able to work fully in the world—as business person, as parent, as artist, or as professional regardless of the field—without being distracted, drained or thrown off balance by it. This means that we do not get caught in the many snares of survival anxiety, or the ongoing seduction of speeding through life to get things done, or the sometimes painful interactions with others with whom we have "difficult" chemistry—people with whom we want to argue and polarize, or for whom we are unable to feel anything but resentment or contempt. To work fully in the world but with balance means that we do not end our day completely exhausted, frazzled and worried. Instead, we work passionately while also being nonattached to results—to success or failure at any level. Easy or difficult relationships can be based in compassion and understanding, even in the face of extreme differences. One of the elements here is working for the sake of work itself and to benefit the whole, rather than working to strengthen our individual position in some way, or out of fear of not surviving.

Bringing the spacious capacity of the contemplative spirit to bear on the travails of modern life is incredibly liberating. When one has a basic—though not necessarily perfect—ability to work in this way, then a foundation has been built for formal retreat and solitude. When we are ready for retreat, support can be provided by the community in the form of food, facilities and whatever else is needed—each community will support its members' desires for solitude in different ways. Going into retreat within the container of community can also give us an added boon: knowing that what feeds the individual also feeds the

300

group, the community's awareness of our intention to retreat is a source of care and attention that will enhance our ability to gain strength and clarity from our solitude.

Communities that do not meditate together may want to consider establishing this as a formal way to participate in the contemplative spirit. Group meditation helps us maintain motivation for practice, something we can easily lose on our own. It has a different "chemistry" than that of solitary meditation. In group meditation one has the energy and alchemy of the larger body upon which to build. A synergy is produced that can directly benefit everyone who participates, while providing intangible benefits to those in community who do not choose to meditate with the group. Group meditation is not exclusive to residential communities; non-residential communities can create a space, even in someone's home, where people can gather at designated times for meditation. Such a gathering may be the first step toward bringing contemplation and silence into the group context and practical effort.

Religious communities often provide more formal and extended retreat opportunities for those who do not live in the community, but who want to set aside time for contemplation and solitude. The Spiritual Life Institute, located near the Sangre de Cristo Mountains in Colorado, is one good example of this. Small cottages that blend invisibly with the ecology of the surroundings are available for retreatants, who may participate in the daily rituals and prayers of the monastery along with the Carmelite nuns and monks who live there, or remain completely solitary during their stay.

Many spiritual communities provide retreat possibilities more informally for their members. One might take a week alone in silence in a small cabin or teepee on an ashram or other community property. In one model that encourages silence and contemplation, designated community members will prepare meals for retreatants, leaving food and water at the retreatant's door. If the retreatant needs anything, he or she can leave a note for the attendant. The structure of time and activities throughout a retreat is highly personal; it may be a time to write, to pray, to meditate, to observe nature, to sing or chant, to do yoga or just to sit in silence and watch the clouds moving through the sky. It may be a time to wrestle with inner conflicts or personal demons, to make a difficult decision, or it may be a time of simple praise and gratitude. For an artist or writer, it can be a time to connect with the creative fires, a time to renew one's own creativity.

Whether or not we have the privilege or opportunity for extended retreat periods, we need to have "mini-retreats" on a regular basis—a short period of silence and solitude or study and contemplation programmed into the day is necessary to feed the soul. In her work as a writer, Alice speaks about what happens when she doesn't create this for herself.

Alice Speaks About the Need for Silence and Solitude

The more communally you live, the more you need solitude. In the midst of a happy but chaotic day of community celebration, a friend of mine once said, laughingly, "I've had all the communion I can take!"

Balance is always needed. Time spent in solitude does not need to be equal to the amount of "togetherness-time," but it should be quality time. Even ten minutes of some kind of solitude in which you connect with your inner life can be enough, even if you're involved with other people all day long.

If I don't take that time for myself, then my art suffers—my poetry, my writing, the creative dimension. I'm very creative in brainstorming with groups, but if that isn't balanced with periods of solitude in which I can be nourished with a different kind of food, then I suffer.

There are many types of solitude that I find nourishing. Solitary study for example is such an enrichment, where I just pore over a text and allow myself to be saturated in it. That solitary feeding enriches and expands me, and because I have been nourished I can then nourish other people with it. I am actually more dynamically in relationship with people because I have been fed. I become someone who has resources to give to others. I notice with others who are doing the same that they become very attractive in community because they supply a unique kind of food. They are desirable in this way because they are just very juicy people.

If I don't take time for solitude my dreams start showing up with images of being lost or not being able to find where I'm supposed to be. When I start feeding that need for solitude again, my dreams change. I was noticing this a few months ago; night after night I was dreaming of being lost, and I realized it was because I had neglected my personal writing time, and when I do that I just get dried out. It's far too easy to neglect this need because I have all these deadlines and projects that have to be completed, but I have to make the time or I lose a connection to the Muse. She, the Muse, requires consistent feeding. If she's missing any of the essential nutrients needed for her diet, then I have to get them back! But this is often a struggle, living in community as I do. There are so many demands on my time! I have to make it a conscious choice and commitment, and sometimes it means that I have to sacrifice sleep or some other activity.

In the Western world, solitude is greatly feared. Facing the void of silence, we become anxious and afraid. We are habituated to distractions and noise because we have denied the life of the soul and have repressed our own feeling life out of fear. Most Westerners will go to any lengths to avoid being silent, alone or introspective because these states bring us into confrontation with our own mortality and the impermanence of life—death too is silent and solitary, and we cannot help being reminded of this fact when solitude and silence are resounding all around us. Our modern lifestyle is, for the majority, a very extroverted affair, which for the most part is geared toward avoiding this kind of deeper self-reflection. Shyness, for example, is practically a stigma for children in our public schools; those who are not at least somewhat aggressive and gregarious are considered different or withdrawn, when in fact they may simply have a naturally contemplative nature. Many children have suffered the pain of being labeled and treated as "outsiders" or "black sheep" among their peers.

Since most children spend up to eight hours a day in front of a television set (the perpetual babysitter), it is no surprise that we are so addicted to noise, input, distractions and constant fascinations of one kind or another. I am always shocked when I visit family members who keep their television and/or radio going twenty-four hours a day. Many homes have televisions in numerous rooms, including kitchen and bathroom, and these too gabble and babble endlessly. Where is the opportunity for inner silence or solitude at home if one is constantly bombarded with the crudest and most inane images, meaningless words and scenarios of petty human interactions? Once we are in the car, where many people spend several hours per day, it is more of the same with the incessant bleating of the radio. This unrefined and insidious noise makes it impossible for the finer, more subtle dimensions of the life of the spirit to dawn upon us, or to pierce through the dense cloud of confusion, trivia and ennui.

When Anne's mother lay dying at home, with her bed set up in the family den, the television ran incessantly, as was the household's habitual way of life. One night Anne's mother weakly lifted her head to look at the actors on the screen, who were enacting a sitcom. In a quiet tone of incredulity and amazement she whispered "Those people are crazy!"

"You're right Mother, they are crazy," Anne affirmed.

For the dying woman the television had finally become not only irrelevant but absurd. It took the demand to turn inward in solitude, which impending death makes, for her to perceive the noise of the constantly droning television set as something intrusive to her basic sanity. Anne watched many similar insights dawn for her mother in the last weeks of her life, as the presence around her became more deeply contemplative day by the day.

No one else can do this work for us; it is we who must face ourselves. No one can die for us, no one can live for us. Understanding this can be one of the great gifts of solitude. We cannot face our own fears and enter into solitude *for* each other but we can support one another going through the process, and this is in place where the understanding and support of community can be a tremendous help in our spiritual life. By looking into the depths of ourselves, we support others in doing the same. And when we know ourselves better, we are able to serve others. There is freedom in knowing ourselves.

At Medicine Pipe Ranch individuals who wanted to spend a day in silence without retreating to complete solitude would hang a small sign around their necks which said "Silence," as a way to remind their companions. My friend Erin made a commitment to be silent for six weeks in the community in which we live. During that time she interacted with everyone, and she was actively involved in many events of the days, but she never spoke a word. Not at any time did she feel out of relationship with anyone because of her practice; in fact, she came more deeply into relationship with others, and communicated quite clearly through other channels—a look, a smile, a gesture. We enjoyed her quiet company a great deal. I found her presence to be a comfort and a constant and benevolent reminding factor to be mindful and thoughtful, to take my speech more seriously, to remember my purpose in the moment, even as I hurried around and chatted, too often mindlessly, with others.

Most indigenous traditions utilize solitude as a primary ingredient of the initiatory experience for adolescents. The Native American tradition of the vision quest is an example of solitude used for transformative purposes. Vision quests were used both as rites of passage for young people entering the adult world, and for adults seeking visions and guidance from the spirit world. Often vision quests also involved austerities such as fasting from food and/or water for three days or more. The Xhosa dancers of Kentani, South Africa, as reported by *National Geographic* in 1925, would initiate their young men by a circumcision ceremony followed by three months of isolation from their families. When the young men appeared within the society again, it was in reed masks and dried palm-leaf skirts, which were then set on fire to signify their new adult status. This tradition continues today in a modified form.[6]

Solitude Feeds the Community

The internal work that one does in community nourishes the whole. While some individuals spend the majority of their lives in solitude and in so doing serve all the world, most monks and nuns, as well as yogis and Eastern ascetics, have come to the conclusion that one must re-enter the marketplace (that is, the community) in some way, not only to test what has been earned in solitude, but to serve others.

The early Christian desert fathers and mothers were examples of this inner journey, as was Henry David Thoreau, who believed that although we are born into community that nurtures and defines and molds us up to a point, we are also obligated to respond to an inner call for solitude and authenticity. Buddha also spent time in solitude, and Jesus Christ is another example of this. He spent forty days and nights in solitude in the desert fasting, but after that returned to Galilee to teach and heal. In an article titled "Surrounded by Water and Dying of Thirst," Lambros Kamperidas discussed this issue of withdrawal and re-entry:

We can only be of use to our community if we withdraw from it and start a pilgrimage of self-discovery. It is only by retreating from the community and distancing ourselves from it that we come to an understanding of ourselves and our potential . . . . This understanding brings about a transformation of our old selves, previously defined—ill-defined perhaps—by the community which gave us our identity, and this transformation allows us to realign ourselves to the world beyond the confines of our community and to rediscover our place in it. Only in this sense can our solitude bear fruit and can our solitary state become public domain. In any other respect our solitude is unproductive and leads merely to depression . . . . Indeed, the solitary who does not return to his community, to enlighten and serve it in a selfless way, may be rightly regarded as having forsaken it and lived in solitude for several years. St. Anthony of Egypt, an inspiration to anchorites of all time, returned to Alexandria after twenty years of seclusion spent in a ruined fortress in the desert. Then, realizing that to continue living in the city would be comparable to the life of a fish on dry land, he decided to go back to the desert, but to make a commitment to see all those who flocked to his cell.[7]

This kind of inner work is not without its difficulties. In fact, in the early Christian era, the word *agon* was commonly used to describe the spiritual struggle of the soul in solitude. This agony was not of a purely psychological nature, but a divine struggle to "overcome" the passions. By this we may assume that the passions are brought into alignment with their divine purpose through the transformative fire of contemplative self-knowledge. As Kamperidis wrote: "In his extreme solitude in the presence of God, the solitary's heart is purified and his senses are restored to

their original purity." [8] Through this kind of tempering in the fires
of interior work, the alchemizing of emotions and feelings (both
so-called *positive* and *negative* emotions and feelings) are transformed in a way that returns them to the organic innocence that
is our God-given birthright. Love, which can be selfish and self-
serving, becomes spontaneous *agape,* or ultimately other-ori-
ented and altruistic; anger and hate, which are bitter, violent and
destructive, become an expression of our ability to make appropriate distinctions, and of our caring and commitment when we
sense or see that a necessary boundary or principle has been
intruded upon or violated; depression, which can be the result of
meaninglessness, boredom and abstract angst at the inner emptiness that is basic to human nature, can become a conscious relationship to true emptiness, what the Buddhists call *shunyata,* or
the rainbow-like void out of which all life arises. Silence is the
sound of *shunyata,* and it is a silence that can be heard within
the midst of the noisy display of life running rampant. Silence is
the core, the seed within solitude that blossoms into emptiness;
the divine state so sought after in all of the world's great spiritual
traditions.

Emptiness

> Achieving emptiness means emptying ourselves of what-
> ever is standing between us and community . . . Once a
> group becomes sufficiently empty, then community comes
> in as a gift of the spirit.
>
> —M. Scott Peck

M. Scott Peck, psychiatrist and noted author on
psychology, spiritual life and community, spoke in an interview of
the basic phases in the building of community. The first he calls
pseudo-community: in this phase members usually mask their
deeper, genuine feelings with pleasantries and small talk.

We chit-chat about the weather, about our teenage daughter's high-school football team, about our college years long past, or about a movie we saw recently. We often "hide out" in this kind of ostensibly easy-going, light but superfluous level of relationship because of our fears of intimacy and of unleashing our own inner demons. The second phase comes when the members tire of superficialities. Now they allow conflicts to emerge, make attempts to change each other, and the result is chaos as the walls and barriers of the socially correct *persona* come tumbling down. In this stage we struggle and argue, judge each other and project our own shadows onto the other. We fear that our group will not make it; we suddenly don't like each other so much. We become psychologically constellated by the habits and personalities of others. We are still attempting to be individually "right" and "on top" of the situation, to defend our personal territory. Community is still defined, though unconsciously, by the politics of social domination, selfishness and greed—which is a contradiction in terms and cannot work for very long because the innate impulse of community is toward unity and the common good.

According to Peck, communities that function as open systems will survive the chaos and breakdown of this second stage and re-order at the next evolutionary stage. In this third stage members begin to set aside their preconceived prejudices, biases, defenses and other barriers to real relationship, intimacy and communion. In this setting aside of the "ten thousand things" that crowd and cloud our vision, an inner emptiness begins to dawn. We have used up the games we play with one another—the dramas, the niceties, the fighting, the flirting. All of the games of ego have been emptied out and our instinctual draw toward one another as human beings becomes present. Out of emptiness, real community can begin to blossom. Unmotivated by self-interest, relationship begins to take on the shine of real essence, and communion arises spontaneously in moments when we least expect it, sometimes with those that we had the most difficulty with before.

But this can only happen when we begin to empty ourselves of the assumptions, prejudices and conclusions we have drawn that obscure reality as it is. When we empty ourselves of all of this, it allows room for the miraculous, the extraordinary, the breathtakingly new and possible to arise.

In my experience, moving through these stages is not a strictly linear process. In fact, we may weave in and out, and repeat the stages again and again in a spiraling dance in which we continually refine and go deeper together. Community, like all natural systems, reflects the pattern of the physics of the universe, which expands and contracts in pulsations of cyclic time. So, even (or especially) after a time of breakthrough and expansion, when the nectar of communion has flowed like wine among us, we may well find ourselves back at what seems like the beginning—contracted, superficial and scared to trust. We should not be discouraged by this, but should realize the nature of evolution. In an open system we constantly purify, clarify and distill the essence of our lives together.

Community is a natural expression of the interconnected patterns of life, and its inherent possibility is always present as soon as we empty ourselves to receive it. As Westerners, and particularly as consumer-mad Americans, we are filled up, stuffed to overflowing with anything and everything. We are so full that we have no room left inside for anything new, and life holds no surprises for us. There is a parable that speaks symbolically of this overblown, grandiose and stuffed existence, and why we might want to consider emptiness as a necessary part of our evolutionary process. A brilliant intellectual decided that he wanted enlightenment, and so sought to become the disciple of a Buddhist teacher. The man was escorted into the master's quarters to take tea with him. Holding his cup out, the man watched as the *roshi* poured tea, filled the cup, and then kept pouring and pouring while the tea overflowed copiously. The would-be disci-

ple put the cup down. "Why did you do that?" he asked in aston-
ishment.

The master replied, "You came here seeking a teaching, but
your cup is too full to receive anything. If you want the teaching,
you must first empty your cup." His action was the concrete
demonstration to the student that before he could begin his quest
for enlightenment and wisdom, he would have to become empty.

Like the student in this story, we all find ourselves in a similar dilemma. We begin to enter into contemplation and meditation only to find that our minds are glutted with trivialities and
conflict, and our bodies are caught up in the chemistry of nervous tension and the fight for survival—mind and body feeding off
each other in an endless cycle of overwrought activity. Slowly, as
we divest ourselves of assumptions, presumptions and the assurance that we know—and therefore control—everything in ourselves and in our environment, an openness begins to dawn
within us. We suddenly have room inside for something completely new. A simple spaciousness begins to spread within, making room for the refreshing wind of innocence to blow through.
This is a process of deconstruction, which takes conscious
thought, effort and self-knowledge. We cannot live in a psychological bubble of denial, projecting all of our unknown aspects
onto others, and still create the kind of inner emptiness that
makes us receptive to radical change. As we deconstruct the
habits and false beliefs gathered and fortified from childhood on,
we begin to wonder who we are. This can be a terrifying experience, but trust and faith in the goodness and ultimate divinity of
our own human nature will see us through.

In the Buddhist tradition, all phenomena, or the manifest
world, is considered to be essentially empty; this emptiness, or
shunyata, is the enlightened perspective—not a nihilistic emptiness, but a divine emptiness that is also, paradoxically, often
described as rainbow-like, luminous, clear. When *shunyata*
dawns within the soul, the individual becomes transparent to the

Divine in a way that produces an inner radiance, and one acts spontaneously from instinctual wisdom which is at the same time empty but completely whole, in relationship and responsible to the environment.

This sounds great, but again it takes hard work and self-discipline. Becoming empty is a process of deconstructing the illusory nature of one's separative identity, which at a practical level may begin with close observations of one's habits. This might involve learning to refrain from habitual talking, which many of us use as a way to defend ourselves from reality. Through constant, habitual chatter, joking, teasing, laughter or gossip, we are distracted and self-absorbed in a way that keeps us from being truly present with what is arising in the moment. To deconstruct this habit, we might decide that when we disagree with what someone is saying we will choose to stay quiet rather than respond or straighten the person out on our personal view of things. Seeking emptiness, we often find that we must let go of our most treasured opinions and aspects of ourselves, and for many people who believe they are being jovial and spontaneous, the behavior is really an obsession run by a deep-seated need to be at the center of group attention. In order to break through this kind of psychological obsession, we may need to become less demonstrative and visible. On the other hand, someone who tends to shy away from the group and always wants to be alone may have to become more involved and present in group discussions. Another person who loves to dominate through always knowing the right way to do things may have to let others do things in their own way without voicing any criticism. Making these kinds of personality changes creates an inner friction and tension that can lead to a radical kind of letting go; as the inner friction mounts, it becomes so dissonant and unpleasant to our true impulse of being that we reach the point where we have to let go of our old structures and habits. In this way we are deconstructed and left empty for the newly arising, essential self.

312

Emptiness makes room for a sense of the Divine to come in. It makes room for spirit; before that we are too often filled up with our own illusions. Two things can't occupy the same space at the same time; when selfishness is there, selflessness can't be. One thing that I have found in community is that each time we cycle through falsity and chaos into emptiness, we are at a more mature level of understanding, and therefore we have a greater capacity to capitalize on the potential at hand. As we cycle through each series of stages, after a certain number of rounds on the wheel of community experience, the stage of chaos doesn't last so long because we are able to go through it with self-assurance.

Simplicity

Simple things are always the most difficult. In actual life
it requires the greatest art to be simple.

—Carl Jung

As we begin to catch glimpses of inner silence and emptiness, we may find that we just naturally stop neurotically amassing things. Simplicity becomes the natural outgrowth of a life that has slowed down and become more inwardly focused in an attitude of quiet. Raised within the opulence and unconscious greed of a consumer lifestyle, many Americans may think of simplicity as being the starkest austerities—a crust of bread, a tin cup of water, a bowl of gruel—but life can be very rich and full and yet extremely simple in form.

A few years ago I started asking myself the question, what do the Christian ascetics mean by true poverty? I cannot pretend to know the answer to that question, but I have come to understand that poverty in this sense is meant symbolically, and infers a blessed state of being. Perhaps true poverty has to do with simplicity, which to me means living with elegance—not taking more than is needed of anything, conserving energy and resources, respecting ourselves and others, maintaining an attitude of sensitivity and alert receptivity to spaces, places, people and things. Simplicity brings natural beauty into our lives—into what we create and into the smallest actions we take, and penetrates as well into the psychological realm. Simplicity itself becomes an intangible food source, a great pleasure and joy as we drop the shackles of meaningless complexities and our search to get more from the convoluted labyrinth of accessories and other useless stuff and junk—not to mention the worry and guilt, which are the irksome, heavy, sometimes agonizing but always unnecessary, psychic baggage of our times.

Often, my excesses stem from my haste—when I am running from being with myself. When I am hurrying around the most is when I tend to seek more extravagant foods, entertainment to the point of satiation and distraction from any real meaning or purpose, impulsive purchases of things I do not really want or need. I am not suggesting that we should never have beautiful possessions or good entertainment or sumptuous desserts, but that the motivation behind acquiring them could spring from real enjoyment and appreciation rather than from a desperate attempt to avoid becoming more self-aware.

Mass mindless consumption of products is our culture's illusory search for something that we already have. It prevents us from being present in the moment because we are too busy seeking the next brief high of acquiring or consuming yet another thing. Consumerism clutters our lives and makes junkyards of our psyches, whereas simplicity lends a physical and psychic spaciousness to our lives and connects us with nature. A room that is well-appointed with a few exquisitely placed pieces of furniture or decorative touches—a room that is also kept clean and orderly—evokes a very different response from us than a room that is disheveled and messy, where piles of discarded clothes, books, papers, used dishes or toys are heaped up without thought or care.

Community is often a call to downsize, or cut to the bone. If we live in a residential community, we often give up having a much larger range of territory in which we can multiply and hoard our possessions, like a dragon sitting on a pile of gold. Community asks us to be more simple, to simplify our lifestyles because now each decision we make must consider the whole group, and involves a context of selflessness, whereas previously we could think only of ourselves and our psychologically driven needs systems. Community calls us to an ecology of elegance— not only to support the ecological concerns of our planet, but the ecological concerns of the soul, which are intricately connected and mutually supportive.

Just by considering what simplicity might be and applying that inquiry to every area of our lives, we develop conscious awareness as to where changes can be made. For instance, we can start by looking objectively at one room in one building, asking ourselves how to create more space there—space that makes room for silence, reflection, contemplation. For example, maybe our looking will inspire us to take a course in Zen flower arranging so that we can create arrangements for the community meditation hall or meeting room.

I remember with great joy the times when I have traveled and lived cheaply, having little in the way of personal possessions to buffer me from raw experience. This recollection provides an excellent point of reference for me in considering how to apply simplicity to my life in community. With clothing, for instance, a valuable piece of advice once came to me from a businessman who said, "If you haven't worn it in the last six months give it away!" For those of us who live in community, another practical approach to simplifying our lives may mean that we limit our trips around town, letting one designated person take care of individual errands, or at least joining with others in limiting the use of vehicles. Not only does this conserve energy more wisely, but it also relaxes personal tension and helps creates more psychic space—one small step in cutting back on the onrush of speedy activity that can dominate our lives. Certainly country life supports simplicity more than urban life because nature is a perfect expression of simplicity and harmony within cycles of creation and destruction, but even in an urban environment we can find many ways to practice simplicity.

Contemplation in resonance with nature can be our inroad into a deeper ecology of the heart, mind and soul, to a wholeness found in perfect simplicity of form and function. Thoreau said it this way: "The indescribable innocence and beneficence of Nature—of sun and wind and rain, of summer and winter—such health, such cheer, they afford forever! . . . Shall I not have intelligence with the earth? Am I not partly leaves and vegetable mould myself?" Through a conscious relationship to ourselves, to others and to our activities we can stay in relationship with the Earth.

Simplicity helps bring our attention to an awareness of the deeper presence that imbues each moment. In the Vajrayana Buddhist tradition there is a principle of creating sacred spaces or relating with the environment that involves our ability to perceive and draw out the *drala* of all things. *Drala* refers to the deepest nature and energy of any object, person, thing or place, which is perceived by means of placing one's focused attention. Attention, when purified, simplified and focused, brings one into direct contact with an extraordinary richness of perception and experience that does not depend on concrete terms or material opulence. This *drala,* or the magical essence of all things, is what can be discovered through simplicity of life; rather than rendering life stark and bare, we have the marvelous opportunity to see and perceive the beauty and wonder underlying and inherent within that which is ordinary in life—the droning bumble bee who happily robs the complice flower of her nectar, the children playing on the grass, the steam arising from a full teacup, the curve of our lover's neck.

316

This new perception brings a passion and a depth to our life in community as well, because suddenly the simplest acts, the simplest things are imbued with great pleasure. In this way, working side by side in the garden or chopping vegetables in the kitchen, our communion and shared understanding of this very simple pleasure becomes something much greater and more fulfilling than a hard workout in the morning sun or yet another plain meal in the communal kitchen. We can come to treasure and deeply appreciate the salad and simple soup, rather than always having to have the six-course gourmet meal; then, when the time for grand celebration comes, the enjoyment of the feast is heightened a hundred-fold.

Service—The Art of Giving

> Freedom of will is the ability to do gladly that which I must do.
>
> —Carl Jung

When the separative walls break down, we begin to realize that serving others is serving ourselves. But this is not an easy process, because although the impulse to serve is natural to the human spirit, we have been trained in a paradigm that says service is demeaning. This prejudice against serving is not without good reason, because for thousands of years those with the privileges of wealth and societal power have exploited those without. Servitude in abject slavery and/or oppressed poverty has tainted thousands of years of human interactions throughout the world's cultures, the memories of which lay dormant but very present within the cells of the human body. Here is another area where re-visioning is necessary in order to glean the gifts of the spirit, in which service to others plays an integral role.

We may also feel resentful that some are more able or willing—for whatever reason—to serve the common good than others are able or willing. In the Rule of St. Benedict, a guideline for life in religious community, we read the following wise words: "Whoever needs less should thank God and not be distressed . . . whoever needs more should feel humble because of his weakness, not self-important because of the kindness shown him." [10] Taking this advice to heart, we might find the humility, in the face of the grand design of life, to suddenly realize how unusual it is to have the opportunity to really serve another human being. As Kathleen Norris writes, "None of us can understand what possible use we are in this world; it's one of the deeper mysteries. Rarely, grace comes to us in the form of another person who tells us we have been of help." [11]

Bob Dylan once wrote a song that exhorted his listeners to face the fact that we've all got to serve somebody. The idea is that everyone serves some principle of life, whether it is devil or angel. If we are all serving something or someone—the question is, who or what? Are we only self-serving? Do we serve unconsciousness, or do we serve the impulse toward evolution through growing consciousness? Do we serve the idols of success, wealth, status, achievement, recognition? Do we serve the dark lords of power, fear, anger and pride? Or do we serve a more altruistic purpose? This is an area in which it is easy to fool ourselves. It takes a tremendous commitment to self-honesty to answer that question for ourselves with a bone-hard truth. How can we get clear about who and what our lives are dedicated to serving? One way to investigate this is to look at the details of our daily lives. Do we make time for others, or are we just too busy to help out our partners, our children and friends, or even a stranger? The last time someone asked you to do something for them, did you say yes or no, and for what reason? What principle or ethic is important to you, what is it exactly that informs your decisions?

A Dagara elder once said to Malidoma Somé, "The sweat of one person has significance only when it serves everybody." [12]

Perhaps in these jaded and decadent times, ideas like altruism, devotion, surrender of self to serve the good of another or of the whole are not considered "politically correct," but the prevailing attitude of nihilistic cynicism is deadly to the life of the soul. How can we possibly expect to save our severely endangered planet if we are not able to stop serving our own comfort and gratification with the wanton abuse of resources? How can we expect the flame of consciousness to catch on fire if we are unwilling to do our part toward building a world that is based on a vision of the sacred, and then take practical steps toward embodying that?

Once we get clear about what we *are* serving in our daily lives, then we can begin to make necessary adjustments. We can begin to open up and become more available to the needs of others. We can extend ourselves to be of assistance in a hundred ways, many of them quite invisible. No one is going to give us a medal for serving invisibly and quietly, for picking up the tasks that have been dropped by someone else, for soothing the anxious child; no one is going to put our picture in the paper for finally making the time to set up that recycling system for our household or community. We are not going to get fame and fortune through our efforts to be of help, but these small acts of generosity and kindness have much bigger repercussions than we can imagine.

The Sanskrit word *seva* translates as service, but infers the work of a disciple who, hoping for spiritual realization, chooses to prove herself or himself worthy through selfless service. In English, the verb *to serve* has at least fifteen different definitions, but the one we are considering here is that of bringing aid, assistance or help to another, or to pay reverent honor to another, as in an act of devotion to a higher purpose or vision. Service is an opportunity given to us in community to deeply feed the soul. If we are honest with ourselves, we find that the times we are truly happiest are times when we are serving others. As we find joy in giving a special gift to someone we love, service is also a gift given, whether it is making a tired partner a cup of tea, giving a massage, cooking a meal, or running an errand.

In community, opportunities to serve in small ways abound throughout our day: providing extra help on a project whose deadline is encroaching on a busy co-worker; offering to be with the children while a weary mother takes a much-needed nap; listening quietly and offering non-judgmental understanding to a friend; driving our teenagers around town, or playing Monopoly for two hours with a restless nine-year-old when we have a thousand other pressing things to do. It is also a form of service to offer non-judgmental honesty to a friend who is asking for feedback. Through service we are given the chance to be used completely in a way that engages our hands and heart in right activity that feeds the soul.

Consciously directed service springs from compassion, and demands that we focus our attention on something bigger than our own petty problems and agendas. This focus enables us to serve something greater than even the individuals involved; our service can be bigger than people and places—it can be a vehicle for serving the immanent Divine that resides within all forms.

I have asked myself questions about service for years: Is service solely the physical actions done to benefit others? Are we serving in times of solitude, prayer or even rest? Can every action we make be an action done in service? Is it possible to serve the Divine in ordinary life? I think there are no straightforward answers to them. However, when I keep the questions "cooking" inside, while I honor the place in myself that instinctively knows when and how to serve, I am most satisfied. Sometimes the most obvious way I can serve those I love is to take an afternoon nap, or spend an hour reading or regenerating my own energies in some way that refreshes my own capacity to give. In order to freely give, we must also be able to freely receive, so it is equally important that we be able to see and receive the gestures of generosity and care that are extended to us in and by our community.

At some point, considerations about service all seem to overlap and weave together. The distinctions are no longer important; what is important is that I simply serve, for that is where my heart lies, and is a tangent point to the life of the soul.

I am also spiritually fed by the many demonstrations of service that I witness in others. When I see my friends taking the time to serve one another or myself, I am deeply moved. Within community, the mutual caring and concern that informs our acts of service are felt as a connecting flow of energy, a circuitry of shared life. Each act of service builds upon the last, and a momentum is created which carries the group forward into greater heights of compassion, generosity and kindness.

The need for service in community can seem endless. While I have certainly complained about this constant draw on my energies, I have also been grateful. When I am faced with my own neurotic dramas, I want to pull back from everyone and collapse. But if I know that thirty hungry people are depending on me to cook their lunch, then I am drawn out of my self-obsession and by necessity thrust back into relationship with others. It is common to feel conflict around sacrificing one's own needs or private time to serve others, but the miraculous thing about serving others is that it all comes back in multiplied blessings in one form or another, often nonlinearly.

Sometimes we serve others by simple acts of surrender which are necessary to keep community running smoothly. Our preferences of how we would set up our own living situation, how we might run many things, when we might want quiet, when we might want conversation or not, when to eat, what to eat and how it's prepared—all these things may need to be sacrificed in community in order to participate in what works best for the group as a whole. Of course, these small surrenders are called for in all walks of life—in the workplace, certainly in the singular family and in all kinds of relationship—but community can often force these issues out into the open where a spotlight gets put on them. This is a principle connected to the ideals and reality of transcendence, to the gifts of the spirit, and yet it is practiced through simple daily decisions. In talking about going out to dinner with her husband, my friend remarked that in choosing where to go, it is more important to have communion between them than to have her preferences "win," so she happily surrenders to her partner.

Service and sacrifice are often inextricably intertwined. As we put aside total self-absorption and self-interest, we discover the true meaning of sacrifice—"to make sacred." Carl Jung once wrote, "From that sacrifice we gain ourselves—our 'self'—for we have only what we give." [13] We build community in this dance of service, surrender and sacrifice. The gift lies in the conscious choice to surrender and serve. When we choose communion with others over and against a self-centered, isolated existence, we are building a foundation that supports the full flowering of a unified and blessed life, and we are reminding ourselves of the distinction between that which is real and endures, and that which is the passing illusion. This is part of how community connects the individual with the sacred.

Prayer

> To explore into God is prayer.
>
> —David Steindl-Rast

Considering prayer is the strongest antidote to a lack of faith. Prayer is vital to our lives. Genuine prayer is the single most important ingredient in the survival of the sacred elements of humanness that are still existing, however tenuously, in our world today. Genuine prayer is a matter of heart, not mind. It is perhaps not so much about asking for boons and blessing, but about praise and adoration of the splendor and magnificence of the Divine in our lives. Prayer may be intangible to many of us, but it literally has substance and force, and physically affects the nature of life on the face of the planet. In one form or another, every community should be involved at heart with prayer. It could be traditional and ritualistic, or very formal in the context of ceremony and symbol and so on, but prayer could also simply be the compassion with which one serves others. Genuine service always has some element of prayer in it, even if there is no conscious acknowledgement of that. When there are numbers of people involved, as in communal prayer, the energy of the group magnifies whatever real prayer is going on. If only one person in the group is genuinely praying in relationship to the Divine, then the energy of the group magnifies that. Group prayer is sort of like the difference between a 5000-watt transmitter and a 50,000-watt transmitter.

Amazing Grace, a book by Jonathan Kozol, gives a wrenching description of life among the poor in the South Bronx, New York. It is not only an account of the adversity, brutality and prejudice faced there daily, but also a commentary on the resilience and power of the human spirit, and the community that has been created in the midst of this violent microcosm of the human condition in the modern world. When Kozol was interviewed on National Public Radio he was asked what he thought one could do to serve the people of this South Bronx community. He recommended that one attend his or her local church more.

Why would a man like Kozol who was not necessarily deeply "religious" by his own admission give an answer like that? Perhaps because while social action is of great value, the suffering of humankind originates at a much deeper place—the same place that the longing for the sacred, for the Divine, issues from. In the same spirit, many poets, theologians, artists and scientists from all fields—physicists, biochemists, ecologists, psychologists—are saying that we cannot save our world at this point by directing our efforts at remedial actions which attempt to alleviate

323

any one aspect of the overall problem. According to these "movers and shakers," it is going to take a much deeper view of the holistic and sacred nature of life itself to catalyze change.

In their book, *Belonging To The Universe*, Fritjof Capra and David Steindl-Rast share their conversation about many things, including asceticism and prayer. At one point, Capra asks Steindl-Rast, "How do you understand asceticism?' to which Steindl-Rast replies, "As practices which help to prepare oneself for religious experience. Various meditation experiences, for example. Of fasting, which is gaining new popularity today. Or simply the cultivation of a sense of gratefulness in one's life, gratefulness for colors and sounds and smells and textures. Here the goal is to make one more alive by making the senses more alive." [14] This is a prelude to religious experience, and is connected to bringing prayer back into the life of the body.

Gratitude, reverence and the mood of devotion or worship invokes the ecstasy of the body, and it is this full spectrum of prayer that shouts from every cell of the body that is necessary to the hope of the world.

Bernadette Speaks About Prayer

Hatha yoga opened up a whole new domain of prayer for me; I literally had no idea that prayer could be the full expression of the body. Even though I knew philosophically that all of our daily work could be prayer, I wasn't liberated enough in the body to know that the body itself could be prayer. Through my experience in spiritual communities, from convent to ashram, I have learned that if the body, mind and heart are connected, then everything can be prayer. Over the years my relationship to prayer, both solitary and communal, has become much more all-encompassing and organic.

My life now incorporates many experiences of prayer in daily communal periods of meditation, group chanting and celebratory song in praise of the Divine. Every practice of my day, either alone or with the people I work with in community, is a form of worship and prayer. This is not formalized in ritual, but is a mood and intention that one is called to embody through remembrance of the Divine.

As for personal prayer, Mother Tessa of the Spiritual Life Institute talks about "stealing time for our prayer." For most of us busy people the only time we're going to be able to steal for solitary contemplation is from our sleep. Because we are so active—working in the world and with our families—we are not going to have the kind of contemplative opportunity we need and hunger for if we don't do that. I've heard stories of women with three or four children who have to get up an hour or more before the children arise if they want to have any kind of personal time to feed themselves with silence, solitude, prayer or meditation. That's not easy to do when many nights the children may also have been restless or sick or just needing mother's presence. But this is the kind of commitment it takes for us to have prayer in our lives.

In other words, monks and nuns have been doing this kind of committed spiritual life for hundreds of years, and quite well. They've really got it down! When I was a nun, there was always lip service paid to the fact that everyone should be doing this kind of constant prayer within home and family. But to actually bring consciousness to one's daily life in the raising of children or working to support home, family and community is incredibly demanding—it really is an intensive spiritual practice.

Several members of our community write, compose and perform rock and roll and blues songs—which for me is a form of communal worship through dance, music, ecstasy. There have been many times when I have found myself in a profound state of prayer during these celebrations of music and dance. This is prayer in the body. One can easily make a case for whatever music is contemporary to the times and culture being the form that is used for prayerful invocation in any given religious society. Rock & roll, for

325

example, is connected to the very rich tradition of music, song and dance that can be abundantly found in holy life. For example, the psalms of David were songs, accompanied by the lyre, which addressed many facets and dimension of earthly life—love, war, sorrow, anger, worship and prayer. The Islamic Sufis whirl and dance in prayer to drum-based music that some would consider quite erotic, and the Hindus also have religious music that is sensual and evocative of many different emotional states. The African-American Christian charismatic church is another great example of an effortless, spontaneous and natural expression of ecstatic prayer through dance and song. Many Christian churches today are looking toward contemporary music as the musical expression that speaks most directly and effectively to their congregations.

As a student of Osho Rajneesh I got the first inkling that to be a sexual being was possibly sacred. This understanding was incredible to me because there was so much fear of sexuality in my Catholic upbringing—it was all so fear and guilt-associated. That realization is being offered to me now within my present community—that sexuality can be prayer. Obviously I am not talking about communal sex, but sexuality as prayer experienced as an ongoing dimension of relationship within a couple can feed the whole community in many intangible ways. This too is an important way in which we must bring prayer back into the body in radical terms.

If we bring prayer back into the body then there is a clearer recognition of our bodily connectedness to the Divine, which is absolutely necessary to our evolution as creatures. How can we respect the Earth when we are so out of touch with our own bodies? How can we find the Earth sacred when we don't know that our own bodies are sacred? The elements of the Earth are flowing through our very veins—our tears are salty, our blood is salty like the ocean—but most of us just don't really make the connection at a gut level. Our ability to move and work and participate on the Earth with creativity and ultimate sanity depends on a deepening of this context and understanding. Although one's specific path may not involve political or ecological activism, it still must come out of a context of ultimate respect for and recognition of one's connection to the Earth.

Larry Dossey, M.D., and others are proving that the people who are prayed for—even if they don't know that they are prayed for, and even at a distance—have a higher success rate in their operations and in their cancer therapy. What is that saying? That there is a dimension in which our prayer is affecting the world. Many people have known that for thousands of years, but now we are proving it in the laboratory, in scientific terms. Someone like Thomas Merton would have been insane to sequester himself away for an entire lifetime if it were not possible that such a life could change the world. His writings reveal a deeply sane person of great wisdom, of profound conscience and concern for all of life. The spiritual communities, the monasteries and ashrams of the world have not abandoned the world to destruction, but have become more deeply committed, have in fact dedicated their lives to the salvation of the world, the planet, humanity. That tradition of conscientious renunciation within spiritual community is found in every great religion that has a branch of mystics and contemplatives. When we study them it is very rare to find that they stay only in the mystical ethereal realm of relationship to a Divine Beloved. Most of them that I've studied or personally known have a vision of the sacred that is inclusive, unifying and all-embracing. There is a conscious awareness that they are actually bringing the world to a place of greater sensitivity and greater consciousness through their own inner life.

Organized religion today has lost, to a great degree, this understanding of prayer as spontaneous mystery, which is a whole body experience. Carl Jung said, "For living matter is itself a transformer of energy, and in some as yet unknown life participates in the transformation process," pointing toward the mystery also of the human body and its capacity for transformation of a kind that cannot be understood rationally. [15] By associating it with sin, the bodily experience of ecstasy was effectively outlawed by Christianity, and particularly Protestantism, hundreds of years ago, and in its place we have been given a very limited relationship to what prayer can be. Or, as in Islam, Judaism and Hinduism, ecstasy has been designated the exclusive territory of men, while women are expected to sit elsewhere, tend the children and the hearth, and carry out their spiritual impulses in private. So many people have been turned off to the idea of prayer because of the dogmatic, stultifying forms in which it is found is many religions.

Prayer is a universal act of the human spirit that cannot be legislated in religious terms. It is an impulse of the heart that is more than supplication and complaint. Prayer is poetry; it is gratitude, praise and awe. Prayer is song and dance and rapture and ecstatic witness to the beauty and divinity in life. Worshipful prayer is not the exclusive domain of any particular tradition. Rather, it is our birthright as human beings to reflect, converse, commune and even dance with the Divine in whatever form is authentic to us.

In communal or shared prayer, we speak in the language of the heart, in silence or in song, and find that our hearts can beat as one. The force of our combined prayerful mood in community has far-reaching effects that are unmeasurable and completely intangible, and yet one can sense into and intuit that some universal, vast Presence hungers for our combined prayers, and is calling them forth in these dangerous times. It is going to take much more than trying to fix or remedy the world's problems one at a time to create a world worthy of our great grandchildren. It is going to take a radical shift, a fundamental change, a miracle fueled by many people who have combined their hearts and prayers and energies in a common goal, a common vision. It is our prayers—in song and dance, in lovemaking, in meditation, in solitude, in gratitude and praise, and even in washing the dishes or planting the garden—that can make a difference in the world as it is today.

The Navajo people have many beautiful and complex ceremonial songs, chants and prayers that mirror the complex relationship between human beings, nature and the Divine. This relationship seems to be captured in the Navajo word *hózhó*, which, although not translatable into English, generally refers to the radiance and profound attributes perceived in nature and of humankind's relationship to it.[16] The prayer ceremony *hózhóójí*, or Blessingway, can be translated as "the way to secure an environment of perfect beauty," and at the heart of which are a number of chants addressed to the spirit that dwells in all forms, most obviously in all things living.[17]

> The so-called "Navajo Prayer to the Internal Forms of the Earth," also known simply as the "Earth's Prayer," is a pivotal world-rejuvenating prayer to the vital spiritual core of each element in nature. The proper recitation of its sacred passages returns the environment in its totality to a primal state of hózhó. Through its reenactment, the original acts of creation are repeated and the world is re-created . . . Thus, in the minds of many traditional Navajo, the "Earth's Prayer" resonates throughout the whole world and across boundless expanses of time, summoning forth the sacred beauty and innate harmony that existed in primordial earth during the era of creation . . . In the Western literary tradition, the microcosm of a single grain of sand can resonate [symbolically] with the

meaning of the whole cosmos; just so in Navajo prayer the blessing of a tiny part of the universe is sufficient to bless the whole.[18]

Similarly, the Kayapó of the Amazon in Brazil come together to dance in a ceremonial circle, "they know that they are dancing to preserve and sustain the structure and integrity of the entire natural world." [19]

The Western world must enter into the sacred knowledge held for so many thousands of years by indigenous people, combine it with the knowledge of science and the arts that are the signposts our times, our culture and consciousness, and then allow this to evolve as a cohesive whole. We have got to come back together, to gather our scattered fragments and coalesce as an organic, interconnected totality.

Community in the postmodern era of Western culture is a necessary part of this gathering back together, this sense of belonging and therefore of responsibility. This may sound ridiculously idealistic in the face of global destruction and wide scale war and suffering, but as Buckminster Fuller once said, "The world is now too dangerous for anything less than Utopia." We really have no choice but to go forward with a radical vision of what is possible. Community enjoined within the context of the ultimately sacred is necessary to restore the natural order. What else is going to make it possible for humanity, in this moment of chaos—poised as we are at the brink of possible extinction—to reorder at a higher and more complex level of functioning?

Black Elk said, "It may be that some little root of the sacred tree still lives. Nourish it then, that it may leaf and bloom and fill with singing birds." The sacred tree is a universal metaphor for the world axis, the center of the world that has its roots in the earth and its topmost branches in heaven. The still living roots of the sacred tree lives in the soil of every community; if we nourish it through conscious acts—which may lead to a deep sense of unity and transformation as the organic foundations of our lives—it will blossom and produce the fruits of spiritual evolution within individuals who have bonded together in community, in an ever-widening circle of life and wholeness.

> *OM*
> *That is the Whole.*
> *This is the Whole.*
> *From wholeness emerges wholeness.*
> *Wholeness coming from wholeness,*
> *wholeness still remains.*
>
> —*The Upanishads*

ENDNOTES

CHAPTER 1

[1] Durning, A.T., *How Much is Enough* New York: W.W. Norton and Co., 1992, p. 23.

[2] Ibid., p. 38.

[3] Ibid, p. 43.

[4] Ibid, p. 46.

[5] Ibid, p. 73.

[6] Mariana Caplan is the author of seven books including: *Untouched: The Need for Genuine Affection in an Impersonal World* (1997), and *Halfway Up the Mountain: The Error of Premature Claims to Enlightenment* (1999) and *The Way of Failure* (expected Spring, 2001).

[7] Suzuki, D. and P. Knudtson *Wisdom of the Elders: Honoring Sacred Native Visions of Nature* New York: Bantam Books, 1992, pp. 58-59.

[8] Ibid., p. 58.

[9] Ibid., p. 61.

[10] Devall, B. and G. Sessions *Deep Ecology: Living as if Nature Mattered* Layton, Utah: Peregrine Smith Books, 1985, p. 8.

[11] Capra, F. and D. Steindl-Rast *Belonging to the Universe* San Francisco: HarperSanFrancisco, 1991, p. 70

[12] Lozoff, B. *Human Kindness Foundation Newsletter*, Fall 1996.

CHAPTER 2

[1] Suzuki, D. and P. Knudtson *Wisdom of the Elders: Honoring Sacred Native Visions of Nature* New York: Bantam Books, 1992, p. 123.

[2] "Touching the Mystery. An interview with Miriam MacGillis." In: Dellinger, D. (ed.) *Universe / Earth / Human: Reflections on the New Cosmology* Prescott, Ariz.: unpublished manuscript, 1999, pp. 49-50.

[3] Shaw, M. *Passionate Enlightenment: Women in Tantric Buddhism* Princeton, N.J.: Princeton University Press, 1994, p. 104.

CHAPTER 3

[1] Liedloff, J. *The Continuum Concept* New York: Viking-Penguin, 1975 and 1986, pp. 26-27.

[2] From an interview with James Carville, Democratic Party champion and campaign manager to Bill Clinton's 1996 Presidential Election.

[3] From a brochure of the Spiritual Life Institute, Nada Hermitage, Box 119, Crestone, Colorado, 81131, p. 3.

CHAPTER 4

[1] Ratushinskya, I. *Grey is the Color of Hope* New York: Alfred Knopf, 1988, pp 101-102.

[2] "Ethical Principles and Procedures for Grievance and Reconciliation," San Francisco Zen Center, 300 Page St., San Francisco, California, 94102; (415-863-3136). Used with permission.

[3] "Code of Conduct," Rochester Zen Center, 7 Arnold Park, Rochester, N.Y. 14607 (716-473-9180). Used with permission.

[4] Russell, P. *The Global Brain* Los Angeles: Jeremy P. Tarcher, 1983, p. 65.

[5] Ibid., p. 64.

[6] "Birth of a Salon," *Utne Reader*, July/August 1992, p. 54.

CHAPTER 5

[1] Becker, B. "Making It On Our Own," *Communities Magazine* Spring, 1997, pp. 49-50.

[2] Trungpa Rinpoche, C. *Shambhala: The Sacred Path of the Warrior* Boston: Shambhala Publishers, 1984, pp. 42-44.

[3] Miller, A. *For Your Own Good* New York: Farrar, Straus and Giroux, second edition 1984 pp. 6-7.

[4] Levine, S., *Who Dies? An Investigation of Conscious Living and Dying* Garden City, N.Y.: Anchor Press / Doubleday, p. 188.

[5] Ibid., p. 90.

[6] O'Brien, E. "Community Redux," *The Philadelphia Inquirer* Sept. 15, 1996, pp. G1-G5.

[7] Young, A. "Boss? What Boss?" *Communities Magazine* Spring 1997, p. 31.

[8] Greenleaf, R. K. "The Leader as Servant." In: Whitmyer, C. (ed.) *In the Company of Others*, New York: Jeremy P. Tarcher / Perigee Books, 1993, p. 56.

[9] Eisler, R. *The Partnership Way: New Tools for Living and Learning* San Francisco: HarperSanFrancisco, 1990, p. 183. Permission applied for.

[10] Ibid, p. 183.

[11] Peterson, J. V. "The Rise & Fall of Shiloh," *Communities, A Journal For Co-operative Living,* Fall, 1996, p. 60-62.

[12] Ibid, p. 65.

[13] Ibid, p. 53.

[14] Ibid, pp. 53-54.

CHAPTER 6

[1] Rogers, C. *On Becoming a Person* Boston: Houghton-Mifflin, 1961, pp. 333-334.

[2] Bradshaw, J. *Healing The Shame That Binds You* Deerfield Beach, Florida: Health Communications, Inc., 1988, p. 32.

CHAPTER 7

[1] Pearce, J. C. *Magical Child Matures* New York: Dutton, 1985, p. 25.

[2] Ibid, p. 34.

[3] Ibid, p. 37.

[4] Caplan, M. *Untouched: The Need for Genuine Affection in an Impersonal World* Prescott, Ariz.: Hohm Press, 1998, p. 48.

[5] Ibid, p. 49.

[6] Ibid, p. 50.

[7] Ibid, p. 116-118.

[8] Ibid, p. 118.

[9] Jung, C. G. *Psychological Reflections: A New Anthology of His Writings, 1905-1961* Princeton, N.J.: Princeton University Press, 1978, p. 239.

[10] Jung, C. G. *The Portable Jung* (Edited with Introduction by Joseph Campbell) New York: Penguin Books, 1976, p. 145.

CHAPTER 8

[1] Grifalconi, A. *The Village of Round and Square Houses* Boston: Little, Brown and Company, 1986.

[2] Somé, M. P. "Creating a Sense of Home. The Tribal Community of the Heart." Audiotape, produced by Oral Tradition Archives, P.O. Box 51155, Pacific Grove, Calif., 1993.

[3] Ibid.

[4] Norris, K. *The Cloister Walk* New York: Riverhead Books, 1996, p. 117.

[5] Ibid.

[6] Ibid., p. 118.

[7] Ryan, R. S. *The Woman Awake: Feminine Wisdom for Spiritual Life* Prescott, Ariz.: Hohm Press, 1998, pp. 363-366.

CHAPTER 9

[1] Maybury-Lewis, D. *Milennium: Tribal Wisdom and The Modern World* New York: Viking-Penguin, 1992, pp. 109 and 112.

[2] Ibid., p. 134.

[3] Ibid., 136.

[4] Lozoff, B. *Human Kindness Foundation Newsletter*, Fall 1996.

[5] Ibid.

[6] Somé, M. P. *Of Water and the Spirit: Ritual, Magic, and Initiation in the Life of an African Shaman.* New York: Penguin/Arkana, 1994, p. 23.

[7] Lieblich, A. "The Economics of a Kibbutz," in: Whitmyer, C. (ed.) *In the Company of Others*, New York: Jeremy P. Tarcher / Perigee Books, 1993, p. 75.

[8] Ibid, p. 76.

[9] Liedloff, J. *The Continuum Concept* New York: Viking-Penguin, 1975 and 1986, p. 141.

[10] Ibid, pp. 140-141.

[11] Somé, p. 3.

[12] Ibid, p. 23.

[13] Lozoff, B. *Human Kindness Foundation Newsletter*, Fall 1996.

CHAPTER 10

[1] Jaffe, D. *Healing From Within.* New York: Knopf / Random House, 1980, p. 143.

[2] Ibid.

[3] Ibid.

[4] Ibid, p. 146.

[5] Ibid.

[6] Ibid.

CHAPTER 11

[1] Norris, K. *The Cloister Walk*. New York: Riverhead Books, 1996, p. 51

[2] Somé, M. P. *Of Water and the Spirit: Ritual, Magic, and Initiation in the Life of an African Shaman* New York: Penguin/Arkana, 1994, p. 61.

[3] Ibid, p. 173.

CHAPTER 12

[1] Norris, K. *The Cloister Walk*. New York: Riverhead Books, 1996, pp. 41, 43.

[2] Jung, C. G. *Psychological Reflections: A New Anthology of His Writings, 1905-1961*. Princeton, N.J.: Princeton University Press, 1978, p. 351.

[3] Norris, p. 125.

[4] Somé, M. P. "Creating a Sense of Home. The Tribal Community of the Heart." Audiotape, produced by Oral Tradition Archives, Pacific Grove, Calif., 1993.

[5] Fourteenth Dalai Lama of Tibet, quoted in Hillman, J., *A Blue Fire: Selected Writings by James Hillman* New York: Harper Perennial: 1991, p. 115.

[6] "Flashback from the Geographic Archives: Swept Out of Childhood in South Africa," *National Geographic*, July 1996, p. 132.

[7] Kamperidis, L. "Surrounded by Water and Dying of Thirst," *Parabola*, Spring 1990, pp. 13-14.

[8] Ibid, p. 16.

[9] Thoreau, H. D. *Walden*, Princeton University Press, Princeton, N.J., 1971.

[10] Norris, K. *The Cloister Walk*. New York: Riverhead Books, 1996, p. 19.

[11] Ibid, p. 208.

[12] Somé, M. P. *Of Water and the Spirit: Ritual, Magic, and Initiation in the Life of an African Shaman* New York: Penguin/Arkana, 1994, p. 40.

[13] Jung, p. 332.

[14] Capra, F. and D. Steindl-Rast *Belonging To The Universe* San Francisco: HarperSanFrancisco, 1991, p. 31.

[15] Jung, p. 146.

[16] Suzuki, D. and P. Knudtson *Wisdom of the Elders: Honoring Sacred Native Visions of Nature* New York: Bantam Books, 1992, p. 203.

[17] Ibid., p. 204.

[18] Ibid., pp. 204-206.

[19] Ibid, p. 207.

BIBLIOGRAPHY

Anundsen, K. and C. R. Schaffer *Creating Community Anywhere: Finding Support and Connection in a Fragmented World.* N. Y.: Putnam Publishing Group, 1993.

Bly, R. *The Sibling Society.* Reading, Mass.: Addison-Wesley, 1996.

Capra, F. and D. Steindl-Rast *Belonging To The Universe.* San Francisco: Harper SanFrancisco, 1991.

Communities, *A Journal For Co-operative Living.* Fellowship for Intentional Community, Rt 1, Box 155, Rutledge, MO 63563, (828) 863-4425; www.ic.org.

Davidson, G. and C. McLaughlin *Builders of the Dawn: Community Lifestyles in a Changing World.* Walpole, N.H.: Stillpoint Publishing, 1985.

Devall, B. and G. Sessions *Deep Ecology: Living as if Nature Mattered.* Layton, Utah: Peregrine Smith Books, 1985.

Durning, A.T. *How Much is Enough.* N. Y.: W.W. Norton and Co., 1992.

Eisler, R. *The Chalice and The Blade: Our History, Our Future.* Cambridge, Mass.: Harper and Row, 1987.

_____. *The Partnership Way: New Tools for Living and Learning.* San Francisco: Harper SanFrancisco, 1990.

Forsey, H. *Circles of Strength: Community Alternatives to Alienation.* Philadelphia, Penn.: New Society Publications, 1993.

Grifalconi, A. *The Village of Round and Square Houses.* Boston: Little, Brown and Company, 1986.

Helminski, K. "Grapes Ripen Smiling At One Another: Leadership and the Group Process in Sufism," Gnosis, Fall 1992, pp. 50-55, P.O. Box 14217, San Fransisco, Calif. 94114, (415) 255-0400.

Holt, J. *Escape From Childhood: The Needs and Rights of Children.* N. Y.: Ballantine Books, 1990.

Liedloff, J. *The Continuum Concept*. N.Y.: Viking-Penguin, 1975 and 1986.

Lozowick, L. *Conscious Parenting*. Prescott, Ariz.: Hohm Press, 1997.

Maybury-Lewis, D. *Milennium: Tribal Wisdom and The Modern World*. N.Y.: Viking-Penguin, 1992.

Miller, A. *Banished Knowledge: Facing Childhood Injuries*. N.Y.: Doubleday, 1990.
_____. *For Your Own Good: Hidden Cruelty in Child-Rearing and The Roots of Violence*. N.Y.: Farrar, Straus, Giroux, 1984.

_____. *The Drama of the Gifted Child: Prisioners of Childhood*. N.Y.: Basic Books, 1981.

_____. *Thou Shalt Not Be Aware: Society's Betrayal of the Child*. N.Y.: Meridian (Penguin), 1990.

Pearce, J. C. *Magical Child: Rediscovering Nature's Plan for Our Children*. N.Y.: Bantam Books, 1986.

_____. *The Magical Child Matures*. N.Y.: E.P. Dutton, 1985.

Peck, M. S. A Different Drum: Community Making and Peace. N.Y.: Simon & Schuster, 1987.

Rogers, C. *On Becoming a Person*. Boston: Houghton-Mifflin, 1961.

Shaw, M. *Passionate Enlightenment: Women in Tantric Buddhism*. Princeton, N.J.: Princeton University Press, 1994.

Somé, M. P. "Creating a Sense of Home. The Tribal Community of the Heart." Audiotape, produced by Oral Tradition Archives, Pacific Grove, Calif., 1993.

_____. *Of Water and the Spirit: Ritual, Magic, and Initiation in the Life of an African Shaman*. N.Y.: Penguin/Arkana, 1994.

Suzuki, D. and P. Knudtson *Wisdom of the Elders: Honoring Sacred Native Visions of Nature*. N.Y.: Bantam Books, 1992.

Whitmeyer, C., ed. *In the Company of Others*. N.Y.: Jeremy P. Tarcher / Perigee Books, 1993.

ADDITIONAL TITLES FROM HOHM PRESS

THE SHADOW ON THE PATH
Clearing the Psychological Blocks to Spiritual Development
by VJ Fedorschak
Foreword by Claudio Naranjo, M.D.

Tracing the development of the human psychological shadow from Freud to the present, this readable analysis presents five contemporary approaches to spiritual psychotherapy for those who find themselves needing help on the spiritual path. Offers insight into the phenomenon of denial and projection.

Topics include: the shadow in the work notable therapists; the principles of inner spiritual development in the major world religions; examples of the disowned shadow in contemporary religious movements; and case studies of clients in spiritual groups who have worked with their shadow issues.

Paper, 300 pages, 6 x 9, $17.95   ISBN: 0-934252-81-5

• • •

HALFWAY UP THE MOUNTAIN
The Error of Premature Claims to Enlightenment
by Mariana Caplan
Foreword by Fleet Maull

Dozens of first-hand interviews with students, respected spiritual teachers and masters, together with broad research are synthesized here to assist readers in avoiding the pitfalls of the spiritual path. Topics include: mistaking mystical experience for enlightenment; ego inflation, power and corruption among spiritual leaders; the question of the need for a teacher; disillusionment on the path . . . and much more.

"Caplan's illuminating book . . . urges seekers to pay the price of traveling the hard road to true enlightenment." —*Publisher's Weekly*

Paper, 600 pages, $21.95   ISBN: 0-934252-91-2

• • •

**TO ORDER PLEASE SEE ACCOMPANYING ORDER FORM
OR CALL 1-800-381-2700 TO PLACE YOUR ORDER NOW.**

ADDITIONAL TITLES FROM HOHM PRESS

THE JUMP INTO LIFE: *Moving Beyond Fear*
by Arnaud Desjardins
Foreword by Richard Moss, M.D.

"Say *Yes* to life," the author continually invites in this welcome guidebook to
the spiritual path. For anyone who has ever felt oppressed by the life-negative
seriousness of religion, this book is a timely antidote. In language that translates the complex to the obvious, Desjardins applies his simple teaching of
happiness and gratitude to a broad range of weighty topics, including sexuality
and intimate relationships, structuring an "inner life," the relief of suffering,
and overcoming fear.

Paper, 278 pages, $12.95   ISBN: 0-934252-42-4

• • •

THE ALCHEMY OF LOVE AND SEX
by Lee Lozowick
Foreword by Georg Feuerstein, Ph.D.

Reveals 70 "secrets" about love, sex and relationships. Lozowick recognizes
the immense conflict and confusion surrounding love, sex, and tantric spiritual
practice. Advocating neither asceticism nor hedonism, he presents a middle
path—one grounded in the appreciation of simple human relatedness. Topics
include:* what men want from women in sex, and what women want from men
* the development of a passionate love affair with life * how to balance the
essential masculine and essential feminine * the dangers and possibilities of
sexual Tantra * the reality of a genuine, sacred marriage. . .and much more. " ...
attacks Western sexuality with a vengeance." —*Library Journal*.

Paper, 300 pages, $16.95   ISBN: 0-934252-58-0

• • •

**TO ORDER PLEASE SEE ACCOMPANYING ORDER FORM
OR CALL 1-800-381-2700 TO PLACE YOUR ORDER NOW.**

ADDITIONAL TITLES FROM HOHM PRESS

CONSCIOUS PARENTING
by Lee Lozowick

Any individual who cares for children needs to attend to the essential message of this book: that the first two years are the most crucial time in a child's education and development, and that children learn to be healthy and "whole" by living with healthy, whole adults. Offers practical guidance and help for anyone who wishes to bring greater consciousness to every aspect of childraising, including: • conception, pregnancy and birth • emotional development • language usage • role modeling: the mother's role, the father's role • the exposure to various influences • establishing workable boundaries • the choices we make on behalf of our children's education ... and much more.

Paper, 384 pages, $17.95   ISBN: 0-934252-67-X

• • •

THE WOMAN AWAKE: *Feminine Wisdom for Spiritual Life*
By Regina Sara Ryan

Though the stories and insights of great women of spirit whom the author has met or been guided by in her own journey, this book highlights many faces of the Divine Feminine: the silence, the solitude, the service, the power, the compassion, the art, the darkness, the sexuality. Read about: the Sufi poetess Rabia (8th century) and contemporary Sufi master Irina Tweedie; Hildegard of Bingen, Mechtild of Magdeburg, and Hadewijch of Brabant: the Beguines of medieval Europe; author Kathryn Hulme (*The Nun's Story) who* worked with Gurdjieff; German healer and mystic Dina Rees ... and many others.

Paper, 35 b&w photos, 520 pages, $19.95   ISBN: 0-934252-79-3

• • •

**TO ORDER PLEASE SEE ACCOMPANYING ORDER FORM
OR CALL 1-800-381-2700 TO PLACE YOUR ORDER NOW.**

ADDITIONAL TITLES FROM HOHM PRESS

THE YOGA TRADITION: *Its History, Literature, Philosophy and Practice*
by Georg Feuerstein, Ph.D.
Foreword by Ken Wilber

A complete overview of the great Yogic traditions of: Raja-Yoga, Hatha-Yoga, Jnana-Yoga, Bhakti-Yoga, Karma-Yoga, Tantra-Yoga, Kundalini-Yoga, Mantra-Yoga and many other lesser known forms. Includes translations of over twenty famous Yoga treatises, like the *Yoga-Sutra* of Patanjali, and a first-time translation of the *Goraksha Paddhati*, an ancient Hatha Yoga text. Covers all aspects of Hindu, Buddhist, Jaina and Sikh Yoga. A necessary resource for all students and scholars of Yoga.

Paper, 708 pages, Over 200 illustrations, $39.95   ISBN: 0-934252-83-1
Cloth, $49.95   ISBN: 0-934252-88-2

• • •

**WHEN SONS AND DAUGHTERS
CHOOSE ALTERNATIVE LIFESTYLES**
by Mariana Caplan

A guidebook for families in building workable relationships based on trust and mutual respect, despite the fears and concerns brought on by differences in lifestyle. Practical advice on what to do when sons and daughters (brothers, sisters, grandchildren...) join communes, go to gurus, follow rock bands around the country, marry outside their race or within their own gender, or embrace a religious belief that is alien to yours.

"Recommended for all public libraries."—*Library Journal.*

"Entering an arena too often marked by bitter and wounding conflict between worried parents and their adult children who are living in non-traditional communities or relationships, Mariana Caplan has produced a wise and thoughtful guide to possible reconciliation and healing...An excellent book."
—Alan F. Leveton, M.D.; Association of Family Therapists, past president

Paper, 264 pages, $14.95   ISBN: 0-934252-69-6

• • •

**TO ORDER PLEASE SEE ACCOMPANYING ORDER FORM
OR CALL 1-800-381-2700 TO PLACE YOUR ORDER NOW.**

ADDITIONAL TITLES FROM HOHM PRESS

WE LIKE TO NURSE
by Chia Martin
Illustrations by Shukyo Lin Rainey

Research has documented that the advantages of breastfeeding far outweigh the disadvantages in the overall health of the child. This unique children's picture book supports that practice, as it honors the mother-child relationship, reminding young children and mothers alike of their deep feelings for the bond created by nursing. Captivating and colorful illustrations present mother animals nursing their young. The text is simple and warmly encouraging.

"A delightful way to remind the very young of our species' natural heritage as well as our deep kinship with other mammals." —Jean Liedloff, author *Continuum Concept*

Paper, 36 pages, 16 full-color illustrations, $9.95   ISBN: 0-934252-45-9

• • •

WRITING YOUR WAY THROUGH CANCER
by Chia Martin

This book applies tried and true methods of journaling and other forms of writing to the particular challenges faced by the cancer patient. Research confirms that people who write about their upsetting experiences show improvement in their immune system functioning. Thousands of cancer patients today could profit from the journal writing techniques and inspiration offered in this practical, comforting, yet non-sentimental, guidebook. Its wisdom is useful to anyone who faces a personal health crisis; or anyone who wishes to confront their grief, loss or a difficult present reality with less panic, fear and confusion.

"Chia Martin's story is a vivid reminder of the importance of psychological and spiritual issues in healthcare."—Larry Dossey, M.D., author, *Reinventing Medicine* and *Healing Words*

Paper, 192 pages, $14.95   ISBN: 1-890772-003

• • •

**TO ORDER PLEASE SEE ACCOMPANYING ORDER FORM
OR CALL 1-800-381-2700 TO PLACE YOUR ORDER NOW.**

ADDITIONAL TITLES FROM HOHM PRESS

UNTOUCHED
The Need for Genuine Affection in an Impersonal World
By Mariana Caplan
Foreword by Ashley Montagu

The vastly impersonal nature of contemporary culture, supported by massive child abuse and neglect, and reinforced by growing techno-fascination are robbing us of our humanity. The author takes issue with the trends of the day that are mostly overlooked as being "progressive" or harmless, showing how these trends are actually undermining genuine affection and love. This uncompromising and inspiring work offers positive solutions for countering the effects of the growing depersonalization of our times.

"Mariana discusses virtually every significant human need and behavior in a language that abjures all technical terms, and speaks plainly and simply, both to the heart and the mind's consent. This is a considerable achievement."—Ashley Montagu, author of, *Touching, The Human Significance of the Skin*

Paper, 384 pages, $19.95   ISBN: 0-934252-80-7

• • •

NATURAL HEALING WITH HERBS
by Humbart "Smokey" Santillo, N.D.
Foreword by Robert S. Mendelsohn, M.D.

Dr. Santillo's first book, and Hohm Press' long-standing bestseller, is a classic handbook on herbal and naturopathic treatment. Acclaimed as the most comprehensive work of its kind, *Natural Healing With Herbs* details (in layperson's terms) the properties and uses of 120 of the most common herbs and lists comprehensive therapies for more than 140 common ailments. All in alphabetical order for quick reference.

Over 150,000 copies in print.

Paper, 408 pages, $16.95   ISBN: 0-934252-08-4

• • •

**TO ORDER PLEASE SEE ACCOMPANYING ORDER FORM
OR CALL 1-800-381-2700 TO PLACE YOUR ORDER NOW.**

ADDITIONAL TITLES FROM HOHM PRESS

INTUITIVE EATING: *EveryBody's Guide to Vibrant Health and Lifelong Vitality Through Food*
by Humbart "Smokey" Santillo, N.D.

The natural voice of the body has been drowned out by the shouts of addictions, over-consumption, and devitalized and preserved foods. Millions battle the scale daily, experimenting with diets and nutritional programs, only to find their victories short-lived at best, confusing and demoralizing at worst. *Intuitive Eating* offers an alternative—a tested method for: • strengthening the immune system • natural weight loss • increasing energy • making the transition from a degenerative diet to a regenerative diet • slowing the aging process.

Paper, 450 pages, $16.95   ISBN: 0-934252-27-0

• • •

10 ESSENTIAL HERBS, REVISED EDITION
by Lalitha Thomas

Peppermint. . .Garlic. . .Ginger. . .Cayenne. . .Clove. . . and 5 other everyday herbs win the author's vote as the "Top 10" most versatile and effective herbal applications for hundreds of health and beauty needs. *Ten Essential Herbs* offers fascinating stories and easy, step-by-step direction for both beginners and seasoned herbalists. Learn how to use cayenne for headaches, how to make a facial scrub with ginger, how to calm motion sickness and other stomach distress with peppermint. Special sections in each chapter explain the application of these herbs with children and pets too. Over 35,000 copies in print.

Paper, 395 pages, $16.95   ISBN: 0-934252-48-3

• • •

10 ESSENTIAL FOODS
by Lalitha Thomas

Carrots, broccoli, almonds, grapefruit and six other miracle foods will enhance your health when used regularly and wisely. Lalitha gives in-depth nutritional information plus flamboyant and good-humored stories about these foods, based on her years of health and nutrition counseling. Each chapter contains easy and delicious recipes, tips for feeding kids and helpful hints for managing your food dollar. A bonus section supports the use of 10 Essential Snacks.

Paper, 300 pages, $16.95   ISBN: 0-934252-74-2

**TO ORDER PLEASE SEE ACCOMPANYING ORDER FORM
OR CALL 1-800-381-2700 TO PLACE YOUR ORDER NOW.**

RETAIL ORDER FORM FOR HOHM PRESS BOOKS

Name_____ Phone ( )_____

Street Address or P.O. Box _____

City _____ State _____ Zip Code _____

	QTY	TITLE	ITEM PRICE	TOTAL PRICE	
1		THE SHADOW ON THE PATH	$17.95		
2		HALFWAY UP THE MOUNTAIN	$21.95		
3		THE JUMP INTO LIFE	$12.95		
4		THE ALCHEMY OF LOVE AND SEX	$16.95		
5		CONSCIOUS PARENTING	$17.95		
6		THE WOMAN AWAKE	$19.95		
7		THE YOGA TRADITION: PAPER	$39.95		
8		THE YOGA TRADITION: CLOTH	$49.95		
9		WRITING YOUR WAY THROUGH CANCER	$14.95		
10		WE LIKE TO NURSE	$9.95		
11		WHEN SONS AND DAUGHTERS CHOOSE...	$14.95		
12		UNTOUCHED	$19.95		
13		NATURAL HEALING WITH HERBS	$16.95		
14		INTUITIVE EATING	$16.95		
15		10 ESSENTIAL HERBS	$16.95		
16		10 ESSENTIAL FOODS	$16.95		
17		WIDENING THE CIRCLE	$17.95		
			SUBTOTAL:		
			SHIPPING:		
			TOTAL:		

SURFACE SHIPPING CHARGES

1st book $5.00
Each additional item $1.00

SHIP MY ORDER

☐ Surface U.S. Mail—Priority   ☐ UPS (Mail + $2.00)

☐ 2nd-Day Air (Mail + $5.00)   ☐ Next-Day Air (Mail + $15.00)

METHOD OF PAYMENT:

☐ Check or M.O.   Payable to Hohm Press, P.O. Box 2501, Prescott, AZ 86302

☐ Call 1-800-381-2700 to place your credit card order

☐ Or call 1-520-717-1779 to fax your credit card order

☐ Information for Visa/MasterCard/American Express order only:

Card #_____ – _____ – _____ – _____

Expiration Date_____

ORDER NOW!

Call 1-800-381-2700 or fax your order to 1-520-717-1779.

(Remember to include your credit card information.)

www.hohmpress.com